THE EDGEWATER
SANDWICH
AND
HORS D'OEUVRES
BOOK

JOHN EARL of SANDWICH

Engrav'd by J. Corner.

Published by J. Sewell, Cornhill.

Arnold Shircliffe

THE EDGEWATER
SANDWICH
AND
HORS D'OEUVRES
BOOK

Dover Publications, Inc., New York

Published in Canada by General Publishing Company, Ltd., 30 Lesmill Road, Don Mills, Toronto, Ontario.

Published in the United Kingdom by Constable and Company, Ltd., 10 Orange Street, London WC 2.

This Dover edition, first published in 1975, is an unabridged and unaltered republication of the text first published in 1930 by the Hotel Monthly Press under the title *The Edgewater Sandwich Book.* The halftone illustrations have been deleted in this edition.

International Standard Book Number: 0-486-23131-3
Library of Congress Catalog Card Number: 74-84005

Manufactured in the United States of America
Dover Publications, Inc.
180 Varick Street
New York, N. Y. 10014

Foreword

✓ ✓ ✓

"And with some it will always be that sandwiches will be more in want than the instructions of how to make them."

✓ ✓ ✓

THE sandwich, like the salad, has become an American institution. People are seeking less food, lighter food, reasonable prices and instant service; and it is the sandwich shop that is delivering such a service. A well ventilated, colorful, clean shop serving a variety of sandwiches, salads, desserts and beverages, made from high grade materials at a reasonable price, is bound to prosper; also the housewife who serves these delicacies in an appetizing manner will have her friends making a beaten path to her door.

The word sandwich is quite elastic, as it may mean two slices of bread with a filler of meat or other material; one slice of bread with an attractive topping, or a filling between ice cream slices, cake slices, pancakes, crust slices, etc. So popular has the sandwich become that special bread and toasting machines are made to handle it.

Pressed cheeses, hams, etc., are made to fit the bread slices, this to aid the quick making of good-looking and tasteful sandwiches. Practically everything that enters into the composition of a salad can be worked into an eye-pleasing and tasty sandwich. Bread enters into the making of practically all sandwiches. Sandwiches, made with a meat filling or peanut butter and served with a simple salad and a glass of milk, make an excellent light luncheon. The partaking of such a fare cannot bring but the best results insofar as health is concerned and practically everything necessary to maintain life is wrapped up in the above simple fare.

Many of the recipes given are the result of various experiments which have suggested themselves to the writer at different times. Certain standard dishes have been turned into sandwich fillings, and last, but not least, many friends have sent in the recipes of their best sellers, and to these due credit is given.

The Art of Making Sandwiches

✦ ✦ ✦

SANDWICHES may be as elaborate or as simple as one wishes to make them, and as liberal or dainty as the trade, occasion or home folks require. They may contain one ingredient or six, but the filling should not be less than one-fourth of the sandwich. The highly imaginative one can perhaps improve or may mar (no matter); the experience gained will be worth it. The author of that delightful little book, "Clarisse," says "You are invited to modify the recipes and to think out your own variations. For culinary laws are no more fixed than those of chemistry, and a natural gift is a treasure compared with which science is often of trifling account." This is very true, for one with the natural gift can almost always improve upon any fixed scheme. Give the man who knows a well-made and well-served article and he will shout your praises from the house-tops.

To make a first class sandwich it is important that you have the correct tools and proper materials in the best of shape to work with. Without these necessary items, the art of sandwich making, even in the hands of the experienced, cannot be anything but a dismal failure. Bread should be at least twelve hours old (and of a fine grain texture) unless, for certain reasons, bread or rolls freshly made are required. Unless otherwise stated crusts are to be removed. If sandwich bread is trimmed before sandwiches are made, it will prevent waste of butter and filling. However, for daintiness and attractiveness they are to be trimmed after lettuce, butter and fillings have been placed. Squares, fingers or triangles make least waste; cut bread thin and have no ragged edges. For quantity production cut the entire loaf lengthwise and keep slices together so they match. When fancy cutters are used, use the same cutters for bread and meat. Meat scraps can be ground up and utilized for other sandwiches.

Breads used for sandwiches:

Barley	Fruit	Pumpernickel
Black	Graham	Raisin
Bran	Half rye	Rice
Buckwheat	Nut	Rye
Corn	Nut and fruit	Salt rising
French	Peameal	White
French rye	Potato	Whole wheat

Bread or toast may be cut into the following shapes:

	Eggs	Rings
Circles	Crescents	Roll
Clubs	Fingers	Rounds
Hearts	Funny faces	Squares
Spades	Horseshoes	Stars
Diamonds	Lozenges	Triangles
Doughnuts	Oblongs	

When cut with a doughnut cutter the lower slice may remain uncut, and center hole of top slice filled with crushed pineapple, jam, rubyettes, etc. This sandwich should be of a small type. Rings may be cut from rolls and tied with white, silver, gold or tri-colored ribbon.

If wet garnishes, such as slaw are used, they should be well drained or the sandwich protected from the juices, as there is nothing that I know of that will bring more unfavorable comment than a soaked sandwich.

To keep sandwiches from drying out, wring out a towel which has been soaked in ice water, until it is just damp to the touch, and lay this over the sandwiches; and over this another which is just a little more moist. (See recipes for Rolled Sandwiches.) Sandwiches should be moist and not smeary; mayonnaise, if used, should be thick, not thin. A smeary, dry, clumsy, raggedy sandwich is everything but what a sandwich should be. The word sandwich suggests something light, fancy, appetizing; and if anything but that, they fail in their mission.

A sandwich should be seasoned, not insipid, so that when one bites into it one should find it a moist, savory, snappy, appetizing combination.

Hot sandwiches should be served as soon as made, and should not be trimmed unless so requested.

Banquet rolls, finger rolls, or small French rolls should be baked until rather crisp. These can be hollowed out and filled with whatever savory mixture you may wish. The crust end of the plug removed can be reinserted without the crumb.

Butter should be whipped with a spatula or wooden spoon until creamy, and a little whipped or raw cream added to reduce it to a consistency that is easily handled (one pound of butter to one cup of whipped cream). Butter can then be used on the thinnest slices of bread without crumbling or breaking the slice. A few drops of chervil, tarragon, parsley, garlic, mint, thyme, borage, violet, nasturtium, lemon, lime, pineapple or onion juice, or a little dry mustard or grated horseradish added to the butter used for various sandwich fillings gives an added zest.

All meats must be thoroly cold before slicing, unless for hot sandwiches, and they also should be cut thin.

In all the recipes for scrambled egg sandwiches, use one-third the amount of garniture to eggs used, plus the seasoning. A tablespoon of raw cream added to the eggs will give a better looking dish. Eggs should be whipped up with cream first and then dropped into a hot, clean, well buttered pan and stirred constantly until cooked. Do not cook eggs too dry. Garniture can be added to eggs after they are in the pan; this will give a brighter, cleaner item.

In making egg sandwiches the author advises leaving out truffles and other expensive or hard-to-procure items. The same recipe can be used if poached eggs are called for as scrambled or fried. The manner of cooking eggs should be controlled by the desire of the guest. When a desire is not expressed the cook should use the method he excels in, or the one preferred by most guests. Poached eggs are not suggested unless the eggs are perfectly fresh, as the time consumed, and the waste in their preparation warns against this. These egg combinations are not new, but some are, however, new to the realm of sandwiches; and if handled right should gain immediate favor, as they must be cooked to order to be right. They will undoubtedly give Friday lunch and Lenten days enough variety to please the most fastidious.

In restaurants or sandwich shops the egg sandwiches can be turned out quickly and in good shape by having the necessary garnish ready when the meal starts; a jar of good espagnole or brown sauce, a jar of veloute sauce, and other various garnitures called for, in bowls, already cut and ready for a moment's notice. Six, eight or ten of these various sandwiches, not too complicated, can be handled on a Friday menu, and possibly two or three during the week. These sandwiches were created mostly for the sandwich shop and should be used at supper time when more time can be taken to prepare them. If used in a home some more suitable decoration or garniture should be added, and, of course, instead of two eggs, one should be the service.

Do not season fried eggs unless they are to be turned over or a sauce is to be poured over them, as the condiments detract greatly from the appearance. Eggs can be cut into desired shapes and arranged on various cuts of toast for all open sandwiches.

Contents

{Complete Indexes are on Pages 247 to 260}

The Edgewater Sandwich Book

◆

Adamneve Sandwich

*White bread, butter, lettuce, apple sauce, Galax
leaves, apple*

On a thin slice of buttered white bread spread a
thin layer of well drained and seasoned apple sauce
or apple butter. Press on upper slice, trim in apple
or fig-leaf or fancy shapes and arrange on lettuce
and galax leaves on plater around a red delicious
apple.

These sandwiches mixed with an assortment of
meat and salad sandwiches are always appreciated.

Aeroplane Sandwich
Lindbergh Sandwich

*Toast, butter, hard-boiled eggs, ham, cress, mayon-
naise, pickles, pimentoes, olives .*

On a slice of buttered toast, one and one-half by
five inches, arrange a mixture of hard boiled eggs
(whites and yolks chopped separately) and chopped
ham, each item mixed with mayonnaise separately.
Place on toast in following order: Whites of eggs,
ham, yolks of eggs. Cut a slice of toast in half and
place at either side of center slice. Garnish top of
each wing with chopped lettuce or cress mixed with
mayonnaise. Cut small aeroplanes of whites of hard
boiled eggs and pimentoes. Garnish the white and
red parts of sandwich with white aeroplanes and the
two green parts with red ones. Garnish with lettuce and four-leaved clovers, cut out of cucumber
rings.

Afternoon Sandwich (Open)

*Turkey, bread, butter, marmalade, olives, pimentoes,
lettuce*

On two slices of bread spread with butter place
one slice in center of plate and cover with slices of

white meat of turkey, boiled and cold. Cut second slice in half and place one-half slice at either end; spread half slices with marmalade. Garnish with olives, pimentoes and lettuce.

Agostini Sandwich—I

Sausage, eggs, toast, tomato sauce, butter

Poach six thin slices of frankfurter sausage in chicken stock. Whip up one egg with a little cream and scramble egg lightly. While egg is cooking add slices of sausage. Turn sausage and egg over and then place between two slices of trimmed hot buttered toast. Cut sandwich in two diagonally, place on a platter and pour a hot tomato sauce over. Serve hot and at once.

Agostini Sandwich—II (Open)

Toast, Lyons or Cervelat sausage, eggs, tomato sauce

On two rounds of toasted bread place a few slices of poached Lyons or Cervelat sausage. Arrange two poached eggs on top of sausage and pour a well seasoned tomato sauce over eggs. Serve at once. This is an extremely fine and tasteful sandwich.

Slices of cooked frankfurters may be used in place of imported sausage.

Albert Sandwich

French rolls, creamed chicken, bread crumbs, bacon, olives, radishes, lettuce

Cut off the upper part of a French roll lengthwise, about one-fourth inch from the top and remove the crumb. Fill center with diced white meat of chicken creamed. Sprinkle with bread crumbs Polonaise and place under hot broiler and brown. Strip with bacon and serve at once. Garnish with olives, lillied radishes and lettuce.

Sweetbreads, capon, turkey or any sea food mixture can be handled the same way. Mixture should be sufficiently moist.

Almond Sandwich

See Chicken and Almond

Alpha-Omega Sandwich—I (Open)

Toast, chicken paste, eggs, tomato sauce

On rounds of toast make a border of chicken paste. In center place a poached egg, well trimmed and drained. Sprinkle with butter and place in oven a few moments, then pour hot tomato sauce over the egg and serve at once.

Alpha Omega Sandwich—II

*Toast, butter, ham, chicken, Thousand Island dress-
ing, cress, hard boiled egg*

Cut two slices of bread thin and toast on both
sides, then spread with butter. Fry thin slice of
boiled ham on both sides and place it on toast, cover
ham with three thin slices of boiled breast of
chicken or turkey (cold), then press on upper slice.
Trim and cut the sandwich into four squares. Place
the four squares on a hot plate in shape of a cross,
leaving a center square open. Then pour a little
Thousand Island dressing over each square. In center place a pom pom of fresh watercress and garnish
top of each square with a slice of hard-boiled egg.

Alpine Sandwich

*Swiss cheese, cress, half rye bread, dill pickles,
lettuce*

Spread extremely thin slices of pumpernickle or
half-rye bread with a water cress butter (chopped
cress and creamed butter) and place a thin slice of
Gruyere (Swiss) cheese on top. Press on upper slice
and cut into desired shapes. Garnish with lettuce
and sections of fanciful cut dill pickles. Serve mustard on side.

Swiss and Switzer was originally made in Emmenthal, Switzerland. A first class Emmenthal
is never less than four months old when exported,
will keep for several years, uncut, and under favorable conditions. It has a nutty, tangy flavor, is'
somewhat dry but tender. The holes or eyes, tho
generally characteristic, are not necessary to qualify
for many good cheeses are blind, as dealers describe
them. The Gruyere is an example of the blind type.

Alsatian Sandwich (Open)

*Eggs, toast, butter, chicken, goose or turkey livers,
brown sauce*

Place two poached eggs on buttered rounds of
toast spread with a finely ground and seasoned paste
of chicken, goose or turkey livers. Pour over a thin,
well seasoned, rich brown sauce and serve at once.

Amandine Sandwich

*Chicken, almonds, mayonnaise, bread, lettuce, cress,
gherkins*

Mix equal amounts of white meat of boiled chick-
en and chopped blanched almonds and mash to a
paste. Season and add enough mayonnaise base
No. 3 to make it the right consistency to spread.

Spread on thin slices of white bread, press on leaf of lettuce and upper slice. Trim and cut into desired shapes. Garnish plate or platter with clusters of water cress and fanned gherkins.

Chicken amandine can be turned into an appetizer by using toast and adding ground capers or ground sour gherkins to paste; or by spreading toast with anchovy butter and the mixture, just enough to give it a tang. Serve on rounds, diamonds or short sticks of toasted bread and decorate with red, brown or green butters.

American Sandwich
Ham, egg, toast

Place a horse shoe cut of ham in a small skillet and brown on one side, turn slice over and break a raw egg in on top of ham. Finish cooking in oven until egg is done, baste with butter and turn out on a freshly made and trimmed slice of toast; press on upper slice and serve hot and at once.

Sandwich can be garnished with American fried potatoes and lettuce.

This makes a real American dish and whenever in doubt this is the sandwich to order.

American Cheese Sandwich
See Toasted Cheese

Andalousian Gaspacho Sandwich

Toast, butter, tomatoes, cucumbers, green peppers, Bermuda onions, French dressing, Herkimer cheese

On two full slices of trimmed whole wheat bread, toasted and spread with butter, place a mixture of thinly sliced and peeled tomatoes, squeezed cucumbers, green peppers and sweet Bermuda onions. Serve two or three slices of each vegetable on each slice of toast and pour over a liberal amount of French dressing, Base No. 5. Sprinkle with finely grated Herkimer cheese and serve. This is called a salad. I have made a sandwich out of it, but it is really a soup! Try it and see what you think about it.

If French Dressing makes sandwich too soupy use mayonnaise or Thousand Island Dressing. Vegetables should be arranged on toast in a pleasing manner. The two slices of toast to be placed lengthwise on platter.

Anglaise Sandwich (Open)

Toast, lobster paste, shrimp, veloute sauce, eggs

On two rounds of toasted bread, spread with lobster paste, place two poached eggs trimmed to shape. Cover it with a good hot creamy veloute sauce garnished with finely diced shrimp. Serve hot.

Antipasto Sandwich
Antipasto, mayonnaise, toast, lettuce

Drain off the moisture of a small can of Antipasto, chop the solids up fine and drain again. Add enough mayonnaise to bind and spread on thin slices of freshly made toast, press on upper slice and cut into desired shapes. Serve on leaves of lettuce.

Antipasto chopped, drained and mixed with cream cheese or butter makes an excellent filling.

Antipasto is an Italian product and can be procured at any first class delicatessen store.

Apicius Sandwich
Bread, butter, apple-sauce, country sausage

Spread a slice of toasted bread with butter and apple-sauce. Press on a thin cake of freshly fried country sausage and upper slice. Trim and serve hot. This makes an excellent, tempting tidbit, an item for a winter's day luncheon.

Apple Sandwich
See Sliced Apple

Arabian Sandwich
Bacon, mayonnaise, horseradish, toast, tomato, lettuce

Chop two thin slices of broiled bacon and mix with enough mayonnaise to bind; then add one teaspoon of grated horseradish (strained). Spread mixture on thin slice of toast, and place two thin slices of peeled ripe tomatoes on top of mixture. Season, press on leaf of lettuce and upper slice, trim and cut in two diagonally. Serve on leaves of lettuce.

Argenteuile Sandwich (Open)
Toast, ham, eggs, Hollandaise sauce, bread crumbs, potatoes

On two rounds of toast place thin slices of boiled ham, cut to shape. On top of ham place a fried egg trimmed to shape. Pour over eggs a little Hollandaise sauce and sprinkle with bread crumbs Polonaise. Surround sandwich with Long Branch potatoes. Sandwich after it is made to be placed in an oven for a few minutes to heat. In place of ham three or four asparagus tips can be placed on each round of toast. Toast may be cut in squares, if desired.

Aromatic Sandwich—I
Grinner Sandwich
Bread, butter, cream cheese, aromatic vinegar

On thin slices of bread spread with butter and then cream cheese (which has been reduced to the proper consistency by the addition of aromatic vinegar Nos. 1, 2 or 3), press on leaf lettuce and upper slice, trim and cut in desired shapes. Serve on bed of lettuce.

Chopped tarragon, sorrel, chives, sweet basil, or chervil added to sweet butter or cheese gives an aromatic flavor to the sandwich. Sandwiches should be cut in fancy shapes and served in conjunction with jellied and assorted meat sandwiches.

Grinning parties made up part of pleasures our forefathers indulged in—the ugliest grinner receiving a prize. The aromatic vinegar helped the following grinning sinner to carry off the prize.

Aromatic Sandwich—II
Cream cheese, aromatic vinegar, bread, lettuce, bar le duc

Reduce cream cheese to proper consistency with a mixture of one-half aromatic vinegar and one-half bar le duc. Spread on thin slice of white or brown bread. Arrange a little shredded lettuce over cheese. Press on upper slice, trim and cut diagonally or in fancy shapes. Serve at once. Vinegar may be omitted and lemon juice added.

Artist Sandwich
Eggs, hicory nuts, mayonnaise, lettuce, olives

Rub the yolks of two hard boiled eggs through a sieve and add to it an equal amount of chopped green olives and hicory nuts. Bind together with mayonnaise base No. 3 and spread between thin slices of white bread. Trim and cut in diamond shape. Serve on leaves of lettuce.

Pickles can be used in place of olives.

Athletic Club Sandwich
Anchovies, chicken, pickles, toast, cress, mayonnaise, lettuce

Pound to a paste in a mortar one-half ounce of boned anchovies and two ounces of white meat of chicken.

Add a little mayonnaise to give paste the right consistency and spread on thin slice of freshly made toast. Sprinkle with a little chopped pickle and shredded lettuce. Press on upper slice, trim, cut into desired shapes, garnish with cress and serve.

This combination makes a splendid filling.

August Savory Sandwich (Open)

Onion, green pepper, tomatoes, eggs, toast, butter, Herkimer cheese

Dice finely one small onion and one green pepper. Then saute until cooked and brown. Add one cup of canned tomatoes and reduce to half. Fry two eggs and place on two pieces of buttered toast, freshly made. Pour sauce over eggs, season and sprinkle with grated Herkimer cheese and butter. Place under a hot broiler to melt cheese; serve at once and very hot.

Aurora Sandwich—I (Open)

Toast, butter, eggs, cream sauce, tomato sauce, bacon

On a slice of toast, buttered and cut diagonally and then placed in diamond shape arrange several slices of hard boiled egg. Place the small ends of egg at small ends of toast and overlap slices so that large slices are in the center. Garnish sides of eggs with a strip of broiled bacon. Bacon should cover edges of toast on either side and nestle close to eggs. Over eggs and bacon pour a rich, well seasoned cream sauce, just enough to coat the eggs. Around base of toast pour a well seasoned tomato sauce. Serve hot.

Aurora Sandwich—II (Open)

Toast, eggs, tomato sauce, cream sauce, hard boiled egg yolks

Pour a little hot tomato sauce in a platter and place two rounds of toast in the center. Put a poached egg on top of each round of toast and pour a little cream sauce over the eggs. Sprinkle with chopped hard boiled egg yolks. This is an excellent open sandwich for Friday, good looking and easy to prepare.

Avocado Sandwich

Avocado, bread, lemon, lettuce, French dressing

On thin slices of white or brown bread, spread alligator pear, or avocado, which has been worked into a fine paste and seasoned with salt and lemon juice or mixed with a little French dressing or chili sauce. Press on upper slice and leaf of lettuce, trim and cut in fancy shapes.

AUTHOR'S NOTE: The avocado, or ahuacatl, contains from 15% to 20% easily digested vegetable oil or fat, making its flesh exceptionally nutritious. The protein content is high and when eaten with lemon juice or a little good French dressing it is a feast for the gods as well as a real health giving item.

"Avocado" was the name given by the Spanish Conquistadores to the *Persea Gratissima,* whose fruit is the "alligator pear." M. Turiault again traces the Spanish word back to the Carib word "Aouacate."

Babylon Sandwich

Lettuce, toast, mayonnaise, pineapple, chicken salad, hard-boiled egg, caviar, cress, pickles, tomatoes

On leaves of lettuce place a rounded slice of toast spread with mayonnaise and on it lay a slice of fried pineapple, warm. Cover with second round slice of toast. Make a second round sandwich out of brown or graham bread, toasted, and fill center with chicken salad. Place this sandwich on top of pineapple one. The salad sandwich should be less in circumference than pineapple sandwich. On top of salad sandwich place a half hard-boiled egg filled with caviar. Garnish with cress, fanned pickles and tomatoes. Serve a little mayonnaise on the side.

This is really a three-course luncheon, the appetizing caviar, the salad sandwich with the relishes of pickle and tomatoes and the dessert of pineapple. It is a unique, tasty sandwich luncheon.

The lower toast should be cut the same size as slice of pineapple.

Bacon Sandwich

Bacon, white bread, mayonnaise, butter, tomato, potatoes, lettuce

On a thin slice of white bread, toasted and spread with sweet butter or mayonnaise or both, place a leaf of lettuce and then three thin strips of broiled bacon. Press on upper slice, trim and cut in squares, half or diagonally. Serve on leaves of lettuce and garnish with Long Branch potatoes and quartered tomatoes.

Bacon and Lettuce Sandwich
See Lettuce and Bacon

Baktom Sandwich

White and whole wheat bread, bacon, tomato, cucumber, lettuce, mayonnaise, butter

On a thin slice of toasted white bread, spread with sweet butter, place three slices of crisp bacon, freshly broiled. Press on a slice of whole wheat bread, toasted, spread with mayonnaise and lettuced. On lettuce and mayonnaise place in center a slice of red ripe tomato, peeled; around tomato arrange several thin slices of squeezed cucumber. Press on a third slice of white bread, toasted. Trim edges and cut in two diagonally. Place on plate in diamond shape on leaf of lettuce and serve at once. A little Thousand Island or sour cream dressing can be served on side.

This is a very well balanced, economical dish and a real item for the sandwich shop or tea room. Bread should be cut thin and toasted fresh. The three layers should not be over one inch high.

Season tomato and cucumbers.

Balzac Sandwich

Tongue, mushroom, eggs, toast, butter, cream sauce

Julienne one slice of cooked smoked beef tongue and one medium sized mushroom. Cook mushroom in butter and when done add tongue to heat. Whip up two eggs into an omelet mixture, add tongue and mushroom, season and cook mixture the same as you would fried eggs over. When done, place on a thin slice of buttered toast. Press on upper slice, trim, cut in two diagonally and arrange on a hot platter in diamond shape. Pour over it a light cream sauce flavored with onion. Serve hot and at once.

Banana Sandwich—I

White bread, bananas, lemon juice, orange juice, lettuce

On thin slice of white or whole wheat bread, spread with mayonnaise, spread finely mashed or pureed bananas which have been thinned with orange juice. Press on upper slice, trim and cut into fancy shapes. Serve on bed of lettuce. After bananas are peeled and sliced they should be bathed in lemon juice so they do not turn black. These sandwiches should be served as soon as made. Crushed pineapple may be added to the puree for variety and flavor.

Banana Sandwich—II

Toast, bananas, cheese, bacon, mayonnaise, lettuce, butter

Make a paste of raw, ripe bananas. Spread slices of white bread with butter and paste. Cover with thin slices of bananas, sprinkle with cheese and finely chopped broiled bacon. Melt cheese under hot broiler, or use two slices and brown in toasting machine. Serve with mayonnaise on the side and garnish with lettuce.

Banana Sandwich III

See Ripe Banana

Barbecued Sandwich—I

Barbecued meat, drippings, seasoning, bread

On white or whole wheat bread place a slice of barbecued meat. The bread should be lightly dipped in the juices which have dripped out of the joint while on the spit roasting. On this are placed thin slices of barbecued meat. The sandwich is to be eaten out of the hand and untrimmed.

Barbecued Sandwich—II

See Charles Lamb

Bar Le Duc Sandwich (Open)

Whole wheat bread, butter, bar le duc, cream cheese, lettuce

Cut thin slices of whole wheat bread in diamonds, hearts or rounds; spread with butter and pipe edges with thinned-down cream cheese. Fill center with bar le duc. Serve on leaves of lettuce.

Any jelly may be used to form center garnish.

This makes an ideal afternoon tea item. Toasted white bread can be used in place of the whole wheat bread.

Bayonne Sandwich

Ham, egg, toast, tomato sauce, parsley

Fry a horseshoe cut of ham on one side, turn it over and break an egg on it. Place in oven to finish cooking egg. Have two slices of trimmed toast ready; place one on plate and cover with the cooked ham and egg. Press on upper slice and pour over it a well flavored, light tomato sauce. Garnish with parsley and serve at once.

Ham and egg should be cooked in a very small pan to keep egg from spreading out too much; this will give sandwich a better appearance.

AUTHOR'S NOTE: Mayonnaise was at one time called bayonnaise, the word supposedly to have originated in the city of Bayonne, a city in southern France, famous for fine hams, and from which the word bayonet is derived.

Beach Walk Sandwich

Toast, turkey, butter, lettuce, Russian dressing,
hard-boiled egg

Butter two slices of thin toasted white bread. Cover the lower slice with cold roast turkey, season and press on lettuce leaf and upper slice. Cut sandwich into four squares and arrange on plate. Underline with lettuce and pour over the squares a Russian dressing. Garnish tops of squares with slices of hard-boiled egg. Serve at once. This is a very tasty and very well liked sandwich—one of the finest items in the book so far as popularity is concerned.

"Cookery is eminently an experimental and practical art."

Bean and Sausage Sandwich

See Sausage and Bean

Bean Major Sandwich

Toast, mayonnaise, string beans, hard-boiled eggs,
lettuce, tomato

Trim two slices of toast. Place one slice in center and cut the other slice in four and surround center slice with four triangles. Spread toast with mayonnaise. Garnish center slice with marinated string beans (not fried) and sides with the fried beans. Garnish the two triangles of toast at ends with slices of hard-boiled egg, and side triangles with slices of tomato covered with mayonnaise. Serve on bed of lettuce. This makes an unusual sandwich.

The entire sandwich may be garnished with the fried beans and sprinkled with chopped bacon for variety.

NOTE—To French fry beans: Use a can of De Luxe or tiny French string beans. Dry carefully, roll in flour, season and immerse in hot grease. A French fryer is necessary for this, or two are better. Place beans in one and give them a hot dip for a few seconds, then finish in the next fryer of smoking grease.

Bearnaise Sandwich

Eggs, toast, butter, Bearnaise sauce

Cook a light omelet mixture on both sides, like you would fried eggs over. Do not cook too hard.

Place egg mixture on a thin slice of buttered toast, press on upper slice, trim and cut in four squares. Place squares on a hot platter and pour a hot Bearnaise sauce over. Serve at once.

Bechamel Sandwich

Toast, eggs, Bechamel sauce, paprika, bread crumbs, butter

Make toast as in Aurora. Fry two eggs separately and trim in round shape. Pour over a well made Bechamel sauce (not too thin), season, sprinkle with paprika, bread crumbs and butter. Brown quickly and serve.

Beef Sandwiches
See also

Chipped Beef
Cold Roast Beef
Corned Beef
Grilled Roast Beef

Hot Roast Beef
Raw Beef
Sirloin of Beef

Beef Combination Sandwich

Beef, egg, lettuce, pickles, mayonnaise, bread

Chop or grind one cup of cold roast beef, add one chopped hard-boiled egg, one-half cup of chopped lettuce, two small sweet pickles chopped, and enough mayonnaise to bind. Spread on thin slices of bread, press on upper slice, trim, and cut into desired shapes.

Beef Hash Sandwich

Beef hash, tomato, toast, watercress

Arrange hot roast beef hash on two trimmed slices of toast, garnish with two slices of fried tomato and a pom pom of watercress. Serve hot.

Cold roast beef hash can be put thru a grinder and then spread on trimmed slice of toast, the upper slice pressed on and then toasted in an electric toaster. Garnish with Long Branch potatoes and slices of fried tomato.

Drain off surplus moisture before using ground hash as a filler.

Beef Heart Sandwich

Beef heart, savory, mayonnaise, bread, lettuce

Grind cooked beef heart and season with chopped savory, salt and pepper. Bind with mayonnaise and spread on thin slices of bread. Place on leaf of lettuce or sprinkle with chopped cress. Press on upper slice, trim and cut into desired shapes. Garnish with braized onions. Serve warm.

Slices cut from a roast beef heart (cold) with the addition of a thin slice of boiled ham or a few strips of broiled bacon makes an excellent combination for a sandwich filler.

Beef Loaf

One pound finely ground raw beef; 3 yolks of eggs; 1 cup bread crumbs; 1 tablespoon butter; pepper, salt and chopped celery leaf to season; enough cream or milk to moisten. Mix above ingredients together in roll or loaf and bake.

When cold, slice and use with mayonnaise and lettuce as filling for sandwich.

Beef a la Mode

Potato pancakes or rye bread, beef a la mode

On a freshly made four-inch potato pancake place two thin slices of tender beef a la mode, press on upper pancake, pour some of the sauce around the sandwich and serve at once. Be sure to serve a beef a la mode sauce well garnished with vegetables. Slices of rye bread can be used in place of pancakes.

AUTHOR'S NOTE: "Farthing Pie Houses were common in the outskirts of London a century ago. Their fragrance caught the sharp set citizen by the nose and led him in by that prominent member to feast on their savory fare." This early pie house was nothing more than an early sandwich shop, the only difference there was, one sold meat between pie crusts while the latter placed his meats between bread slices.

Beet Combination Sandwich

Beets, horseradish, mayonnaise, bread, bacon, lettuce, cress

Bake three or four beets and allow to cool. Chop fine and mix in one tablespoon of horseradish. Strain off surplus moisture and add enough mayonnaise to bind. Spread slices of white or whole wheat bread with mixture and sprinkle with finely chopped broiled bacon. Press on upper slice, trim and cut into desired shapes. Serve on lettuce and garnish with cress. Chopped pickled beets, cold boiled potatoes, chopped chives bound together with mayonnaise make a tasty combination. Baked beets are far superior to boiled ones in flavor as they retain all their mineral content.

Benedict Sandwich

Toast, ham, egg, hollandaise sauce

On a horseshoe of toast place a slice of ham, fried or broiled, cut in same shape. In center of ham place a well drained poached egg. Over egg pour a hot hollandaise sauce. Serve at once. A raw egg can be placed on top of ham, then put in oven and cooked. Egg can also be covered with a creamy Veloute sauce, sprinkled with cheese and browned in a medium hot oven or under broiler.

Egg to be cooked by time the browning is complete.

Toasted English muffin can be used in place of toast if desired.

Bercy Sandwich

Sausage, eggs, cream, toast, tomato sauce

Split and broil two links of farm sausage. Whip up two eggs with a tablespoon of cream and scramble. Arrange the links of sausage on a piece of thin trimmed toast and cover with eggs. Press on upper trimmed slice. Cut into three finger sandwiches. Arrange on platter and pour a light tomato sauce over the top. Serve at once while hot.

Biloxi Sandwich

*Whole wheat or white bread, pineapple, butter,
lamb chop, cress*

On a slice of white or whole wheat bread, toasted and spread with finely chopped pineapple mixed with butter, place a loin lamb chop, grilled. Lamb chop should be cut one inch thick, boned and split in half but not severed, then broiled between a fine wire broiler over a hot fire. Garnish with cress and serve with a glass of buttermilk. This constitutes a well balanced luncheon; is a tasty combination and if handled right is a real picture. A little melted butter to be poured over chop just before serving. A second slice of toasted bread spread with grated pineapple and butter should be served on same platter with chop.

Black Walnut Sandwich

*Whole wheat bread, cream cheese, black walnuts,
pickled walnuts, lettuce, celery, French dressing*

On thin slices of plain or whole wheat bread spread cream cheese which has been thinned down with French dressing; sprinkle chopped black pickled walnuts, or arrange thin slices of same on top of cheese. Cover with lettuce and press on upper slice. Cut in fanciful shapes and garnish with quartered pickled walnuts and branches of hearts of celery.

Cheese can be omitted and chopped nuts mixed with mayonnaise and shredded lettuce.

Bohemienne Sandwich—I (Open)

Eggs, Piquant sauce, mushrooms, potatoes, toast

Fry or poach two eggs and place on toast as in Aurora. Make a Piquant sauce, add a few chopped mushrooms to it and pour a little over the eggs. Serve a few chateau potatoes as a garnish.

Bohemienne Sandwich—II

Eggs, tongue, cream sauce, toast

Poach two eggs and place on round pieces of toast. Add a little finely chopped tongue to cream sauce and mask eggs; or pour the cream sauce and finely chopped tongue on the toast and set the eggs on top. Serve hot.

Boiled Vegetable Sandwich

Toast, Thousand Island dressing, beets, carrots, potato salad, cauliflower, Hollandaise sauce, lettuce

Spread two slices of thin toast with Thousand Island dressing and arrange on platter. Chop one pickled beet finely, mix with mayonnaise and spread on center slice. Arrange a row of thinly sliced baby carrots on top of beets. Cut second slice of toast in two and place on one triangle of toast finely chopped potato salad; on second triangle of toast place very small rosettes of cauliflower, masked with Hollandaise sauce. Garnish with lettuce. In place of cauliflower, chopped boiled onions, green cabbage, broccoli or, in fact, any fresh vegetable with good color effect may be used. Triangles of toast to be placed at either end of center slice.

This is a very tasty vegetable sandwich.

Bon Bouchee I

Puff paste, crab flakes, lettuce, mayonnaise, black and green olives

On rounds of puff paste, browned, place a small mound of marinated crab meat flakes, finely cut lobster or shrimp mixed with a very little shredded lettuce. Cover or mask completely this bouchee with a red or yellow mayonnaise (mayonnaise mixed with a little red paste and aspic or yellow paste and aspic). Garnish top of bouchee with round of black olives centered with red butter, and the sides with very thin slices of fluted green olives, centered with red butter. Serve on doily or leaf of lettuce. This bon bouchee can be placed on a butter cracker or on a freshly toasted round of bread. Pile crab, lobster or shrimp in a pyramid about one-half inch

high. This should be made so that one can pick
it up with the fingers. Do not come to edge of puff
paste or toast with the sea food and make the
bouchee no larger than a silver dollar.

Bon Bouchee II
Puff paste, jam or preserves, nuts

Between thin slices of puff paste, cut in rounds
or finger shapes, spread apricot, peach, strawberry,
marmalade, quince jam or loganberry preserves
mixed with a little ground Canton ginger or
blanched chopped almonds. Serve on lace doilies as
a dessert with cocoa, chocolate or milk. The puff
paste bouchees should be very small and the mixture should be thick so it does not run.

Boneless Pike Sandwich
Pike, toast, butter, tartar sauce

Handle the same as Fried Smelt No. 1 or No. 2.
Boneless pike makes one of the best fish sandwiches
in the whole category of lenten or Friday dishes.
Use the fillets out of a one pound pike.

Borage Sandwich
Borage, butter, salt-rising bread, lettuce

On thin slices of salt-rising or milk bread spread
a mixture of sweet butter and chopped leaves of
borage. Press on upper slice and garnish with
leaf of lettuce. This is an excellent herb sandwich.
    AUTHOR'S NOTE: It was customary in olden times,
as well as to-day, to communicate flavor to drinks,
sauces and salads by means of different herbs.
Among the first in point of flavor is borage. This
is mentioned as growing in herb garden of John
de Garlande as early as the thirteenth century and
at that time was held in high esteem by doctors,
botanists and health seekers.

Bordelaise Sandwich
Eggs, toast, bordelaise sauce, tomato

Fry or poach two eggs and place on pieces of
toast, cut round or square. Pour over a good
bordelaise sauce and garnish with two fried slices
of tomato.

Bourguignon Sandwich
*White bread, ham, currant jelly, vinegar, curry
powder, potatoes*

Cut a slice of ham from the horse-shoe about
one-fourth inch thick. Fry in a very little bacon
grease until brown. Remove ham and add to the

grease one tablespoon of currant jelly, one teaspoon
of vinegar, a dash of pepper, one-sixth of a teaspoon of curry powder or mustard. Stir well to
dissolve jelley and add ham again. Stew in this
sauce a few seconds. Place ham on square piece
of toast and pour over the sauce. Press on upper
slice, trim and serve at once. Garnish with Long
Branch potatoes.

Horse-shoe cut comes from the thick part of the
leg and starts just above the knuckle.

Braized Ox Joints Jardiniere Sandwich

Ox joints, toast, onions, carrots, brown sauce

Trim meat from braized ox joints when cold and
heat. Place a trimmed slice of toast on a hot plate
and cover with the heated meat. Press on upper
slice. Garnish with small braized onions and baby
carrots, which should completely encircle the sandwich. Serve a light sauce on the side or pour over
sandwich just before serving. Serve at once. This
is a very tasty sandwich and one that is appreciated
whenever served.

The trimmed meat can be placed between two
trimmed pieces of white bread and then toasted in
a patent toaster. The thick sauce or gelatinous substance adhering to flesh when trimmed off of bones
should not be removed. This is the substance which
adds flavor to the sandwich and makes it worth
while.

A dish of slaw or a green salad should accompany this sandwich.

AUTHOR'S NOTE: After trimming all meat from
the bones, the meat as well as the vegetables can be
run thru a grinder and then spread on slices of
toast, then sprinkled with chopped pickles, the top
slice pressed on, trimmed and served. This left-
over stew sandwich if handled properly is a real
revelation in the realm of sandwiches. If some of
the jellied gravy adheres to the vegetables or meat
particles, pass that thru the machine also, for
therein lies the soul or flavor of the dish. And as
Sam Weller the Lesser said, "It's the gravy as
does it."

A postponed stew is best ground up and then
spread on toast. Postponed or left over stew handled
in this manner as a sandwich filling when sprinkled
with chopped pickles makes an appetizing item.

Bread and Butter Sandwich

Cut very thin slices of white, whole wheat or
brown bread and spread with fresh or salted butter,

press on upper slice, trim and cut into desired shapes.

AUTHOR'S NOTE: Slices of white or brown bread spread with butter, then sprinkled with brown sugar, and pressed together, made one of the Laguiappe's doled out by an early New Orleans grocer. This sandwich was often made open type out of a split biscuit sprinkled generously with brown sugar.

Lagnappe, a familiar word to every child in New Orleans years ago, signifies the little present given to purchasers of groceries, provisions, fruit or other goods sold at retail stores. Grocers, especially, sought to rival each other in the attractive quality of their Lagnappe, which consisted of candies, biscuits, fancy cakes, etc. The chief purpose was to attract the children. The little one sent to the grocery never failed to ask for its Lagnappe.

Breakfast Sandwich—I (Open)

Toast, eggs, tomato sauce, tomato, bacon

On two rounds of toast place two trimmed fried or poached eggs. Pour a little tomato sauce around the base of toast and garnish two center sides of eggs with a slice of fried tomato. Curl around each egg a strip of bacon which has been broiled underdone. Serve at once. This makes a real artistic looking sandwich.

Breakfast Sandwich—II

Toast, egg, bacon, tomato, watercress

Fry one egg and three strips of bacon country style and place on slice of toast. Press on upper slice of toast, trim and cut in two diagonally. Serve on platter and garnish with slice of fried tomato and watercress.

"Sunshine in a breakfast room in winter, is almost as glorious a thing as the fire itself. It is a positive tonic; it cheers the spirits, strengthens the body, and promotes digestion."

Breakfast Sandwich (Open)—III

Eggs, toast, ham, chicken, peppers, mushrooms, anchovy butter

On two rounds of toast, spread with anchovy butter, place two poached eggs. Garnish a rich, tomato flavored, brown sauce with finely chopped ham, white meat of chicken, green peppers and mushrooms in equal proportions. Pour a little of this sauce over eggs and serve at once.

Breakfast Sandwich—IV (Open)

*Whole wheat bread, butter, eggs, bacon, cress,
tomato*

On a slice of untrimmed, buttered whole wheat
bread place finely diced bacon and scrambled eggs.
Garnish each end of sandwich with rosettes of cress
and each side with a slice of fried tomato. Serve
hot.

Breast of Chicken Sandwich (Open)

Chicken, butter, toast, sauce, mushrooms

Brown a boned breast of chicken quickly in butter
and then smother in covered pan slowly until done.
Place breast on piece of trimmed toast three and
one-half by two inches, spread with sweet butter.
Make a light sauce out of one teaspoon butter, one
teaspoon flour, one-third cup of cream and one-third
cup of chicken stock. Melt butter and add flour,
stir a few minutes until thoroughly smooth and
flour is well cooked, add hot cream and stock slowly
and incorporate thoroughly. Cook for five minutes,
strain and season. Pour sauce over chicken. Garnish each end of center slice with a second slice of
toast cut in half diagonally. On top of cut pieces
of toast place two fried mushrooms. Serve at once.
See note on breasting out a capon—(Chicken Virginia).

Breast of Guinea Sandwich (Open)

*Toast, butter, guinea hen, currant jelly, wild rice,
bacon, cress*

Arrange in center of platter on a thin slice of
well trimmed, buttered toast a breast of guinea hen,
which has been previously sauted and smothered
in butter until brown and done. Cut a second slice
of toast in half and trim. Garnish one-half with
currant jelly and place at one end of center piece
of toast. Garnish the other half of slice with wild
rice, boiled and then browned. Criss-cross breast
of guinea hen with two strips of broiled bacon.
Garnish with cress. Arrange rice and jelly on toast
in an attractive manner.

Bretonne Sandwich

Onion, eggs, cream, toast, Espagnole sauce

Julienne or chop one small onion and fry in butter
until done. Whip up two eggs with onion and one
tablespoon of cream. Fry mixture lightly like you
would fried eggs over. Place on a thin piece of
freshly made toast, press on upper slice, trim and

cut in two diagonally. Place on a platter in form of
a diamond and pour over sandwich a very thin
Espagnole sauce, highly flavored with tomato.

Bride's Sandwich

*White bread, orange butter, turkey or capon, lettuce,
orange blossoms, beets*

Cut thin heart-shaped pieces of plain white bread
and spread with orange flavored butter or orange
flavored mayonnaise. Cut thin slices of cooked turkey or capon (white meat) with the same heart-
shaped cutter used in cutting bread. Place a slice
of turkey on lower slice of bread and press on upper
slice. Arrange sandwiches in a heart-shaped mound
on a cold plate on leaves of lettuce. Garnish border
with orange or nasturtium blossoms and center with
a mound of shredded lettuce filled with heart and
arrow-shaped pieces of red beets. The hearts and
arrows should be cut with small cutters from thin
slices of strawberry beets.

Bridge Luncheon Sandwich (Open)

*Toast, butter, rye, graham and white bread, caviar,
lettuce, anchovy, cream cheese, mustard, Switzer
cheese, pickle, turkey, gherkin, strawberry
jam, peaches, apricot sauce, olives,
cress, radishes*

On a silver platter or fancy plate, garnished with
lettuce, place a heart, club and diamond shaped
pieces of toast; also a thin spade-shaped piece of
rye bread. Spread the three pieces of toast with
butter and spread the rye bread with French mustard. Cover the heart with caviar, pipe edges with
a little cream cheese and garnish top with a curled
anchovy. Cover the club with cold roast turkey.
Press on upper slice and garnish top with fanned
gherkin. Cover the spade of rye bread with a thin
slice of Switzer cheese. Press on upper slice and
garnish top with a club-shaped piece of pickle.
Spread the diamond with strawberry jam and garnish top with slices of fresh peaches and paint top
surface with apricot sauce. Garnish with cress,
green and ripe olives and lillied radishes. This
sandwich takes time to make and should constitute
the main dish of a luncheon. The filling for sandwiches may be varied to suit taste and the garnish-
ings also. The cutters for making shapes are made
of tin and can be purchased thru wholesale pastry
supply houses. Cut cheese and meat with cutters so
that they are uniform. Do not make the sandwiches
too far ahead nor attempt them for large parties,

unless you have plenty of skilled help. The toast may be of graham or white bread.

Brie Sandwich

Brie cheese, rye bread, lettuce, olives, mustard butter

Spread thin slices of rye bread with a light flavored mustard butter. On lower slice place thin slices of trimmed Brie cheese. Press on upper slice, trim and cut into fingers, squares or diagonally. Serve on lettuce leaves and garnish with green olives.

White bread spread with sweet butter, to which has been added a little bar le duc, makes a tasty item.

Brie cheese cut in very thin slices and to shape, served on round butter wafers, makes a real afternoon treat. Brie cheese is yellowish white and comes in rounds about two inches thick and twelve to fourteen inches in circumference.

Brochette Sandwich (Open)

Chicken livers, bacon, bread crumbs, toast, butter, tomato, cress

Trim chicken, turkey or goose livers in pieces of uniform size. See that the gall is not broken on any and, if it is, trim very carefully or discard. Throw out all livers that are not firm and of good color. Broil several strips of bacon underdone and cut in one and one-half inch pieces. Pierce a piece of liver and then a piece of bacon in center and continue until the needle or skewer is full. Season, roll in bread crumbs and broil slowly or place in pan in oven and cook slowly. When they are cooked (not dried out), toast a slice of plain white, whole wheat or rye bread, butter it and set the skewer of livers in center. Pull out the skewer and pour a little melted butter over. Garnish with a slice of broiled tomato and cress. Skewer may be left in if a fancy one is used. This makes an ideal supper sandwich.

Brocoli and Chicken Sandwich
See Chicken and Brocoli

Broiled Cheese Sandwich
See Cheese Broiled

Broiled Hamburger Sandwich
Round steak, onions, bread, pickle, lettuce

Put round steak thru a food chopper twice. Remove sinews. Season with salt, pepper, and finely

chopped onions or chives. To one-half pound of
steak use one tablespoon of chopped chives or onions.
Press into thin, flat cakes and broil quickly. Place
cake on a thin slice of bread and press on upper
slice. Surround sandwich with small glazed onions
and decorate top with a slice of dill pickle. Serve
on hot plate garnished with lettuce.

Broiled Rump Steak Sandwich (Open)

*White bread, butt sirloin, Bermuda onion, dill
pickle, butter*

On a slice of toasted white bread, buttered, place
a slice of grilled sirloin butt, well seasoned. On
a second slice of white bread, buttered, place two
slices of broiled Bermuda onion. Brush hot butter
over meat and onion. Garnish sides of sandwich
with slices of dill pickle and serve at once.

A steak cut from the inner side of a sirloin butt
is considered by some to be the finest and best flavored piece of meat on the entire steer carcass.

Bruxelloial Sandwich

*Eggs, toast, sprouts, cream sauce, paprika, Parmesan
cheese, crumbs*

Arrange two poached eggs as in Bruxelloise.
Around each egg make a border of cooked brussels
sprouts, cut in half. Pour over sprouts a light cream
sauce, well seasoned. Sprinkle with paprika, bread
crumbs and Parmesan cheese. Brown quickly and
serve.

Bruxelloise Sandwich

Eggs, toast, sprouts, cream sauce, Parmesan cheese

Prepare two rounds of toast. Fry two eggs barely
done and place on toast. Encircle eggs with cooked
brussels sprouts cut in halves. Cover the sprouts
with a light cream sauce. Sprinkle eggs and sprouts
with Parmesan cheese and butter and brown quickly
under a hot salamander.

Bryn Mawr Beach Sandwich

*Bread (rye and white baked together), mayonnaise,
Swiss cheese, chicken, bacon, tomato, cole slaw*

Cut two slices of this bread and spread with
mayonnaise. Press on a slice of Swiss cheese, then
three slices of white meat of chicken and then
2 strips of broiled bacon. Press on upper slice. Cut
in two diagonally and garnish with a hollowed out
tomato filled with cole slaw. Serve on leaves of
lettuce.

Half rye and half white bread dough placed in the same pan and baked makes a fine combination bread.

AUTHOR'S NOTE: "In compelling man to eat to live Nature gives appetite to invite him and pleasure to reward him."

Buerre Noir Sandwich

White bread, eggs, butter, vinegar, parsley, Worcestershire sauce

On two rounds of bread or toast place fried or poached eggs trimmed to shape. Pour over eggs a Buerre Noir sauce or brown butter.

BUERRE NOIR SAUCE: Brown two prints of butter in a small frying pan. Add a few drops of tarragon vinegar or lemon juice and Worcestershire sauce to hot butter and work around and around to incorporate. Pour sauce over the eggs and serve at once. A little catsup added to butter gives it an added tang and better color. Sprinkle eggs with chopped parsley or chives.

Butcher Sandwich (Open)

Bread, butter, mutton, caper sauce, turnips

On slices of toasted or plain bread, buttered, place thin slices of boiled or roasted mutton. Mask mutton with a light caper sauce and garnish side of sandwich with a spoonful of mashed turnips. Serve piping hot.

Buzz Bee Sandwich—I

White bread, honey, lemon, butter

Spread the lower thin slice of white bread with strained white clover honey, to which has been added a little lemon juice, and the upper slice with sweet butter. Lettuce and press together. Cut in fancy shapes and serve. Sandwiches may be garnished with small cubes of comb honey or small nests of cream cheese filled with honey or bar le duc. Honeysuckle, nasturtium or clover blossoms make an attractive garniture.

Buzz Bee Sandwich—II

White bread, honey, bar le duc, cream cheese, butter, cress

On thin slices of bread spread butter and a little strained honey. Press on second slice spread on one side with cream cheese thinned with bar le duc. Then press on third slice spread with butter and insert a leaf of lettuce. Cut in fancy shapes and serve on bed of lettuce. Garnish with nests of cream cheese filled with strained honey. Decorate with cress and clover blossoms. This is an afternoon item. Cut bread very thin; the three slices with filling should not be over half an inch high. Center slice may be brown or whole wheat bread.

Buzz Bee Sandwich—III

White and graham bread, butter, honey, cress, clover and nasturtium blossoms

Cut thin slices of white and graham bread into horseshoe or beehive shapes. Spread the white slice with butter and arrange very thin slices of comb honey on top, or spread with butter and then strained honey. Press on brown slice and arrange hives or sandwiches in a standing position with brown sides out around a clump of sprigs of cress. Place cress in center of platter. Around the sandwiches place clover and nasturtium blossoms. Sandwiches will have a straight bottom and a rounded top. This makes a pretty, novel morsel.

Slices of honey comb must be cut very thin. Honey should not ooze out on plate or platter.

Cadmus Sandwich

Rye bread, mustard, turkey, ham, Swiss cheese, lettuce, ripe and green olives

On a very, very thin slice of rye bread, spread with French mustard, place a very thin sliver of cold white meat of turkey. On turkey place a very thin slice of cold Virginia ham. Now press on a second slice of very thin rye bread spread with French mustard, and press on top of second slice a thin slice of Swiss cheese and an inner leaf of lettuce. Cover with third thin slice of rye bread, press flat and cut in half. Serve on leaves of lettuce. Garnish with ripe and green olives.

Calf's Brain Sandwich (Open)

Brains, chicken stock, vinegar, onion, eggs, cream, toast, cress

Stir together what you wish,
'Twill be an appetizing dish.

Soak a set of calf's brains in cold, salted water for twenty minutes. Drain and place them in enough chicken stock to cover. Add a teaspoon of vinegar and two slices of onion. Boil five to ten minutes until done; drain and wipe. Remove connective skin and blood clots. Cool them. Cut into small pieces. Whip up two eggs and a tablespoon of cream, season with salt and white pepper and mix carefully with the brains. Heat bacon grease in frying pan, then place a number of small spoonfuls of mixture in it to fry. Do not place them too near together. Turn gently and brown on the other side. Serve on small rounds of toast garnished with cress.

One lobe of the cooked set of brains can be whipped up with one egg and a tablespoon of cream, seasoned and scrambled. This can be used as a filling for a toasted sandwich and garnished with bacon, fried tomatoes and cress.

Calf's Brain Combination Sandwich
Calf's brains, slaw, toast, butter

Chop cooked calves' brains, season, and add an equal amount of finely chopped cold slaw. Spread mixture on thin slice of buttered toast, press on upper slice, trim and cut into desired shapes.

Calf's Head Sandwich
Calf's head, vinaigrette, mayonnaise, toast

Boil calf's head or feet and allow to cool. Put thru a grinder or chop real fine. Add enough finely chopped vinaigrette sauce garnish to calf's head to flavor, season, spread mayonnaise and then mixture on thin slices of toast. Trim and cut into desired shapes.

Camembert Cheese Sandwich
Butter-crackers, Camembert cheese, lettuce

Toast small, round butter-crackers and spread with soft Camembert cheese. Arrange on leaves of lettuce. Camembert to be good should be just soft enough to run. Camembert served on very thin slices of French rye bread, untrimmed, makes a very tasty item. These are open style sandwiches. A very small Bar le Duc or Tart Jelly sandwich may be served as an accompaniment with this tasty morsel if desired. Serve as quickly as made. It is an excellent item for a late supper party.

Cheese is supposed to be extremely hard to digest, but this is an exploded theory. (See note on "Camembert" and "Bar le Duc.")

NOTE ON CAMEMBERT: As the Camembert penicillium mold is essential to the manufacture of Camemberts, and as they do not grow in this part of the world, it was necessary to establish culture in our factories. The originals of the cultures being molds taken from imported Camembert. The special cultures are added to the first batch of cheeses, before salting, and if temperature, humidity, and other conditions are suitable and are kept so, the molds will not only do their work in the cheese to which they have been added, but their spores will so plentifully pervade the factory that, unaided and undirected, they will impregnate all future batches. Great skill is required to manufacture Camembert cheese, whether the result of exact methods based on scientific research, or of long practice based on experienc of generations. It requires for the regular repeated production of a certain required flavor and consistence, several forms of microscopic life, whose correct balance must be maintained. In Camembert, three chief biological factors are lactic acid bacteria, the omnipresent milk mold, and a foreign penicillium mold (the penicillium genus includes the blue-green bread mold.) If the lactic acid bacteria are permitted to develop in too great numbers before the curding, a true Camembert becomes impossible. If the milk mold overcrowds the penicillium the correct consistence will not be obtained. If the penicillium overcrowds, the milk mold consistence may be good, but flavor will be lacking. Micro-organisms are necessary for the production of special types of cheese — numerous variations of style and flavor, and it is flavor, when all is said and done, that wins the many millions of people over to a certain article. Flavor creates the demand and flavor makes a market.

Cannibal Sandwich
See Raw Beef—II

Canton Ginger Sandwich
Cream cheese, cream, Canton ginger, almonds, lemon juice, toast, lettuce, cress

Thin down three ounces of cream cheese with raw cream and mix in one ounce of finely chopped Canton ginger, two ounces of finely chopped blanched almonds, one teaspoon lemon juice, one-sixth teaspoon salt and one-sixth teaspoon paprika. Spread mixture on thin slices of freshly made toast or plain bread and press on upper slice. Trim, cut into desired shapes and serve on leaves of lettuce. Garnish with cress. Mix lemon juice in last.

In case mixture is too thin place in ice-box and thoroughly chill, or add additional cheese.

Cape Riche Sandwich (Open)
Toast, eggs, lobster, tomato sauce

On round pieces of toast place two fried or poached eggs. Add a few pieces of sliced cold boiled lobster to a good hot tomato sauce and pour over the eggs. Serve hot.

Capital Sandwich (Open)

Toast, anchovy butter, eggs, puree of spinach, cream

On rounds of toast, spread with anchovy butter, place two poached eggs. Pour a rich, well seasoned puree of spinach, mixed with raw cream, over the eggs. Serve hot and at once.

Capon Sandwich I

White bread, butter, capon, lettuce

On thin slices of buttered white bread, plain or toasted, place thin slices of capon, boiled or roasted. Lettuce bread and press on upper slice. Cut into hearts, fingers, rounds, diamonds, squares, ovals, clubs or leaves. Serve on leaves of lettuce and garnish with pimolas, olives, gherkins, hard-boiled eggs, stuffed or curled celery, potato chips, lilied radishes, etc. Sandwiches may be spread with mayonnaise, nut, sweet, lemon, cranberry, apple or aromatic butter.

Capon Sandwich II (Open)

Capon, goose liver, egg, anchovy paste, butter, tongue, aspic, toast, lettuce

Pound together two ounces of boiled white meat of capon and a like amount of cooked goose liver, then rub thru a fine sieve. Add one-third teaspoon of anchovy paste and one ounce of butter to the above mixture, season and spread on thin slices of freshly made toast cut in ovals. Garnish top center with a slice of hard boiled egg and criss-cross top with julienned strips of smoked ox tongue. Coat with aspic, chill and serve on bed of lettuce.

Capon Club Sandwich

See Club Capon

Cardinal Sandwich I (Open)

Toast, Lobster paste, eggs, tomato sauce

On rounds of toasted bread, spread with lobster paste, place two poached eggs, well trimmed. Pour over eggs a little tomato sauce. Serve at once.

Cardinal Sandwich II

See Lobster, Cardinal

Caviar Sandwich I (Open)

Caviar (Beluga or Astrakan), white bread, butter,
onions, lettuce, lemon

Spread thin slices of trimmed white bread with
lemon butter. Mix imported caviar with a little
butter and spread on the bread. Garnish edges of
bread with chopped yellow and white of hard-boiled
eggs and finely minced onions, or serve minced
onions on the side. A few drops of onion juice may
be squeezed into the caviar and butter when mixing if raw chopped onions are not desired. If
served on toast cut slice two and one-half inches
square and serve on a leaf of lettuce, or cut into
any fancy shape and garnish with slices of lemon.
Eggs, white and yellow, can be dispensed with if
desired. They are only used for garnish and color.

NOTE ON CAVIAR: The most famous are the Russian sturgeons, particularly the small snooted sterlet,
rarely exceeding three feet in length. This sterlet
is highly prized for its flesh and spawn. The huge
Beluga, Hansen, or white sturgeon will often weigh
as much as a thousand pounds and some have been
known to measure 24 feet in length and weigh a
full ton. A fish of this size will yield as much as
three hundred pounds of spawn or caviar. It is
said that the Beluga is not really old until after
it has passed its second century. In England at one
time the sturgeon was known as the Royal fish and
its consumption was confined to the King's table,
and those who held royal permission to eat it.

Caviar is the salted roe of various fish of the
sturgeon family. Practically all the supply comes
from the rivers of the Caspian and the Black seas.
The finest is that from the Seuruga and Sterlet
species. Fresh caviar, that is mildly salted, for
which only roe in the best condition is suitable, is
salted in the proportion of two to six pounds of
salt to a hundred pounds of roe. It is then drained
and put up in the tin and glass containers. The
mild salting is generally confined to large high
grade roe. The inferior, small sized and off color,
as well as the finest, which is either too far ripened
or too soft, are put up in a ten per cent salt ratio
and repacked in tins for the retail trade. The
eggs or roe vary in size from very small to the size
of a pea. The color is generally black, but may
be shades of grey, green, yellow green, yellow or
a brownish black. The real test is in the flavor and
is as often found in the small as the large, and in
the black as well as any of the other colors. The

grey, yellow and gold are the most rare and, therefore, the most expensive. The Russians consider the
grey and gold the choicest. The Germans favor
the grey, while the Americans the greyish black.
Very little caviar is produced in America.—*From
the Encyclopedia of Food.*

Caviar Sandwich II
Bread, butter, caviar, lemon and onion juice

On thinly sliced trimmed white bread (buttered),
spread enough Beluga or Astrakan caviar to completely cover. Caviar should be mixed with just a
few drops each of lemon juice and onion juice. Serve
these sandwiches or canapes on a lettuced platter with
a few finely minced onions placed in a hollowed out
red ripe small tomato. The caviar should be spread
thin and edges can be garnished with finely chopped
onions if desired. Caviar is often served on an
illuminated masterpiece of ice. A freshly opened
can of Beluga caviar is placed in center of ice; a
small cut glass sauce dish, garnished with inner
leaves of lettuce and filled with finely minced onions,
is placed on one side of caviar while a similar dish
of lemons cut in eighths is placed on the other. (See
Caviar Canape Trimalchio.)

C. C. and L. Sandwich (Open)
*Cabbage, cucumbers, lettuce, mayonnaise, white
bread, hard-boiled eggs, pimolas, red beets*

Chop very fine one-half cup each of raw cabbage,
squeezed cucumbers and lettuce. Mix separately
with enough mayonnaise to bind. Arrange in divisions on a trimmed slice of white bread in order
named. Cut a second slice of trimmed white bread
in four diagonally and spread with mayonnaise.
Arrange one-fourth slice at either end of center
slice. Garnish end slices with a slice of hard-boiled
egg and slices of pimola. Garnish the two opposite
sides with shredded lettuce mixed with chopped
red beets and mayonnaise.

This makes an attractive, unusual and healthful
item.

Celery Roll
See Sandwiches Rolled
*Inner stalks celery, Roquefort cheese, bread, butter,
lettuce, olives*

Stuff small inner stalks of celery with Roquefort
cheese (paste made of Roquefort cheese and raw
cream). Cut freshly made bread very thin and

spread with creamed butter. Roll the thin celery stalk into a cigarette-shaped sandwich. The bread should not break and the celery top of green leaf should protrude beyond the end. Place the rolled sandwiches in a damp napkin to hold in place. Allow to remain in icebox under a slight pressure for two or three hours. Tie with baby ribbon and serve on lettuce leaves garnished with olives.

A number of these tiny tid-bits can be placed in an upright position in the center of a platter and various other kinds of assorted fancy sandwiches piled around to hold them in place. These little pompomed rolls will give platter or plate a unique appearance. The stem with leaf of nasturtium, or flower, or both, and handled in the same way using a cheese spread or filling will bring forth favorable comments.

NOTE: Wrap a freshly baked loaf of bread in a damp towel and place in ice box for at least two hours. Pullman toast or any fine textured white bread is the bread to use. Use a very thin and very sharp knife for cutting. If the bread is not wide enough to give you a decent roll cut the bread lengthwise and then into proper lengths. Have rolls uniform in size, trimmed well and not too large in length or circumference.

In making the celery roll the bread can be spread with a creamed Roquefort mixture and very thin strips of celery rolled in center of bread, allowing the leafy end of celery to be retained on strip. The small inner pieces if too wide can be trimmed to proper sizes.

Charles Lamb Sandwich (Barbecued)

Bread, butter, barbecued pork, fried apple, lettuce

On plain or toasted white or whole wheat bread, spread with butter, place thin slices of barbecued loin of pork. Season with salt and lay a slice or two of fried apple on top. Press on upper slice and trim. Cut in half diagonally and serve on leaves of lettuce.

Hot roast pork can be handled the same way, spreading apple sauce on bread or serving apple sauce or small baked apple on side of sandwich as a garnish.

Chaud et Froid Sandwich (Open)

Oysters, toast, anchovy butter, turkey, lettuce, bacon

Dry one dozen New York counts and cut away the hard part. Bread the soft part and fry brown. Spread rounds of toast with a light flavored anchovy

butter and on it place a round of white meat of
turkey, then on turkey place the soft part or tenderloin of oyster, fried. Arrange at least three or four
rounds of sandwiches on a leaf of lettuce. Garnish
sides of sandwich with small gherkins and two
strips of broiled or curled bacon. Serve at once.
The toast should be warm and the oysters hot. The
tenderloin of oyster can be split nearly in half, then
breaded and fried, which makes a better appearing
open sandwich. This sandwich may be used as
a hot hors d'œuvre.

Chauffeur Sandwich
Ham, bacon, eggs, toast, slaw, lettuce, tomato

Chop or mince one slice of boiled ham and two
strips of broiled bacon. Whip ham and bacon into
two eggs and fry in bacon grease. Turn over and
place on toast. Garnish with slaw, lettuce and
tomato. Serve hot.

Cheddar Cheese Sandwich
Cheese, bread, butter, lettuce

On buttered and lettuced slices of rye or whole
wheat bread place thin slices of Cheddar cheese.
Press on upper slices, trim and cut in desired shape
or arrange on small thin slices of fanciful cuts of
toast or crackers and place under the broiler to
brown. Serve immediately.

AUTHOR'S NOTE: A slice of old American, Herkimer, Cheddar or Stilton cheese with a piece of good
apple pie is a feast for the gods. Cheddar cheese
is neither sweet or overly acid, is of a firm, flaky
texture and has an agreeable nutty flavor. The
cheese is white or of a yellowish tinge and in the
ripening the common lactic acid bacteria are assisted
by the B. Bulgaricus group, both types friendly to
man and do much in the way of freeing the colon
of the B. Welchii, B. Coli, etc. The latter two set
up toxins which are picked up in the blood stream
and multiply rapidly when eliminations are not
regular.

Cheese Sandwiches
See also

Brie Cheese
Camembert Cheese
Cheddar Cheese
Club Cheese
Cottage Cheese
Cress and Cheese
Edam Cheese

Herkimer Cheese
Limburger Cheese
Liederkranz Cheese
Parmesan Cheese
Salami and Cheese
Swiss Cheese
Toasted Cheese

Cheese Sandwich Broiled (Open)
Toast, ham, tomato, cheese

Toast a trimmed slice of bread on one side. Cover the untoasted side with a thin slice of boiled ham or three strips of broiled bacon. Cover ham or bacon with a thick slice of raw, peeled, ripe tomato and season. Cover tomato with chopped old English cheese. Place under hot broiler to melt cheese. Serve hot and at once. This makes a very good open sandwich.

Cheese Combination Sandwich—I
Dates, almonds, American cheese

One ounce finely ground black dates, one ounce finely ground or chopped almonds, one ounce finely ground American cheese. Add enough lemon juice to the above to make it the right consistency to spread. This combination makes a real filling for small, fancy sandwiches.

Cheese Combination Sandwich—II
Tomato, cottage cheese, lettuce, chives

Two ounces chopped connective tissue tomato (without seeds or juice), two ounces cottage cheese, one ounce chopped lettuce, one tablespoon chopped chives, one tablespoon mayonnaise, salt. This makes a real, spring sandwich filling.

Cheese Combination Sandwich—III (Open)
American cheese, tomato, bacon, toast

Two ounces ground American cheese, one ounce chopped connective tissue tomato (no seeds or juice), two strips of broiled bacon, chopped. Mix and spread on rounds or squares of toast. Season, place under broiler and brown. This makes an ideal petit sandwich.

Cheese and Ham Sandwich
Rye bread, mustard, Swiss cheese, chicken, ham, lettuce, mayonnaise

On a very thin slice of rye bread, spread with French mustard, place a very thin slice of white meat of chicken, and on chicken an extremely fine sliver of Westphalian or Virginia ham and Swiss cheese. Press on upper slice and cut sandwich in two. The entire height of the sandwich should not be more than one-half inch. Garnish with lettuce.

Cheese, Nut and Olive Relish Sandwich

Bread, cream cheese, olive relish, nuts

Spread one thin slice of rye or plain white bread with thinned down cream cheese, and the second slice with olive relish. Over the relish sprinkle ground nuts and press both slices together. Trim and cut into desired shapes.

The olive relish may be bought at any first class grocery house. It is put up in small glass jars.

Chef's Special Sandwich—I (Open)

Toast, butter, turkey, Supreme sauce, cheese

On two toasted slices of white bread, spread with butter, place enough boiled and sliced white meat of turkey to cover. Pour over a rich, well seasoned sauce made out of turkey stock, cream, thickened with a roux made of butter and flour. The sauce should not be too heavy. Sprinkle the top of sauce with grated Cheddar or Herkimer cheese. Brown under broiler and serve at once. Slices of toast should be trimmed and placed lengthwise on platter.

Chef's Special Sandwich—II (Open)

Toast, turkey, butter, mushrooms, cream sauce, cheese, parsley

On two pieces of toast, trimmed and buttered, arrange slices of the white meat of roast turkey, and thin slices of fried mushrooms. Over turkey pour a rich cream sauce, not too thin. Sprinkle with Parmesan or Cheddar cheese and a little butter. Brown under a hot broiler. Garnish with parsley and serve at once. This is an excellent sandwich and one that is always liked, if once tried.

Cherry Tomato Sandwich

Toast, bacon, tomato, mayonnaise, lettuce, julienne potatoes

Spread a thin slice of toast with broiled bacon butter. Press on one or two slices of red ripe, peeled tomato, or enough slices of cherry tomato to cover. Press on upper slice of toast spread with mayonnaise and cut in two diagonally. Garnish with lettuce and julienne potatoes. This makes a real tasty treat.

Chesapeake Sandwich

Toast, butter, oysters, bacon, lettuce, cress, dill pickles, chili sauce

Spread a slice of toast with butter and place two or three fried Counts on it. (Do not bread oysters, only dredge them in seasoned flour.) Sprinkle oysters

with chopped broiled bacon, then press on leaf of
lettuce and the upper slice. Trim and cut in half
diagonally. Serve on hot plate garnished with cress
or lettuce and slices of dill pickle. Place pickle on
top of sandwich. Serve a little chili sauce on
the side.

Chestnut Combination Sandwich
*Chestnuts, raisins, lemon juice, mayonnaise, white
bread, lettuce, marshmallows*

Mash or pound in a mortar eighteen roasted chestnuts (not too brown). Mix in one-fourth cup of
seedless raisins, chopped fine, and one tablespoon of
lemon juice. Add enough mayonnaise to reduce to
a consistency to spread. Spread mixture on thin
slices of white bread, cover with a thin layer of
shredded lettuce and press on upper slice. Trim and
cut into desired shapes. Serve garnished with toasted
marshmallows. Use the small, sweet chestnuts.
Raisins may be omitted and cream cheese and bar
le duc added. Chopped chestnuts, butter, lettuce, and
lemon juice make a good combination.

Chicago 1933 Sandwich
*Rye bread, celery, Roquefort cheese, butter, chives,
ripe olives, gherkins, lettuce*

On thin slices of toasted rye bread spread a
mixture made of one-third cup of finely chopped
hearts of celery, two-thirds cup of Roquefort cheese
(mashed to a paste), two ounces of creamed butter,
one tablespoon of chopped chives and one-fourth
teaspoon of paprika. Place the two slices on lettuce,
open faced, and garnish with ripe olives and gherkin. The cheese and celery mixture is enough for
six sandwiches.—*E. E. Amiet, chef, Palmer House,
Chicago.*

Chicken Sandwich—I
White bread, butter, chicken, lettuce

Boiled or roasted chicken may be used. The
roasted gives a more delicious flavored sandwich;
the boiled, a more economical and a better appearing sandwich. Cut thin slices of white meat and
place on thinly cut slices of white bread spread with
butter or mayonnaise. Press on leaf of lettuce and
upper slice. Cut into hearts, fingers, rounds, diamonds, squares, ovals, clubs or leaves. Serve on
leaves of lettuce and garnish with pimolas, olives,
gherkins, hard-boiled eggs, stuffed or curled celery,
potato chips or lillied radishes. Sandwiches can be
spread with mayonnaise, nut, sweet, lemon, cran-

berry, apple or aromatic butter. The sandwiches can be spread with the various butters and served separately or arranged artistically on a large platter. The cutting of these sandwiches into fancy shapes gives considerable scraps from the chicken. Scraps should be ground and mixed with mayonnaise; this will give an additional item to the varied sandwich dish. When lettuce is used in sandwiches with mayonnaise it should be placed in them at the latest possible moment as the vinegar from the mayonnaise dissolves the connective tissue and the salt draws out the moisture, making the lettuce a mass of unsightly pulp.

Chicken Sandwich—II
Toast, chicken paste, butter, egg, cream sauce, asparagus tips

On a round of toast spread a paste of white meat of chicken, well seasoned. Sprinkle with butter, paprika and brown quickly. Place trimmed poached egg in center of paste and place toast and egg on small plate. Pour a well seasoned light cream sauce, garnished with diced asparagus tips, over egg and serve at once.

Use boiled white meat of fowl cut fine, then pounded to a paste, seasoned and moistened with a little 40% cream. Use only the tips of the asparagus cut not over one half inch in length.

Chicken Sandwich III
See Breast of Chicken

Chicken and Almond Sandwich (Open)
Chicken, almonds, mayonnaise, toast, butter, pickles, lettuce

Mince one-fourth cup of white meat of chicken, (cooked) and mix it with one-fourth cup of skinned, chopped and blanched almonds. Add just enough mayonnaise to bind, season and spread on thin slices of buttered toast. Garnish border of sandwich with thin slices of burr pickles. Underline sandwich with lettuce, or sprinkle chicken mixture with chopped pickles. Press on upper slice, trim and serve on leaves of lettuce.

Chicken au Gratin Sandwich (Open)
Chicken, cream, toast, American cheese, butter

Grind the scraps of white meat of chicken, turkey or capon and season with a little salt. Moisten with raw cream; spread enough on a slice of toasted, trimmed white bread to cover. Sprinkle

with American cheese and melted butter. Brown
under salamander on small silver platter or in hot
oven. Serve immediately.

This sandwich, with a little celery salad, a few
olives and a glass of milk, makes an ideal luncheon.

Chicken and Brocoli Sandwich

Brocoli, chicken, toast, cream sauce, cheese, butter

Chop one cup of boiled brocoli and drain off surplus moisture. Mix with enough mortared white
meat of chicken to make a good mixture. Spread
a slice of buttered toast with mixture. Season, press
on upper slice, trim and pour over the top a good
cream sauce. Sprinkle the sauce with grated cheese.
Brown quickly· under a hot broiler and serve at
once. This makes an excellent item.

Chopped, cooked oysters and spinach, or chicken
and spinach, highly seasoned and handled the same
way make excellent combinations.

AUTHOR'S NOTE: The first brewers of tea were
often sorely perplexed with the preparation of the
new mystery. It is recorded that a party of ladies
who sat down to the first pound of tea that came
into Penrith, England, which was sent as a present,
and without directions how to use it, that they
boiled the whole at once in a bottle, and sat down
to eat the leaves with butter and salt, and they won-
dered how any person could like such a diet.

This was the same opinion many people around
Chicago had about brocoli when it was first intro-
duced. The cooks did not peel it before cooking and
in consequence it was a mass of tough fibrous matter
and mush which was thoroly unpalatable. Brocoli,
when handled right, (is, in my opinion), the finest
of all in the vegetable kingdom.

Chicken Chutney Sandwich (Open)

*Chicken, celery, mayonnaise, chutney sauce, white
bread, butter, hard-boiled egg, pimolas,
pimentoes, lettuce, gherkins*

Mix two-thirds cup of finely ground white meat
of chicken with one-third cup of finely chopped
white part of celery. Add enough mayonnaise
base No. 3 to bind, and one teaspoon of English
chutney sauce. Trim and butter two slices of plain
white bread. Cut one slice in four, diagonally, and
arrange one triangle at each side of the second slice.
Second slice to be placed whole in center of dish.
Spread with chicken mixture, garnish triangles with
slices of hard-boiled eggs, pimolas, chopped pimen-

toes, and gherkins. Pimentoes and gherkins are to be chopped separately and mixed with mayonnaise then spread on two triangles. The slices of hard-boiled eggs and slices of pimolas are to be arranged artistically on the opposite two toasted triangles.

Chicken Combination Sandwich
Chicken, tongue, ham, capers, mayonnaise, bread, lettuce

Mix equal amounts of ground white meat of chicken, boiled ox-tongue, boiled sugar cured ham with enough capers to flavor. Add just enough mayonnaise to bind. Spread on thin slices of bread, press on leaf of lettuce and upper slice. Trim and cut into desired shapes.

Chicken, Curried
See Sliced Curried Chicken

Chicken and Grape Sandwich
Toast, chicken, grapes, mayonnaise, lettuce, butter

On slices of toasted white or whole wheat bread, buttered and then spread with mayonnaise, arrange thin slices of white meat of chicken, seasoned. On top of chicken place thin slices of seeded green grapes or Thompson seedless grapes. Press on a leaf of lettuce and then the upper slice. Trim, cut into desired shapes and serve on leaves of lettuce. Garnish with a tiny bunch of Thompson seedless grapes tied with a colored baby ribbon. Grapes may be chopped and sprinkled over the chicken, if desired, or mixed with mayonnaise and spread on toast.

Grapes contain from 12 to 26% grape sugar, 1 to 3% nitrogenous substances, potassium and other salts, also malic, citric and tartric acids.

Chicken Hachee Sandwich
Chicken, gherkins, celery, mayonnaise, toast

Mix one-half cup of finely chopped white meat of chicken, three finely chopped, small, sweet gherkins with one-third cup of finely chopped white stalks of celery. Bind together with mayonnaise. Spread mixture on thin slices of toast, trim and cut into desired shape. This makes an excellent, tasty item. Serve on leaves of lettuce.

Chicken, Ham, and Tongue Sandwich
Chicken, boiled ham, tongue, mayonnaise, white bread, lettuce, cress, pickles

Chop fine one-half cup of white meat of boiled

chicken, one-fourth cup of boiled ham and one-
fourth cup of boiled smoked ox-tongue. Bind together with mayonnaise and spread on thin slices
of white bread. Press on leaf of lettuce and upper
slice. Cut into desired shapes and serve on bed
of cress. Garnish with burr pickles.

Chicken Hash au Gratin Sandwich

Chicken hash, toast, bread crumbs, butter, potatoes,
cress

Handle as in Chicken a la King. Place hash in
center of toast, sprinkle with bread crumbs and
butter and brown quickly under broiler. Serve at
once. Garnish with julienned potatoes and cress.

Chicken a la King Sandwich (Open)

Toast, chicken a la King, Parmesan cheese, mush-
rooms, potatoes, cress, butter

Cut a slice of bread one and one-fourth inches
thick, and carve out center artistically. Spread
bread with soft butter and brown in hot oven. Place
toasted bread on plate or platter and fill center with
chicken a la King. Sprinkle top with Parmesan
cheese mixed with paprika and brown under a hot
broiler. Garnish ends of sandwich with two fluted
mushrooms and the sides with julienned potatoes.
(Potatoes should be drained, floured lightly and
dipped in whipped egg, then put in hot grease
and fried brown). Place a rosette of cress at either
end.

Chicken chop suey can be handled in the same
manner and the noodles placed on side of toast
instead of potatoes. This makes an attractive way
to serve these two items.

In cutting bread for the toast or shell do not cut
thru to the bottom. Leave one half inch walls and
bottom intact.

RECIPE, CHICKEN A LA KING: (Chicken, mushrooms, green peppers, cream): Cut in large cubes
the white meat of a three-pound chicken, boiled.
Heat in small sauce pan with a little butter. Add
enough double cream to cover chicken and simmer
for a few minutes. Season with salt and a little
cayenne. Add one green pepper and three large
mushrooms which have been diced and previously
sauted in butter. Mix and heat all together and
serve as directed.

If a heavy cream is not used, a little cream sauce
should be added.

Chicken Legs, Creole, Sandwich
Chicken leg, butter, Creole sauce, toast

Flour, season and saute one leg of a two-pound fryer until brown on both sides. Remove pan to the back part of the range, add a little stock and cover it, allowing chicken to simmer gently for about ten minutes. Julienne one small onion, one small green pepper, one good sized mushroom and one half ounce of ham. Saute these in a little butter for a few minutes and add them to a No. 1 can of the best tomatoes. Bring tomatoes to a boil, add chicken and simmer down to half, under cover. Season and serve one leg on two toasted slices of trimmed bread. Pour sauce over it and serve at once. Do not cook the chicken too much; in case the chicken is extremely tender, remove legs and reduce the sauce, then just before serving place the leg back in the pan for a few minutes to simmer and moisten. This makes enough sauce for two or three sandwiches. A spoon of mashed potatoes on side of sandwich will help sell the dish.

AUTHOR'S NOTE: In hotels where the breast of chicken is always in demand, the legs can be disposed of in the sandwich Creole, giving profit to hotel, pleasure and satisfaction to the guest.

Chicken Livers Sandwich (Open)
Chicken livers, butter, bacon, toast, onions, tomato

Cut up one dozen chicken livers and cook in butter slowly until done. Cut up four slices of broiled bacon and mix hot livers with them. On rounds or squares of toast, spread with fried onions, arrange livers and bacon. Garnish with two slices of fried tomato and surround toast with a little hot, well seasoned tomato sauce. Serve hot and at once.

Chicken livers, like boiled eggs, to be at their best should be just poached or simmered until heated thru and set. The liver becomes tough and rubbery when cooked for a long time or with intense heat. The same thing happens in cooking eggs.

Chicken and Mushroom Sandwich (Open)
Toast, chicken paste, mushrooms, American cheese, bacon, cress, pickles

Spread two rounds of toast with a paste made of seasoned scraps of white meat of chicken. Cover paste with two large fried mushrooms. Sprinkle mushrooms liberally with good American cheese and brown under a hot broiler. Garnish with bacon, cress and pickles. Serve at once.

Cooked white meat of chicken should be run thru a fine grinder, then pounded to a paste and seasoned well. Broiled ham, chopped mushrooms and American cheese handled as above make a fine combination.

Chicken Pie or Pasty Sandwich
Chicken sauce, pie crust, mashed potatoes,
parsley

On a 5-inch round of pie crust, place several small slices of boiled fowl, pour over fowl a well-made and seasoned fricasse sauce. Garnish with glazed boiling onions, peas, carrots, beans or cauliflower, a spoon of snow or mashed potatoes, and a sprigs of parsley. Serve hot and at once. The pie crust must be short, baked well done and one-fourth inch thick. This pastry sandwich offering is in a class by itself. A fortune can be made on a dish of this kind if handled right and made uniformly according to recipe at all times.

Chicken Ritz Sandwich (Open)
Chicken, butter, cream, toast

Grind white meat of cooked chicken or turkey and season. Place in a small saute pan with a little butter and heat, adding enough raw cream to moisten. Cook about five minutes. Spread on toast, sprinkle with paprika and butter, brown under a hot broiler. Serve at once. This makes a very delicious and tasty item.

Chicken Salad Finger Sandwiches
Chicken salad, capers, pimentoes, hard-boiled egg
yolks, lettuce

Put one cup of chicken salad thru a fine grinder, then cut six finger rolls in half lengthwise. Rolls to be six inches long, one and one-half inches high and three-fourths of an inch wide. Remove crumb and fill lower part with chicken salad, garnish top of salad with four capers placed equidistant apart, surround capers with a strip of red pepper and place a round slice of hard boiled egg yolk in center. Press on upper slice and serve on leaves of lettuce. Garnish with olives.

AUTHOR'S NOTE: A sandwich in the hands of a real cook becomes a masterpiece—in the hands of a plodder a fizzle. The silver platter does not enhance the appearance of an ill-made sandwich; but a sandwich when properly made and garnished does bring out the beauty of the platter and completes the picture.

Splendor of service cannot compensate for inferior or badly cooked food and the finest of cookery is spoiled by inferior service. Dumas said that indifference to cooking indicates neither refinement, intellect nor social eminence.

Chicken Salad Sandwich Molded (Open)

Chicken salad, white bread, slaw, mayonnaise, green olives, radishes, cress, tomato

Place a slice of molded chicken salad in center of two slices of thin white bread. Garnish one end with a little slaw and opposite end with mayonnaise in case. Garnish opposite sides with green olives, radishes, cress, and top of salad with a slice of tomato.

(See recipe for Molded Chicken Salad or Salad en Aspic.)

Chicken Shortcake

Biscuit, chicken, cream sauce, mashed potatoes

On the lower half of a rich baking powder biscuit place diced or sliced creamed chicken well seasoned. Cover with upper half and pour a rich cream sauce over the top. Garnish with a spoonful of snow potatoes and serve at once. As an accompaniment to this sandwich serve a simple salad. It will help to neutralize the acids generated, thereby adding to the pleasures of dining. Sweetbreads, capon, turkey, etc., can be handled in the same way. A few mushrooms or peas added to sauce gives additional life, color and flavor. Chicken may be served on cornbread, Johnny cake, Southern style. Biscuits should be at least 3 inches in diameter.

Chicken Sandwich, Toasted

See Toasted Chicken

Chicken Virginia Sandwich (Open)

Chicken, Virginia ham, mushrooms, toast, butter, Supreme sauce

Bone and skin a breast of a two-pound spring chicken. Turn the skinless side down in frying pan and brown in butter. When brown turn over, add a little stock and smother in covered pan on back of range for ten minutes to moisten and finish. Broil a slice of Virginia ham lightly and place on a slice of trimmed and buttered toast. Place the breast of chicken on top of ham and a broiled mushroom on top of chicken. Place a second slice of toast, cut in half diagonally, one-half at either side of first slice and pour a little Supreme sauce over all. Serve at once.

This makes a real chafing dish item and a Sunday night treat. To bone a breast of chicken, take a small, sharp pointed knife and follow breast and rib bones from the point of articulation with wing down the entire breast, following the boney structure of the body until entire breast is severed. Leave the second section of wing bone on.

Chiffonade Sandwich

Toast, butter, chicory, beets, hard-boiled eggs, tomatoes, chives, mayonnaise

Spread a slice of toasted white, whole wheat or graham bread with butter. Prepare a mixture of equal amounts of chopped chicory, baked beets, yolks of hard-boiled eggs and connective tissue of raw tomatoes. Sprinkle with chopped chives and add enough mayonnaise to bind. Spread mixture on toast, press on upper slice and cut diagonally. Serve with a glass of milk.

This is the kind of sandwich that will help you maintain an alkali reserve in your blood, which is essential to health.

Chipped Beef Sandwich—I

Toast, creamed chipped beef, bread crumbs, butter, cheese

Cover one piece of toast with creamed chipped beef. Sprinkle with bread crumbs, butter, cheese, and brown under a quick broiler or handle like Chicken a la King or Chef's Special.

Chipped Beef Sandwich—II

Chipped beef, butter, cream, toast

Freshen in cold water three ounces of chipped beef; drain and dry. Place one ounce of butter in a small sauce pan, add the beef and toss around until thoroughly heated, then add two ounces of cream and reduce to half. Arrange a thin slice of trimmed toast on a platter and lift beef out with a fork and place on toast. Press on upper slice, cut in two diagonally and thicken heated cream and pour over the top. Serve at once.

Beef may be freshened, chopped and mixed with scrambled eggs, then used as a filling.

One tablespoon of finely minced onion can be added to the butter in the first recipe and sauted until done. Then add a tablespoon of flour and mix well and then three ounces of cream to make a cream sauce. Add the beef last, toss and mix, allow to simmer a few minutes, then pour over the toast. If too thick, thin down with additional cream. Serve at once.

Chipped Beef Sandwich, Marinated

Chipped beef, French dressing, mayonnaise, radishes, lettuce, bread, butter

Freshen chipped beef and dry, then marinate it for several hours in a French Dressing Base No. 5. Grind up beef and squeeze out surplus moisture. Mix with just enough mayonnaise to bind and add a few chopped radishes. Spread white or whole wheat bread with butter and then with beef mixture. Press on upper slice and cut into desired shapes. Serve on leaves of lettuce.

Chutney Sandwich

Butter, cream cheese, chutney, bread, lettuce

Work together one tablespoon each of butter, cream cheese and Major Grey's chutney (chopped). Spread mixture on thin slices of toast or plain bread. Press on upper slice, cut in fancy shape and underline with doily on bed of lettuce. The above recipe will make two sandwiches. Mayonnaise may be used in place of butter and chopped almonds or olives may be added for variety.

Cinara Sandwich

Artichoke tubers, mayonnaise, lettuce, bread

Peel and chop very finely one-half cup of artichoke tubers; add enough mayonnaise to bind. Spread thin slices of white bread with butter, then the artichoke and mayonnaise mixture, press on a leaf of lettuce and upper slice. Trim and cut into desired shapes. An excellent, nutty flavored filling. Season tubers with salt. Tubers to be kept in cold water when peeled to keep them from turning black.

Club Sandwich

See also

Athletic Club   Golf Club
Double Deck   Shrimp Club

Club Sandwich—I

Toast, butter, mayonnaise, turkey, bacon, lettuce, tomato, slaw, olive

Spread a slice of freshly made toast with butter and then with mayonnaise, cover with white meat of turkey or chicken. Season. Press on two thin strips of broiled bacon, a leaf of lettuce, then the upper slice. Trim and cut in half diagonally. Arrange like a diamond, and garnish with a slice of tomato, a little slaw and a green olive or any other relish to suit the individual taste.

Club Sandwich—II

Toast, butter, mayonnaise, turkey, tomato, bacon, lettuce, olives, slaw

Spread freshly made toast with butter and then mayonnaise. Cover toast with thin sliced white meat of chicken or turkey. Butter a second slice on both sides and press on top of turkey. Cover second slice with thinly sliced peeled tomato, two strips of bacon and lettuce leaf. Cover with a third slice spread with mayonnaise. Trim and cut in half diagonally, garnish with green olives and slaw.

Slaw to be well drained and then placed on leaves of lettuce in basket form so that any surplus moisture that might run out will not soften or spoil toast.

Club Capon Sandwich

Toast, mayonnaise, capon, bacon, lettuce, tomato

Cover with thinly sliced white meat of capon two slices of white bread, toasted and spread with mayonnaise. Lay two strips of freshly broiled bacon on top of fowl, cover with inner leaf of lettuce and press on upper slice of toast. Trim off crust and cut in two diagonally. Underline with lettuce leaves and serve on silver platter. Garnish with half of a peeled, hollowed-out very small tomato, filled with lemon flavored mayonnaise, base No. 3, and lettuce.

Club Cheese Sandwich

Club cheese, cream, horseradish, butter, rye bread, lettuce, mustard, dill pickle

Thin down Club cheese with raw cream and add a little grated horseradish. Spread on thin slices of buttered rye or white bread. Press on a leaf of lettuce and upper slice. Cut into desired shapes.

Club cheese thinned down with cream and a little German mustard added, then sprinkled with chopped dill pickles, makes a unique combination.

AUTHOR'S NOTE: Sandwiches washed down hurriedly at a quick lunch counter with milk, coffee, water and what not will produce, before long, an entirely new form of dyspeptic for which our modern Aescheluses will give a new name. However, the sandwich is almost limitless in form; and if eaten slowly in combination with a leafy salad, a glass of milk or pure water will make an ideal, healthful luncheon.

Club Sandwich, Edgewater Beach

Toast, butter, mayonnaise, turkey, bacon, lettuce, olive, tomatoes, gherkin, slaw, cress

Spread a slice of freshly made toast with butter and then mayonnaise. Cover with sliced white meat of turkey or chicken. Press on two thin strips of broiled bacon, a leaf of lettuce, then the upper slice. Butter and spread with mayonnaise the top of this second slice. Place a second layer with the same ingredients as used for the first. Press on top slice. Garnish with sliced tomato, cress, slaw, gherkin, and olive. This sandwich is simply a doubled deck No. 1 Club Sandwich. Serve mayonnaise on the side.

Club Swiss Sandwich

Toast, butter, mustard, Swiss cheese, tomato, bacon, lettuce

On a thin slice of toast, spread with made mustard and butter, place a thin slice of Swiss cheese. On cheese place a thin slice of peeled tomato and on top of tomato place two strips of broiled bacon. Press on upper piece of toast and cut diagonally. Garnish with lettuce and serve.

Codfish Ball with Bread

Codfish ball, toast, gherkin butter, parsley, bacon

Flatten out a codfish ball and fry brown on both sides. Cut toast round, spread with gherkin butter, lay on codfish ball (flattened out), then press on upper round of toast. Garnish with parsley and two strips of bacon. Gherkin butter and bacon may be omitted and sandwich masked with a good cream sauce sprinkled with bread crumbs and browned. This sandwich when accompanied by a green salad, served on the side, makes a desirable lenten or Friday entree.

Codfish Cakes
Sole Cakes

Fish flakes, potatoes, egg, butter

Mix one-half cup of flaked codfish with one-half cup of freshly mashed potatoes. Bind together with one well beaten egg. Season with salt, paprika and add one tablespoon butter. Flatten out into cakes and fry in shallow bacon grease until brown on both sides.

Salmon, halibut, haddock or flounder can be
handled the same way. Bring fillets to a boil in
salted water. Remove, drain, flake, and handle as
above.

AUTHOR'S NOTE: The best sole comes from the
Devon coast. These are large and called black
sole. The smaller white sole is found on the Dutch
coast and the coast of Sussex.

Codfish Cheeks Sandwich

*Toast, butter, codfish cheeks, tartar sauce, lettuce,
olives, gherkin*

Spread rounds or squares of toast with butter and
then with tartar sauce. Bread and fry codfish
cheeks. Split and arrange them on the rounds of
toast. Lettuce and press on upper slice. Serve at
once. Garnish with olives and fanned gherkins.

AUTHOR'S NOTE: Codfish cheeks can be procured
at various times thruout the year at the wholesale
fish markets. Codfish cheeks and salted salmon
bellies are considered real delicate morsels.

A French lady is said to have exclaimed after
enjoying a morsel such as the above, "What a pity
that this pleasure is not a sin!"

Codfish Flakes au Gratin Sandwich

Toast, codfish, cream sauce, Herkimer cheese, butter

On two pieces of trimmed, toasted whole wheat
or white bread place enough flaked codfish to cover,
pour over the codfish a little freshly made cream
sauce. Sprinkle with ground Herkimer cheese and
butter. Place sandwich in a hot oven or under
broiler and brown. Serve immediately.

The cream sauce is to be made of whole milk,
butter, flour and seasoning, or cream with butter,
flour and seasoning. Simmer the cod slowly until
done with a few slices of onion, herbs and a slice
of lemon. Allow to cool, drain well then break into
large flakes.

Halibut, salmon, trout, finnan haddie, all lend
themselves to the same treatment. Cheese can be
omitted and a few chopped fresh mushrooms, which
have been previously cooked in butter, added to
cream sauce. Then sandwich can be sprinkled with
bread crumbs, butter, paprika and browned. Fish
can be spread on lower slice of toast, second slice
pressed on, then additional sauce poured over top
of all and served hot and at once.

Cold Roast Beef Sandwich—I
Bread, butter, beef, lettuce, potato salad

On a slice of white or rye bread, buttered, place a thin slice of cold roast beef nicely trimmed. Press on upper slice, cut in two diagonally, and serve on cold platter. Garnish with lettuce and potato salad. Have salad dry enough so that moisture does not soak into bread.

Cold roast beef may be made up into small finger sandwiches and used as an item on a platter of assorted sandwiches. Bread, spread with horse-radish butter, adds flavor to the sandwich.

Cold Roast Beef Sandwich—II
Cold roast beef, rye, white or whole wheat bread, lettuce, tomato, cole slaw, butter

On thin slices of plain or toasted rye, white, or whole wheat bread, lettuced and spread with plain or any desired savory butter, place thin slices of cold roast beef. Press on upper slice and cut in fingers, squares, half or diagonally and serve on leaves of lettuce. Garnish with quarterd tomato or lettuce leaf filled with a well drained cole slaw.

Cold Roast Beef Sandwich III
Roast beef, bread, lettuce

On slices of white, rye or whole wheat bread, plain or buttered, place thin slices of cold roast beef, rib, loin or leg. Season, lettuce and press on upper slice. Trim and serve. Medium or well done beef makes the best lunch box sandwich. When beef is rare the bread becomes too soggy unless eaten at once. Lettuce placed above and below beef helps to keep bread dry.

Collegiate Sandwich
American cheese, almonds, pickles, French dressing, bread, tomato, Mexican slaw, lettuce

Grate or mash two ounces of good old American cheese and mix in one ounce of finely chopped blanched almonds and one ounce of finely chopped sweet pickles. Moisten with one tablespoon of French Dressing base No. 5. Spread on thin slices of rye, brown or white bread, press on upper slice, trim and cut into desired shapes. Garnish with a small, ripe tomato hollowed out, filled with Mexican slaw. Serve on leaves of lettuce.

This sandwich, pressed tightly together then dipped in an egg and milk wash and then fried in shallow grease or toasted in patent toaster makes an ideal sandwich.

AUTHOR'S NOTE: This sandwich to be eaten slowly and chewed well. Digestion depends greatly on the frame of mind you are in; laugh and gigger the diaphragm; entertain pleasant thoughts; eat for health; forget professors, studies, allowances.

With diet and patience, Walpole thought all the diseases of man might be easily cured.

Our mental energies, in a great degree, depend upon our physical condition and well being; and the physical condition of that man, be he president, senator, lawyer, doctor, who for half a dozen days, has had an indifferent breakfast or dinner cannot be good.

Combination Sandwich—I

Toast, egg, celery, dill pickle, Thousand Island dressing, lettuce, mayonnaise

On thin slices of toast spread a mixture made of one hard-boiled egg, inner part of one head of celery and one-half small dill pickle, ground or chopped fine, and mixed with enough mayonnaise to bind. Press on upper slice and cut in four squares. Place on plate underlined with leaf of lettuce and pour a little Thousand Island dressing over the squares.

Combination Sandwich—II

Toast, mayonnaise, hard-boiled egg, cole slaw, pickle, celery, lettuce, Russian dressing

On thin slices of toast spread a mixture made of one hard-boiled egg, one heaping tablespoon cole slaw, one-half small dill or sour pickle, one small head of celery all chopped or ground very fine and mixed with enough mayonnaise to bind. Press on upper slice with leaf of lettuce, trim and cut in squares. Pour over squares a Russian dressing and serve at once. Sandwich to be served on leaves of lettuce.

Combination Sandwich—III

Toast, meat mixture, egg, parsley, tomato, potatoes

Cut slices of toasted bread about an inch thick and trim into rounds, squares or ovals. Run the point of a small, sharp vegetable knife around the edge of the bread about one-fourth inch from the edge and about one-half inch deep. Fry in oil or bacon grease until well browned. Remove and cool, then take off the top and remove all the crumb.

Fill with a well seasoned chopped meat mixture and place a poached or fried egg on top. Sprinkle with parsley and garnish with fried tomato and Long Branch potatoes. Corned beef hash makes an ideal filling to use, or Chicken Ritz, or any similar mixture.

Combination Sandwich
See also

Beef	Nut and Olive
Beet	Onion
Calves Brain	Pineapple
Chicken	Potato
Chestnut	Red Devil
Cheese	Roquefort
Cottage Cheese	Russian
Egg	Savory
Fish	Shad Roe
Gooseberry	Special
Ham	Thuringer
Herb and Egg	Turkey
Lettuce	Veal
Mushroom	

Congress Sandwich

Toast, lettuce, Thousand Island dressing, chicken, tongue, butter, tomato

Spread a slice of toast with butter and then Thousand Island dressing and sprinkle with finely shredded lettuce. On this place thin slices of cold boiled chicken and on top of chicken two thin slices of smoked beef tongue. Press on upper slice and cut diagonally. Serve on leaves of lettuce and garnish with quartered tomato.—*Alfred Fries, chef, Pompeian Grill, Congress Hotel, Chicago.*

Cook's Sandwich

Toast, butter, tomatoes, chicory, green pepper, water cress, lettuce, hard-boiled eggs, Thousand Island dressing

On a slice of toasted white, whole wheat or graham bread, buttered, spread a mixture of equal amounts of chopped connective tissue of ripe tomatoes, white leaves of chicory, green peppers, water cress, lettuce, and hard-boiled eggs bound together with Thousand Island dressing. Press on upper slice, cut diagonally and serve at once.

Mix ingredients in a garlic-rubbed bowl. Before adding Thousand Island dressing, drain off surplus moisture. This makes an exceptional salad sandwich and one that needs no garniture. A glass of whole milk makes the luncheon complete.

Ingredients should be cut up very fine.

Cooling Cucumber Sandwich
Bread, butter, cucumbers, cress

Slice cucumbers very thin; soak in a light salt water for a few minutes, then press surplus juice out in towel, by squeezing. Butter thin slices of white bread and arrange cucumbers on bottom slice. Press on upper slice, trim, and cut in finger shapes, three to a slice. Arrange nicely on napkin and garnish with cress. This is an excellent accompaniment for lobster, fish, crabmeat, etc.

Corned Beef Sandwich—I
Corned beef, mustard butter, bread, dill pickle

Slice thin hot or cold corned beef and place on slices of rye, white or brown bread spread with mustard butter. Cut in half and garnish with slices of dill pickle or with a cornucopia of ham filled with cole slaw or kraut. When ground corned beef is used mix with German or French mustard to taste; or add one-third slaw or kraut, finely ground, to two-thirds ground corned beef and bind together with a little French mustard or mayonnaise.

Corned Beef Sandwich—II (Open)
Toast, mustard butter, boiled cabbage, corned beef

Arrange two slices of trimmed or untrimmed toast (as in New Orleans Sandwich), spread with mustard butter on an eight- or nine-inch platter. Cover toast with a thin layer of boiled cabbage (which has been pressed free of moisture and then fried). On top of cabbage arange two or three thin slices of boiled No. 1 corned beef (hot). Serve at once.

Corned beef should be thoroly cooked.

Corned Beef Sandwich a la Harding
Rye bread, mustard, corned beef, cold slaw

Spread a thin slice of rye bread with prepared mustard and place on it enough fatty streaked, thinly cut Harding corned beef to cover. Press on upper slice and garnish with cold slaw. This is a real feast of the connoisseur.

AUTHOR'S NOTE: Recently while attending a convention the author was told this little anecdote about Mr. Harding, the famous Sandwich Shop man, whom the writer knows well. He complained to one of his carvers who was cutting corned beef that the slices were too thick. Mr. Harding said:

"Young man, let me show you how I want that Ambrosian morsel cut," and with that took the knife and steel in hand. Giving the knife a few artistic swings against the steel, he started. An electric fan was located directly behind Mr. Harding and as he carved the delicious fragments they blew away. In the end Mr. Harding was forced to give over the work to the less experienced carver whom he had so recently relieved. The guest who was waiting for the sandwich was pleased with the change of carvers.

Corned Beef Hash Sandwich—I

Corned beef hash, toast, tomato, pickle, chili sauce

Brown an order of corn-beef hash (3 ounces) in a small egg pan make into shape of an omelet and turn out on two well trimmed slices of toasted bread. Garnish either end with a slice of fried tomato and center with slice of pickle. Serve a little chili sauce on the side.

Hash may be browned and placed on slice of buttered toast, then upper slice pressed on and cut in two diagonally. Garnish with fried tomato and pickle.

Corned Beef Hash Sandwich—II (Open)

Toast, corned beef hash, egg, American cheese, tomato, parsley

Spread two pieces of toast with warm corned beef hash and place on platter. Make a hollow in center of beef and drop in a raw egg. Sprinkle top of corned beef with finely chopped American cheese. Place platter in oven, brown cheese and cook egg. Serve at once garnished with two half-slices of fried tomato and parsley. A little paprika added to cheese adds to color effect.

AUTHOR'S NOTE: The author has never been very strong on mixtures and especially on ground pasty food. However, scraps, odds and ends and left overs in meats or vegetables lend themselves singularly or in combination as sandwich fillers in ground up shape. In the early Roman period the cooks were flogged if the things served to their masters were tough and stringy, and to get away from this sort of reward they pounded, mortared, ground, stewed, hashed, seasoned and mixed until nearly all the foods they cooked were messes. If it is possible to use the food in undisguised forms and in combination with other foods that blend well together, it is the thing to do. In case you have scraps and odds and ends to use up, use as few accessories to the one item as is possible to bring out the flavor and make the dish palatable. But to mash up good food which is in the best of shape to a paste and add other pasty stuff to it, reminds one of the man who wanted to or did paint the lily.

Corn Fritter Sandwich

Corn fritters, chicken, mayonnaise, lettuce, celery, tomato

Fry corn fritters well done in shallow grease. Allow to partly cool and split. Cut thin slices of white meat of chicken or turkey, season and dip in mayonnaise. Place turkey or chicken in a small inner leaf of lettuce and insert in the split corn fritter. Serve at once on leaves of lettuce. Garnish with the inner stalks of celery, tomato, etc.

This is rather an unusual combination. The fritter should be made thick enough to split and two fritter sandwiches should be served to the order. Fritters should not be greasy.

Cottage Cheese Sandwich

Bread, butter, cottage cheese, chives, lettuce

On plain or whole wheat bread, buttered, spread a thin layer of fresh cottage cheese. Season with salt and pepper, sprinkle with chopped chives. Press on leaf of lettuce and upper slice. Cut in desired shapes and serve.

Bread may be toasted, if desired.

RECIPE FOR COTTAGE CHEESE

Allow a quart of whole milk to clabber. Pour into cheesecloth and strain. Hang in a cool place and allow moisture to drain out. After the cheese is hung up a few hours it will be dry enough to work. Add cream to give cheese a nice consistency. A few chopped chives gives the cheese an added zest.

Cottage Cheese Combination Sandwich

Toast, butter, anchovy butter, cottage cheese, chives

Spread small rounds of thin buttered toast with anchovy butter and then with cottage cheese mixed with finely chopped anchovies and chives. This may be used as an open sandwich or as a hors d'oeuvre.

Crabmeat Sandwich (Open)

Crabmeat, Newburg sauce, peppers, mushrooms, butter, toast

Proceed as in Lobster Newburg adding a julienned or diced green pepper and a large sized mushroom (sliced) which has been previously sauted in butter.

Crabmeat Newburg Sandwich (Open)

Proceed the same as in Lobster Newburg.

Crayfish Salad Sandwich

Crayfish, lemon, mayonnaise, celery, toast, lettuce, hard-boiled eggs, cress

Wash crayfish and boil slowly in salted water with a few slices of lemon for about twenty minutes. Drain, cool and pick meat out of shells. Clean out the alimentary tract (this can be done after shell is removed by separating or pulling the top part of the tail end back just where it connects with the body). Cut meat in thin slices or dice, salt and mix with finely chopped celery and mayonnaise. Spread mixture on thin slices of trimmed bread or toast, press on upper slice and serve on leaves of lettuce. Garnish with quartered hard-boiled eggs, thin pieces of curled celery and cress. Use one-third chopped celery to two-thirds crayfish meat.

Cream Cheese Roll

Pullman bread, cream cheese, lettuce, radishes

Cut with a very sharp knife extremely thin slices of Pullman bread, freshly made. Cover the entire slice with a thin spread of cream cheese and then roll up very neatly. Trim ends and serve on leaves of lettuce or in fancy folded napkins. Garnish with lillied radishes. The rolls can be tied with various colored baby ribbons. Any fine sandwich paste or mixture may be used as a spread. After sandwiches are rolled they may be wrapped carefully in a damp napkin or cloth and held until needed. The fresh bread may be wrapped in a damp towel, placed in icebox until needed; then when bread is cut it is in a better shape to roll. Caviar and all the herb and fruit flavored butters are excellent fillers for these fancy little bundles of sustenance.

Cream Cheese Sandwich

Cream cheese, cream, white and brown bread, butter, lettuce

Thin cream cheese to proper consistency by adding raw cream. Spread on a very thin slice of buttered white bread, press on leaf of lettuce and then a thin slice of buttered whole wheat bread. Trim and cut into desired shapes. Serve as one of a combination of assorted sandwiches.

Cream cheese thinned with bar le duc and spread on thin slices of white bread makes an ideal sandwich for afternoon teas.

Creole Sandwich I
Eggs, toast, Creole sauce, butter

Place two fried eggs, cooked separately, on two rounds of buttered toast. Pour over eggs a well flavored and garnished Creole sauce. Serve at once on hot platter.

Creole Sandwich II
See Chicken Legs Creole

Cress Sandwich
Bread, butter, cress

Cream two ounces of salt butter and add as much chopped watercress as can be worked into it. Spread on very thin slices of white or brown bread and cut in fancy shapes.

The cress should be freshly washed and picked carefully, then drained, chopped and added to butter just before serving.

AUTHOR'S NOTE: Cress is a highly nutritious herb, containing sulphurated oil and is extremely good to eat. It makes an excellent item to serve with an assortment of meat sandwiches because of its basic qualities and its flavor. Bread spread with mayonnaise, then with cress butter adds flavor and food value to sandwich.

Cress, Chives and Cheese Sandwich
Cheese, French dressing, cress, chives, bread, butter, lettuce, pimolas

Thin one-half cup of cream cheese with an aromatic French dressing, add one-half cup of chopped cress and one tablespoon of chopped chives. Spread on buttered white or graham bread. Press on leaf of lettuce, upper slice and cut in fanciful shapes. Garnish top of sandwich with two or three sliced pimolas or a small fan made out of a sweet gherkin. Serve on leaves of lettuce and garnish with rosettes of cress.

Cress and chives mixed with enough mayonnaise to bind make a very tasty item.

Cress and Egg Sandwich
Bread, hard-boiled eggs, cress, mayonnaise, dill pickles, lettuce

Mix equal parts of chopped hard-boiled eggs and watercress. Bind together with mayonnaise. Spread on thin slices of plain white or whole wheat bread. Sprinkle with finely chopped dill pickles, press on leaf of lettuce and upper slice. Trim, cut in finger shapes and serve on bed of lettuce.

Pickles can be omitted.

Cress, Lettuce and Tomato Sandwich
Whole wheat bread, butter, cress, lettuce, mayonnaise, tomato

On a slice of whole wheat bread, spread with sweet butter, spread equal amounts of chopped cress and lettuce mixed with enough mayonnaise base No. 3 to bind. On top of cress and lettuce place two thin slices of peeled ripe tomatoes, seasoned. Press on upper slice, trim and cut diagonally. Serve on leaf of lettuce. When accompanied by a glass of sweet or acidolphus milk this makes a real healthful luncheon.

AUTHOR'S NOTE: Dr. Robert McCarrison tells us that injections of bacteria sufficient to kill ordinary men in a few hours have no effect whatever upon men who habitually eat the proper foods in correct combinations; also that the incidence of epidemics may be traced and demonstrably proven to keep pace with the eating habits of the people subject to them.

Crust Sandwich
Crusts, butter, Herkimer cheese, tomatoes, onions

Spread with butter the crusts cut from the two ends of a loaf of whole wheat bread. Place one slice on platter and pour over a cheese and tomato mixture. Press on upper crust and pour the additional tomato and cheese mixture over the top. Garnish the side of sandwich with French fried onions. Serve hot and at once.

TOMATO AND CHEESE MIXTURE: Bring to a boil one cup of canned tomatoes, season with salt and white pepper, add two ounces of diced Herkimer cheese and cook from three to five minutes, until cheese is melted, then pour over the crusts as directed.

Cucumber Sandwich
See Cooling Cucumber
See Squeezed Cucumber

Curried Chicken Sandwich
See Sliced Curried Chicken

Danish Sandwich (Open)

Bread, mustard, Swiss cheese, mayonnaise, sardines,
ham, corned beef, turkey, tongue, parsley,
gherkins, slaw, hard-boiled egg

Place a thin finger slice of rye bread spread with
German mustard and covered with a slice of Swiss
cheese on a 7½ inch cold plate. To right of Swiss
cheese place a toasted slice of plain bread spread
with mayonnaise and covered with a boneless
French sardine. To right of sardine place a second
slice of toast spread with butter and covered with
cold, boiled egg. To right of boiled ham place a
thin slice of rye bread, buttered and covered with
cold, boiled corned beef. To right of corned beef
place a slice of plain white bread, buttered and
covered with cold, roast turkey; and last, a slice
of graham bread spread with butter and covered
with cold, boiled smoked ox-tongue. Garnish with
parsley and fanned gherkin. In center place a mound
of slaw and garnish top with a slice of hard-boiled
egg.

This makes a picturesque sort of sandwich and
is much called for when prepared daintily and
artistically. One or two kinds of bread may be
used for economy.

The Day After Sandwich—I

Turkey dressing, toast, butter, cranberry sauce,
lettuce, olives

Use dressing which has been left over from the
Thanksgiving or Christmas turkey. Spread dressing on a slice of toast, spread a second slice with
butter and cranberry sauce and press together. Cut
into finger shapes, garnish with lettuce and olives
and serve on cold plates.

Do not spread dressing on too thick. These sandwiches served with turkey or chicken sandwiches
make an ideal plate combination and a good way
to use up a delicious dressing. Dressing may be
served hot on freshly made toast.

The Day After Sandwich—II

Roast beef trimmings, mayonnaise, pickles, toast,
butter, cole slaw, lettuce

Trim the meat adhering to the bones of roast
beef and put thru a fine grinder. Add three tablespoons of chopped pickles to every cup of meat and

bind with a stiff mayonnaise. Spread on thin slices of buttered toast or plain bread, press on upper slice and cut into desired shapes. Garnish with cole slaw and serve on lettuce leaves.

Trimmings from the turkey or chicken carcasses handled the same way and the liver and gizzard ground with it make a real "Day After" sandwich. Eliminate all surplus fat from beef and grind very fine.

Delicacy Sandwich

Bread, butter, roast lamb, capers, lettuce, mint

On thin slices of whole wheat or white bread spread with caper butter, place thin slices of cold roast leg of lamb. Press on a leaf of lettuce and upper slice. Trim and cut into any desired shape. Garnish with sprigs of mint and serve on cold plates. Bread may be spread with butter and mint jelly for novelty and flavor. Sandwiches can be garnished with small molds of transparent mint jelly.

Demi Deuil Sandwich

Brown and white bread, butter, cream cheese, lettuce, pineapple, almonds, mayonnaise

Spread with butter thin round slices of brown and white bread, cut with a two and one-half inch column cutter. Spread the first slice of brown bread with thinned down cream cheese and place an inner leaf of lettuce on cheese. Next place a thin slice of white bread buttered on both sides on top of lettuce. On white bread place a thin layer of very finely ground pineapple and blanched almonds, in equal amounts, bound together with mayonnaise. Press on a second slice of brown bread and serve on plates, garnished with lettuce. Demi Deuil means in half mourning. This makes a very tasty and attractive sandwich. Sandwich can be cut in two and round sides placed together, which makes an attractive showing. Lettuce should be trimmed to fit sandwich. Pineapple should be drained quite dry before adding mayonnaise.

Deutcher Sandwich

Beef, pork, veal, toast, cream, seasoning

Put two ounces of raw beef, veal and pork thru a fine grinder, season with one-half teaspoon salt, one-quarter teaspoon pepper, two tablespoons of cream, mix and make into cakes, broil or fry, and place on slice of toast. Press on upper slice, trim and cut in two diagonally, and pour a little freshly made cream or fricasse sauce over sandwich. Serve at once.

Devil Sandwich
See Red Devil Combinations

Doctor Sandwich
Toast, butter, tomato, cottage cheese, cress, chives, Lorenzo dressing

On a round of thin buttered toast the size of tomato place a thin slice of peeled, ripe tomato. On tomato place part of a mixture of 2 tablespoons of cottage cheese, two of chopped watercress and one-half teaspoon of chopped chives. Press on upper slice, serve on leaves of lettuce. Pour Lorenzo dressing over sandwich and serve at once.

Domino Sandwich (Open)
Black olives, white of hard-boiled eggs, cress, mayonnaise, bread

Chop one-half cup of black olives, one-half cup of whites of eggs and one-half cup of cress and mix each separately with enough mayonnaise to bind. Spread the olives on one-third of thin slice of bread trimmed and buttered. (Slice to be cut from entire length of loaf of bread.) On the opposite third, spread the whites of eggs, and in the center section place the chopped cress. All three colors should be evenly distributed and a thin line of colored butter should be piped between the olives and cress, and the cress and eggs, as a line of demarcation and to cover up the irregularities. Cut the long slice in as many two-inch wide strips as it will make. Place these finger strips on lettuce and garnish with lilied radishes and olives. Two colors can be used as well as three, as may any other color scheme. Red beets, green peppers, lettuce, caviar, ham, cheese, jellies, etc., all lend themselves to various combinations.

Dorian Sandwich
Bread, salmon, boiled haddock, hard-boiled eggs, mayonnaise

Flake, bone and chop one-half pound of boiled haddock. Season and mix with an equal amount of canned salmon (chopped). Add enough mayonnaise to bind. Spread on thin slices of white bread, season, press on leaf of lettuce and upper slice and trim and cut into desired shapes.

A few chopped capers or pickles added helps flavor.

AUTHOR'S NOTE: "Dorian, who was a notorious epicure, and who was especially fond of fish, had a club foot; and at one time had the shoe that belonged to the deformed foot stolen. He said about his loss, 'I will not wish anything more to the thief than that the shoe may fit him.' This is perhaps where the old adage came from—'If the shoe fits, wear it'."

Double-Decked Club Sandwich

Arrange as in Club Capon only add ⅓ slice of toast, and instead of placing the bacon over the capon place the bacon and a slice of peeled ripe tomato on top of second slice. Cover sandwich with third slice of toast spread with mayonnaise. Cut diagonally and serve as above.

The club sandwich eaten in combination with a glass of milk makes a well balanced luncheon.

Lettuce is rich in Vitamin A which stimulates growth and keeps the body in condition. Tomatoes contain calcium, magnesium, potassium, sodium, chlorine, phosphorus, sulphur and iron and render an alkaline reaction.

Duke Sandwich—I (Open)

Quail, toast, currant jelly, bacon, cress

Place a whole broiled quail on toast in center of platter. Arrange two croutons of currant jelly at either end and strip quail with broiled bacon. Garnish with cress and serve at once.

Croutons should be cut heart-shaped and jelly should be piled high and worked into pleasing shape.

Duke Sandwich—II

Or, spread trimmed thin slices of toast with butter and currant jelly, cover with thin slices of quail cut from the breast, season and press on upper slice, cut in two diagonally and garnish with cress.

Dumas Sandwich (Open)

Toast, Parmesan cheese, eggs, cream sauce, horseradish, paprika, butter

On rounds of toasted bread, place two poached or fried eggs (trimmed to fit toast). Mask top of eggs with three tablespoons of cream sauce to which has been added one teaspoon of freshly grated horseradish. Sprinkle with grated Parmesan cheese (or Swiss), and paprika. Brown quickly. Serve at once. A few drops of butter sprinkled over the cheese will hasten the browning.

Dundee Sandwich

White and brown bread, butter, marmalade, currant jelly, mint

Spread two very thin slices of white and two of brown bread with sweet butter. Spread first slice of white bread with a thin layer of marmalade, then press on a slice of whole wheat spread with a thin layer of currant jelly; now press on the third slice of white bread spread with marmalade and sprinkled with chopped mint, and lastly the other slice of whole wheat bread. Trim crusts and cut into finger sandwiches. They should be served either on a folded napkin or fancy paper doily, garnished with a few sprigs of mint, clover blossoms or nasturtium buds. Cut bread extremely thin or sandwich will be too high and topple over. Sandwich should not be over one-half inch high.

D'Uxelles Sandwich (Open)

Toast, egg, shallots, mushrooms, chervil, sweet basil, butter, brown sauce

On a round of toast place a poached egg. Mince one or two shallots, two mushrooms, two or three sprigs of chervil and sweet basil and smother in butter for a few minutes. Add this garnish to one-third cup of rich brown sauce with a tomato flavor; bring to a boil and pour over the egg. This is an exceptional tasty, open egg sandwich.

Two eggs may be fried and placed on toast and the sauce poured over them, if desired.

Edam Sandwich

Edam cheese, mayonnaise, bread, lettuce

Mash or grate Edam cheese and mix with enough mayonnaise to bind. Spread on thin slices of rye, white or whole wheat bread. Press on leaf of lettuce and upper slice; trim and cut into desired shapes.

Edam cheese can be mashed and then mixed with raw cream, Thousand Island dressing or chutney sauce for variety and flavor.

Author's Note: Edam cheese comes from Edam, Holland, and vicinity. The round or pineapple shapes are obtained by pressure of the curd in iron or wood molds; the color of the outside skin by the use of carmine or a weak solution of litmus and Berlin red. Some markets demand that the skin be colored yellow. The shells are often used to serve spaghetti in. Heat shell and fill with hot spaghetti; trim top of cheese into a fancy border. If the spaghetti is to be browned in shell, a hot salamander will accomplish this.

Edgewater Beach Sandwich
See Club Edgewater Beach

Edgewater Gulf Sandwich (Open)
White bread, butter, Gulf shrimp, mayonnaise, lettuce, pickled beets, piccalily, julienne potatoes

On a thin slice of white bread spread with butter, spread finely ground fresh Gulf shrimp, seasoned and mixed with mayonnaise. Cut a second slice of white bread in half diagonally and place a half at either end of center slice. Place on a silver platter and underline with leaves of lettuce. Garnish the top of one half with chopped pickled red beets mixed with mayonnaise and the other half with squeezed cucumbers mixed with sour cream. At the two opposite sides of square center slice place a little mound of julienne potatoes. Serve on leaves of lettuce.

Egg Sandwich
See also

Cress and Egg
Gravied Egg
Hard-Boiled Egg

Herb and Egg
Spinach and Egg

Egg Combination Sandwich (Open)
Toast, tomato catsup butter, hard-boiled eggs, American cheese

Spread thin slices of trimmed toast with tomato catsup butter. Then cover with thin slices of hard-boiled eggs. Sprinkle eggs with a generous layer of finely grated old American cheese. Place under a hot broiler, melt and brown. Serve on hot plate at once. This is a delectable dish; fit for a bevy of Joves.

In place of hard-boiled egg slices sprinkle toast with noodles, macaroni, finely cut boiled tripe, mushrooms, lobster, crabmeat, shrimp or sardines; and one and all in the eating will make you wish for a neck like a stork or ostrich that you enjoy such food the longer.

Eggplant Sandwich I (Open)
Toast, butter, eggs, eggplant, tomato sauce

On two rounds of buttered toast place two small

slices of fried eggplant, cut to shape. On eggplant place a poached egg. Pour a rich, hot tomato sauce over eggs and serve at once.

Eggplant Sandwich II

Eggplant, bread crumbs, tomato, bacon, Herkimer cheese, lettuce

Cut slices of eggplant, one-half inch thick, and soak in cold salt water for at least one hour. Wipe dry, cut in half, bread and fry brown. Allow slices to partially cool, then split. Insert a slice of raw tomato and a strip of broiled bacon in each half slice of eggplant. Place two half slices on a plate and cover with Herkimer cheese. Brown quickly, garnish with lettuce and serve at once.

This is a very good combination and very tasty.

Eighteenth Hole Pacifier Sandwich

Rye bread, mustard butter, Swiss cheese, lettuce, dill pickle

On very thin slices of rye bread, spread with mustard butter, place a thin slice of imported window Swiss cheese. Press on a leaf of lettuce and the upper slice. Cut in two diagonally and serve with slices of dill pickle on leaves of lettuce.

AUTHOR'S NOTE: The name of this sandwich was taken from the fact that one of Chicago's literati counted eighteen holes in the cheese in his Swiss sandwich.

Eleven P. M. Sandwich

Toast, butter, chicken, mayonnaise, ham, lettuce, dill pickles, tomato

On a slice of white bread, toasted, spread with butter, place a very thin layer of finely ground white meat of chicken mixed with mayonnaise. Press a thin slice of grilled ham (horse-shoe cut) on top of chicken and then upper slice. Trim and cut into desired shape. Garnish with lettuce, dill pickle and a small whole tomato hollowed out and filled with mayonnaise. Serve at once. This sandwich placed between a fine wire broiler and toasted makes a real treat.

El Paradiso Sandwich

Avocado pear, French dressing, bread, peanut butter, pimentoes, toast, lettuce

Marinate thin slices of alligator pear (Avocado) in a strong French dressing for ten minutes. Toast two thin slices of bread on one side, and spread the toasted side with peanut butter. Lay the slices of pear on the peanut butter in a pleasing manner and garnish the top of pear with strips of pimento and serve the two slices (open faced) on leaves of lettuce. Decorate with preserved ginger.—*E. E. Amiet, chef, Palmer House, Chicago.*

Epicurean Sandwich

Rye bread, Roquefort cheese, cream, bacon, mayonnaise, turkey, lettuce, celery, green olives

On a thin slice of rye bread spread with Roquefort cheese, thinned down to a paste with raw cream, place three strips of broiled bacon. Press on a second slice of rye bread spread with mayonnaise. Cover mayonnaise with thin slices of turkey, season, press on third slice and cut in two diagonally. Garnish with lettuce, curled celery and green olives.

E. W. B. Sandwich (Open)

Toast, tomato, egg, cheese, bread crumbs, butter

On a slice of trimmed and buttered toast place a layer of fried connective tissue of fresh tomato, enough to cover the toast except in the center. Crack an egg and place in center of tomato on toast. Sprinkle with cheese, bread crumbs and butter. Cook in oven until brown and done, then serve at once on hot plate.

After removing skin of tomato and seeds, cut connective tissue in strips and fry in hot grease until perfectly dry; drain and place on toast.

Fancy Luncheon Sandwich

Toast, anchovy butter, egg, chicken, mushrooms, cream sauce, parsley

On a round of toast spread lightly with anchovy butter, place a poached egg. Add equal quantities of diced white meat of cooked chicken and mushrooms to a rich cream sauce. Pour sauce, hot, over egg and sprinkle with chopped parsley. Serve at once.

Anchovy butter can be omitted. The sandwich can be sprinkled with grated old American cheese and browned under a hot broiler for variety.

Farm Sausage Sandwich

Sausage, toast, fried apples, cress

Brown two very thin cakes of freshly ground and seasoned pork sausage, and place on two rounds of toast. Press on two cored and fried slices of apple and the upper rounds of toast. Arrange on hot plate and serve at once. Garnish with cress. This is an excellent tasty item.

Links of sausage split and broiled can be used in place of cakes or the whole link just browned in the oven and used as a sandwich filler makes a tasty tidbit. A quartered waffle covered with three links of freshly cooked sausage or strips of broiled bacon with a second quartered waffle pressed on and served with maple syrup on a hot plate will make a hit on a cold night or dreary morning.

Filet Mignon Sandwich I

Beef tenderloin, Pullman bread, Spanish onion, lettuce, potatoes

Cut a slice of beef tenderloin one inch thick and flatten it to one-half inch. Season and grill over a hot charcoal broiler for from four to five minutes. (However, this depends upon the heat of fire and the thickness of fillet.) Place fillet on a toasted trimmed slice of Pullman bread, cut round, and on top of fillet lay a slice of raw or grilled Spanish onion. Press on upper round slice. Garnish with lettuce and Long Branch potatoes. Serve at once.

Tenderloin or fillet should be of sufficient size to cover toast after it is broiled. Slices from tail and neck ends of tenderloins do not make good looking sandwich material.

Filet Mignon Sandwich II
See Grilled Filet Mignon

Filet of Sole Sandwich
See Fried Filet of Sole

Fines Herbes Sandwich

Chervil, chives, sweet basil, parsley, mushrooms, eggs, cream, butter, toast, lettuce

Mix equal quantities of chopped chervil, chives, sweet basil, parsley and fried mushrooms, enough of all to make one-fourth cup. Whip up two eggs with two tablespoons of cream, season and add herbs. Fry mixture in butter and turn over like you would fried eggs over; then place on slice of trimmed, buttered toast. Press on upper slice and cut in two diagonally. Place on platter and garnish with lettuce. Serve hot.

This amount will make four small sandwiches by dropping one-fourth of the amount into the pan at a time, or by frying mixture in four separate cakes.

Finger Roll Salad Sandwich
Finger rolls, chicken salad, lettuce

Split finger rolls and spread liberally with chicken salad. Garnish with lettuce. This is an excellent afternoon tea item.

Chicken salad can be put thru a fine grinder, then placed in a split and hollowed out finger roll. Garnish top of salad with four capers circled with thin strips of pimentoes. Cover with upper slice and place two finger sandwiches on leaves of lettuce. Garnish with a ripe and a green olive.

In putting salad thru grinder be sure not to have mixture too soft or too dry.

Fisherman's Sandwich
Bread or buns, hamburger steak, Bermuda onion, dill pickle

On slice of rye bread or in center of bun place a thin, well cooked hamburger steak. On steak place a thin slice of Bermuda onion and a thin slice of dill pickle. Press on upper slice and serve hot. Bread can be spread with mustard butter.

Five Hundred Sandwich
English walnuts, cream, salt, white bread, lettuce, cress, sweet pickles

Chop one-half cup of blanched English walnuts, pecans or almonds and pound in a mortar. Add to nuts enough 40% cream or butter to make a paste; spread on very thin slices of white bread. Press on leaf of lettuce, upper slice and cut into desired shapes. Garnish with watercress and sweet pickles.

This sandwich should be served on a platter or plate as one of assorted sandwiches.

Flower Sandwich
See Herb and Flower

Foie Gras Sandwich
See Pate de Foie Gras

Fox Grape Sandwich
Fox grape jelly, salt rising bread, butter, lettuce

Spread thin slices of salt rising or milk bread with sweet butter and Fox grape jelly. Press on upper slice, trim and cut into desired shapes. Garnish with leaves of lettuce. The Fox grape is very tart or acid.

Frankfurter Sandwich
Sally in Our Alley Sandwich
Frankfurters, buns or rolls, mustard, horseradish,
dill pickles

Steam frankfurters until thoroly heated thru, or simmer in water for fifteen minutes (do not boil). Split and place between a freshly made bun or roll, oblong shaped. Spread split frankfurter with a little German mustard to which has been added a dash of horseradish. Insert a thin slice of dill pickle, close up the roll and commence the festivities.

Frankfurters on rye are not to be overlooked in the realm of sandwiches.

French Toast Sandwich (Open)
French toast, turkey, bacon, tomato, cress

On a slice of French toast, cut in two diagonally before frying and then placed on a small platter in shape of a diamond, place three slices of cold turkey on one-half of toast and three strips of broiled bacon on other half. Garnish with tomato and cress. Serve a little Thousand Island dressing on side.

Two thin slices of bread spread with cream cheese and bar le duc, then pressed together, trimmed and dipped into egg and milk (like you would in making French toast), and fried like French toast makes an exceptional item. Marmalade and cream cheese makes a good filling also for a sandwich such as the above.

Fresh Pear Sandwich
Toast, cream cheese, bar le duc, lemon juice, pear,
lettuce

On thin slices of toast, spread with cream cheese thinned down with bar le duc and lemon juice, place very thin slices of peeled, fresh Bartlett pear. Cover with second slice and cut in desired shapes. Serve on leaves of lettuce. Bar le duc may be omitted and cheese thinned down with French dressing base No. 5.

Fresh Spinach Sandwich
Spinach, onions, bread, mayonnaise, lettuce

Thoroly drain fresh cooked spinach. Cook in butter (but do not brown) one teaspoonful of finely chopped onion. Add a cupful of spinach to onion (spinach to be squeezed and chopped fine.) Season with salt and a little grated nutmeg. Allow spinach to cool. Spread either plain or toasted whole wheat

or plain bread with butter or mayonnaise, then cover
with a thin layer of spinach. Press on a leaf of lettuce and the upper slice; cut into desired shapes.
Sandwiches may be cut into four squares and top of
each garnished with a slice of hard-boiled egg. A
little French dressing may be poured over squares
at table. Raw spinach can be chopped fine, seasoned
and added to enough mayonnaise to bind, then used
as a spread.

AUTHOR'S NOTE: Spinach is one of the most valuable greens in the vegetable kingdom and should be
included in the dietary of every man, woman and
child.

Fresh Vegetable Sandwich—I

*Cabbage, green peppers, carrots, artichoke tubers,
mayonnaise, graham bread, white bread,
lettuce, tomato*

Mix one-third cup chopped raw cabbage, one-
third of a cup chopped green peppers, one-third of
a cup of new carrots, raw, and one-third of a cup
of chopped artichoke tubers, raw, with enough
mayonnaise to bind. Add seasoning to taste and
mix thoroly. Cut thin slices of graham bread and
white bread. Spread mixture on a slice of graham
bread, press on a slice of white bread, trim and
cut in finger, diamond or diagonal shape. Serve on
leaves of lettuce and garnish with quartered tomatoes. This makes an excellent fresh vegetable sandwich, and if eaten with a glass of milk for a
luncheon it makes an economical as well as a
healthful meal.

Fresh Vegetable Sandwich—II

Dandelions, lettuce, mayonnaise, whole wheat bread

Chop equal amounts of freshly washed, cleaned
young dandelions and lettuce. Add enough mayonnaise to bind and season with just a little salt.
Spread this mixture on thin slices of whole wheat or
white bread. This makes an excellent vegetable or
herb sandwich. Just a very small amount of chopped
green onion tops added to either sandwich adds to
the zest of same.

Friday Sandwich—I

*Two hard-boiled eggs, toast, butter, tomato catsup,
old American cheese (not processed)*

Spread a slice of toast with butter and then with
tomato catsup. Cut hard-boiled egg in thin slices
with egg cutter, the egg slices to be arranged artistically on top of toast. Sprinkle the eggs with grated

old American cheese and place under a hot broiler to brown for a few minutes. Garnish with lettuce and slice of pickle and serve at once. This makes a very tasty, good-looking Friday sandwich. The sandwich should be eaten with a simple herb salad of some kind to balance up the luncheon and help neutralize the acids that are generated thru the bread and egg portion of menu. The bread and egg portion are acid-forming, the simple herb salad alkaline.

Egg slicers can be bought in any 10c store. Cut egg across, not lengthwise.

Friday Sandwich—II

Fish flakes, lettuce, capers, Thousand Island dressing, cress, tomato, butter, toast

Chop one-half cup of flaked lake trout, one-half cup of lettuce, inner leaves, and two tablespoons of capers. Mix in two tablespoons of Thousand Island dressing and one-fourth teaspoonful of salt. Spread this mixture on thinly cut and buttered toast, trim sandwich and cut in four pieces. Place the sandwich on a warm platter. Place these four squares of sandwich in a cross shape and garnish the center with watercress and the four intersections with quartered peeled tomatoes. Pour over top of squares a little Thousand Island dressing and serve immediately.

Left over fish which has been boiled, broiled or baked can be boned, skinned and then flaked. This mixture can be put thru a fine grinder and then spread on very thin slices of fresh bread and the sandwich rolled and tied with colored ribbons.

Fried Sandwich

Herkimer cheese, pickle, bacon, French dressing, bread, egg, cream, cress, Mexican slaw

Mash with a fork one ounce of Herkimer cheese; chop up fine one small sweet pickle, one strip of broiled bacon and add to cheese. Moisten with one teaspoon French dressing base No. 5. Spread on very thin slices of rye, white or whole wheat bread. Press on upper slice, trim and cut in half. Dip in an egg wash made of one egg beaten with two tablespoons of cream. Fry in shallow grease. Brown on both sides. Serve hot or cold. Garnish with cress and Mexican slaw. This is an excellent item.

Sandwiches may be fried without dipping in egg-wash; without wash sandwiches are more crisp, but more greasy in nature. Five or six sprigs of sweet basil, tarragon or chervil chopped and added to mixture greatly enhances the flavor of sandwich. Any sandwich may be handled this way, but it is best to use the egg-wash to hold them together.

Bread must be cut extremely thin and pressed tightly together before dipping into egg-wash. Then they must be fried in hot shallow grease and served at once.

Fried Filet of Sole Sandwich (Open)

Toast, butter, sole, tomato, tartar sauce, lemon, lettuce, parsley

On two slices of buttered toast place two small fried filets of sole, breaded. At either end of sandwich place a quartered tomato. On one side of sole place a small paper cup filled with tartar sauce and on opposite side place a quartered lemon. Garnish with a little lettuce.

Any kind of boned, breaded and fried fish cut in small uniform pieces can be handled in the same way. A small spoon of mashed potatoes may be used as a garnish in place of tomato, if desired. An additional slice of toast can be pressed on and sandwich cut in two diagonally and then masked with tartar sauce.

Fried Mush Sandwich

Fried mush, salt pork or bacon, cress, slaw

Cut four diamond-shaped pieces of cold corn meal mush and fry brown. Arrange two pieces on a hot plate and cover with a piece of fried salt pork or several strips of broiled bacon. Press on two upper slices and garnish with cress and slaw or serve with maple syrup.

Frog Legs Sandwich I

Frog legs, butter, toast, tartar sauce, bacon, lettuce, pickles, tomatoes

Saute one pair of bullfrog legs slowly in butter, smother until done. Allow to cool and bone. Spread thin slices of toast with tartar sauce and arrange flakes of legs on top. Press on a strip of broiled bacon and upper slice. Trim and cut in two diagonally. Serve on leaves of lettuce. Garnish with pickles, cut octopus style and quartered tomatoes.

The flakes from the saddle can be ground, mixed with enough tartar sauce to bind them together, then spread on thin slices of toast. Cut in desired shapes and serve. This is an excellent way of disposing of saddles. By grinding, the objectionable tough sinews are made usable.

Frog Legs Sandwich II

Frog legs, butter, tartar sauce, toast, lettuce

Saute six gras. frog legs in butter and then detach flesh from the bones. Chop flesh finely and mix with enough tartar sauce to bind. Spread on thin slices of toast, press on upper slice, and cut in finger shapes. Serve warm on leaves of lettuce.

The saddles of Jumbo frogs can be simmered in water and when cooked flesh detached from the bones, then chopped and mixed with tartar sauce or mayonnaise and spread on toast or plain bread. This is an outlet for an item which is hard to move. Grass frogs have a much sweeter meat and better flavor than bullfrogs, they are also more tender and luscious.

Do not allow fish or frog legs to soak in water after they are cleaned, as the fine flavor will be materially lessened.

Fruit Sandwich I

Pears or peaches, spices, pound cake, apricot syrup, mayonnaise.

Boil whole pears or peaches until under done in a simple syrup with a few spices. Allow to cool, drain well and cut in uniform slices. Arrange alternate slices of peach and pear, overlapping, on top of a piece of pound cake spread with a lemon mayonnaise. Cake to be cut one-half by five inches and one-half inch thick. Brighten fruit with a little apricot syrup and serve. A second slice of pound cake may be pressed on to complete closed fruit cake sandwich. Sponge cake may be used instead of pound cake. The open fruit sandwich served a la mode is quite acceptable and makes a real satisfying fancy dessert.

AUTHOR'S NOTE: Careme said that the dessert had been elevated into a science with a view to retain girls, young women and children at the table in friendly converse.

Fruit Sandwich II

Pound cake, apricot jelly, peaches, pears, layer cake

Spread a slice of toasted pound cake with a thin layer of apricot jelly or cream cheese and on it arrange very, very thin slices of fresh pears and peaches, alternately. Press on a thin slice of toasted layer cake and cut into small squares. Serve on fancy paper doilies. Thin slices of toast may be spread with mayonnaise and chopped assorted fruit used. Fruit should be drained as dry as possible

before placing on toast. Fruit jams are easier to
handle than fresh fruit. Place the slices of fruit so
that they are practically flat on cake. This can be
done by cutting the slices very, very thin and overlapping them in regular order.

Fruit Sandwich III
See Maple Fruit

Fruit and Nut Sandwich
Bread, butter, mayonnaise, orange (or grapefruit or
pear or peach), almonds, lettuce, olives,
nasturtium blossoms

On very thin slices of bread spread with jelly or
butter and mayonnaise, arrange very thin sections of
orange, grapefruit, fresh pear or peach. Sprinkle
fruit with powdered sugar and chopped blanched
almonds, cover with lettuce and second slice. Trim
and cut into desired shapes. Serve on bed of lettuce
or on folded napkin. Garnish with green olives and
nasturtium blossoms. The sections of orange or
grapefruit should be skinned and then thinly sliced,
lengthwise.

Fruit Sandwich, Spiced
See Spiced Fruit

Fuje Sandwich
Bamboo shoots, bean sprouts, water chestnuts, bacon,
toast, Thousand Island dressing, lettuce

Open a No. 2 can of Fuje Chinese vegetables
(mixed), drain and chop the chestnuts and shoots,
leave the sprouts whole, season, then mix all together. Add to the mixture enough Thousand Island
dressing to bind, spread on thin slices of buttered
toast, press on a strip of bacon, a thin slice of
turkey, a leaf of lettuce, and the upper slice, trim
and cut in desired shapes and serve. Garnish with
lettuce and lilied radishes.

Gambetta Sandwich (Open)
Toast, eggs, brown sauce, calves' brains, mushrooms

On two rounds of toast place one poached and
one fried egg, trimmed to shape. Pour over eggs
a good brown sauce garnished with calves' brains
and diced mushrooms. Serve hot and at once.

Gaspacho Sandwich
See Andalousian Gaspacho

German Sandwich (Open)

*Rye bread, sauerkraut, bacon, pickle, cress, mustard
butter*

On a slice of rye bread, spread with mustard or
a light mustard butter, place a thin layer of boiled
and fried sauerkraut. Strip kraut with two or three
pieces of broiled bacon or two links of split and
broiled sausage, press on upper slice, cut diagonally
and garnish with two slices of dill pickle and a little
cress. Kraut should be boiled for at least two
hours with an onion and in a little chicken stock;
then drained, allowed to cool and all surplus moisture strained out. Press kraut into small round
thin cakes, dip in beaten egg and fry brown in
butter. This makes a real tasty sandwich and if
once tried will always be called for.

This sandwich made on small rounds of toast
with top garnished with short strips of bacon or
thin rounds of sausage and thin small rounds of
kraut makes an ideal appetizer.

Ginger Sandwich
See Canton Ginger

Golf Club Sandwich (Open)

*Toast, lettuce, butter, turkey, tomato, green pepper,
Thousand Island dressing, caviar*

On a round piece of buttered and lettuced toast
place a round piece of white meat of turkey. On
turkey place a slice of ripe tomato, peeled. Around
tomato place a ring of green pepper and fill center
of tomato with a stiff Thousand Island dressing.
Sprinkle a little caviar over the top. Season turkey
with a little salt. Serve on bed of lettuce, with a
glass of buttermilk (fresh and cold).

AUTHOR'S NOTE: As long as cream has been
churned, the health value of buttermilk as a delicious, refreshing drink has been known. Buttermilk is a real food as well as a refreshing drink,
for it contains a very fine quality of protein, valuable mineral salts, sugar and a lactic ferment which
gives its satisfying sharp taste.

The people of Biblical times associated buttermilk
with long life. Nations of today, whose people
drink buttermilk are strong physically and live long
lives.

Doctors recommend buttermilk as a healthful
drink, because it stimulates digestion, acts as a tonic

to the body and helps to correct constipation and other disorders of the digestive tract.

The U. S. government says "Buttermilk is an excellent food alike for old and young. For health and pleasure, few drinks excel pure, fresh, cold buttermilk."

Buttermilk and a sandwich or salad make a nutritious, healthful luncheon, popular with business men.

Gooseberry Combination Sandwich (Open)
Gooseberry relish, cheese, toast, lettuce

Add enough finely grated Herkimer or old American cheese to one-half cup of well strained gooseberry relish to bind. Spread on thin slices of fancy cut toast or bread. Serve on leaves of lettuce. This is one of the most appetizing and best sweet fillings in the book. Strained apple sauce may be handled the same way. Gooseberry relish mixed with cream cheese makes an ideal combination.

Gooseberry Relish Sandwich
Herkimer cheese, gooseberry relish, bacon, toast, lettuce

Make a mixture of three ounces of chopped Herkimer cheese, one ounce of gooseberry relish, three strips of ground, broiled bacon. Spread on thin slices of toast, press on upper slice and serve on leaves of lettuce. Cream cheese may be used in place of Herkimer.

Gooseberry relish can be purchased in any first class delicatessen store. (See gooseberry relish recipe under Gooseberry Combination Sandwich.)

GOOSEBERRY RELISH

Put four quarts of gooseberries, two pounds of seeded raisins and four oranges thru a fine grinder. Then put on fire and boil fifteen minutes. Add one pint of water or fruit juice and four pounds of granulated sugar and cook until the consistency of marmalade. (Cherry juice is very good.)

Gravied Egg Sandwich
Egg, butter, toast, essence of beef or mutton, onions

Fry one egg over in butter and place on round of toast. Press on upper slice. Mix equal quantities of butter and essence of roast mutton or roast beef; slightly thicken, season and pour over toast. Garnish around sandwich with fried onions. Serve hot and at once.

Eggs fried under a broiling steak or chop are, as Brillat Savarin said, quite edible.

Green Sandwich—I

*White bread, lettuce, butter, cress, green olives,
capers, mayonnaise*

Chop equal amounts of cress and green olives
with one-half the amount of capers. Mix with
enough mayonnaise to bind. Spread on thin slices
of buttered white bread. Lettuce, press on upper
slice, cut into fanciful shapes and serve in fancy
folded napkins garnished with cress. A few chopped
chives may be added to give additional zest. Cut
sandwiches in shamrock or clover leaf shapes for
novelty.

Green Sandwich—II

*Green olives, capers, pistachio nuts, mayonnaise,
bread, butter, lettuce, mint*

Chop equal parts of green olives, capers and
pistachio nuts and mix with enough green mayonnaise to bind. Spread mixture on thin slices of
buttered and lettuced bread. Press on upper slice
and cut in desired shapes. Garnish with sprigs of
mint.

Bread can be cut into shamrock or clover leaf
shapes, then spread with mixture and a very thin
border of cream cheese piped around edge of these
open sandwiches to enhance the appearance.

Green Peas and Mint Sandwich

Peas, mint, mayonnaise, white bread, butter, lettuce

Puree a few freshly cooked green peas and add
a little finely chopped mint leaves. Spread thin slices
of buttered white bread with mayonnaise and mixture, season, press on upper slice, cut in diamond
or finger shapes. Arrange on lettuce leaves and
garnish with sprigs of mint.

AUTHOR'S NOTE: New green peas should be
cooked in the least possible amount of water, and
when cooked to be drained very dry. Cook in an
open vessel and add one-fifth or sixth teaspoon of
soda to a quart of water when boiling peas to retain
color. Peas should be drained immediately when
cooked, and chilled in cold water. By doing this
they will retain a fine green color. That is, if they
were of a fine green color to start with.

Green Pepper Sandwich

*Green pepper, celery, French dressing, mayonnaise,
lettuce, ripe and green olives, radishes, bread*

Chop one sweet green pepper and one-third cup
hearts of celery. Marinate in French dressing for

at least three hours. Grind and drain thoroly, then add enough mayonnaise base No. 3 to bind. Spread on thin slices of trimmed bread; press on upper slice, garnish with lettuce, ripe and green olives and lilied radishes. A little grated horseradish adds zest to mixture.

Chopped green peppers mixed with an aromatic mayonnaise and spread on thin slices of buttered bread makes a tasty combination.

Methods of Using Green Peppers for Garnish

1.—Place a green pepper in hot grease for half a minute; remove and rub off skin.

2.—Place pepper in a pan of boiling water with a pinch of soda and salt.

3.—Boil until underdone and allow to cool. Pepper can then be cut in strips, dice, rings, diamonds, etc., and has a bright, good looking color. It will also be tender and still crisp enough to use as a garnish on salads, etc.

4.—Place pepper on broiler or over flame. Turn so all sides of pepper are blistered. Remove and rub off skin.

5.—Use au naturel.

Grill Sandwich

Cheese, almonds, lettuce, green olives, mayonnaise, lemon juice, salt, toast

Chop two ounces old Herkimer cheese, twelve blanched almonds, one-fourth of a small head of lettuce and eight stoned green olives, and mix together. Add lemon juice and salt. Bind with mayonnaise. Spread on toast or plain bread; press on upper slice and cut in desired shapes. The mixture is enough for three sandwiches.

Grilled Filet Mignon Sandwich (Open)

Filet mignon, toast, butter, Bermuda onion, tomato, cress, pickle

Grill a tenderloin steak cut one-half inch thick (medium). Place two pieces of buttered toast on a plate or platter. On one piece put the grilled steak and on the other a slice of broiled Bermuda onion. Garnish either end with a quartered tomato and place a little cress and a fanned pickle in the center. Have everything ready when steak comes off the broiler. Pour a little butter over steak and onion and serve at once.

Grilled Roast Beef Sandwich—I (Open)
Roast beef, toast, butter, tomato, Bermuda onion, parsley

Cut a slice of cold roast beef one-fourth of an inch thick and grill quickly on a hot broiler. Place on two trimmed pieces of thin buttered toast (as in hot roast beef sandwich) and pour over a little melted butter. Garnish sandwich with a slice of fried tomato, a slice of fried Bermuda onion and a sprig or two of parsley. Serve at once.

Voltaire, in a pert remark on English cookery said "that tho they have twenty-four religions they only have one sauce." However, a little melted butter added to the natural roast beef juice and poured over any grilled meat enhances its flavor.

Grilled Roast Beef Sandwich—II (Open)
Roast beef, Pullman bread, tomato, lettuce, French fried potatoes

Grill one-half inch slice of cold, medium roast beef over a hot charcoal broiler for one minute on either side. Serve on plain or toasted slices of Pullman bread. Garnish with lettuce, quartered tomato and French fried potatoes. Serve at once. This is an excellent plan of using up end pieces of cold roast beef.

Grinner Sandwich
See Aromatic

Guinea Sandwich
See Breast of Guinea

Half Moon Sandwich
Almonds, capers, mayonnaise, bread, olives, lettuce

Mince one-half cup of blanched almonds, skinned, and mix with one tablespoon of finely minced capers. Add these to just enough mayonnaise to bind, season with salt and spread on four half rounds of thin white bread. Garnish with olives and lettuce.

White meat of chicken can be used in place of almonds, or two parts almonds, two chicken and one part capers.

Halibut Sandwich
Halibut, lemon juice, paprika, mayonnaise, toast, pickles, lettuce

Drain one-half pound of boiled halibut, flake and rub thru a sieve. Season with salt, lemon juice, paprika and add enough mayonnaise base No. 5 to produce a good spreading mixture. Spread on thin slices of toast or plain bread and sprinkle with finely chopped pickles, sweet or sour. Cover with upper slice and cut into desired shapes. Serve on bed of lettuce.

A thick raw cream, cream or tomato sauce, may be used in place of mayonnaise.

Thin slices of bread spread with halibut mixture, then trimmed and toasted in a patent toaster, makes a real tasty Friday sandwich.

Ham Sandwich
See also

Cheese and Ham	Sugar Cured Ham
Chicken, Ham & Tongue	Toasted Veal Ham
Hot Roast Ham	Virginia Ham
Sardine and Ham	

Ham Sandwich—I
Boiled ham, butter, lettuce, rye bread, dill pickles, mustard, slaw

Between thin slices of rye bread, buttered and lettuced, place cold boiled ham. Cut diagonally. Place sandwiches on a plate and garnish with a ham cornucopia filled with slaw and lettuce, and sliced dill pickle. Serve made mustard on side.

Ham Sandwich—II
Rye bread, butter, lettuce, boiled ham, dill pickle, mustard

Cut rye or half-rye bread in thin slices, butter and lettuce and lay on thin slices of cold boiled ham. (A well cured smoked ham, boiled and allowed to cool in its own liquor and then sliced, is ideal.) Press on upper slice, cut diagonally and garnish with lettuce and slices of dill pickle or small green onions. Serve mustard on the side, if requested. A little cole slaw served in a hollowed out boiled and pickled beet makes an ideal garniture.

Bread may be spread with a mustard butter, but if one is seeking the delicate flavor of the ham eat it au naturel and not with mustard, or any other condiment.

Ham Au Gratin Sandwich (Open)
Ham, toast, cream sauce, butter, Herkimer cheese

Cover two pieces of buttered and trimmed toast with finely diced boiled ham. Pour over ham a light cream sauce and sprinkle top of sauce with grated Herkimer cheese, paprika and butter. Brown

under a quick broiler and serve at once. Use the
same method of arranging as in Chef's Special.

Minced ham, and cooked elbow macaroni (equal
proportions) bound together with a rich tomato or
cream sauce, then spread on toast, sprinkled with
grated Herkimer cheese and browned makes a real
tasty item. Serve hot and at once.

Ham Combination Sandwich (Open)
Toast, ham, egg, Hollandaise sauce

On a round of toast place a round piece of
broiled ham. On ham place a poached egg. Serve
at once. This makes an excellent open sandwich.

HOLLANDAISE SAUCE: Three egg yolks, one-third
teaspoon of salt, one-fifth teaspoon of paprika, one
tablespoon of lemon juice, two tablespoons of cream,
one-fourth pound of butter. Beat eggs, salt, paprika and cream in a bowl and pour into double
boiler. Cook until it thickens. Remove from fire and
stir in lemon juice.

Ham and Pineapple Sandwich (Open)
*Toast, butter, ham, pineapple, strawberry jam,
potatoes*

On a slice of toasted white bread, trimmed and
buttered, place a slice of broiled ham (horseshoe
cut). Cover with a slice of fried pineapple, and fill
center of pineapple with strawberry jam. Sprinkle
ham and pineapple sandwich with a little powdered sugar. Place it under hot broiler for one
minute and send to table piping hot. This makes
a real picture if handled right. Garnish with
julienne potatoes.

Ham Salad Sandwich
Ham salad, bread or toast

Put a ham salad thru a fine grinder. Spread on
thin slices of plain bread or toast. Press on upper
slice and cut into desired shapes. Serve on lettuce
leaves.

Ham, turkey, lobster or in fact any of the meat
salads put thru a fine grinder and worked into a
fine mixture makes an excellent filling for a plain
or toasted sandwich. A lettuce leaf inserted between slices adds to the attractiveness and flavor.

Ham Steak Sandwich (Open)
Toast, ham, tomato sauce, onions

On two pieces of toast, placed end to end and
trimmed, place a horseshoe cut of ham steak, broiled.
Pour over ham a rich tomato sauce. Garnish either

end of sandwich with French fried onions. Ham steak should be cut at least one-fourth inch thick. This makes a very desirable combination.

Ham Sandwich, Unusual

Bread, tomato butter, boiled ham, green peppers, mustard butter, lettuce

Spread a very thin slice of white bread with tomato butter and place on top a thin slice of boiled ham, sprinkled with finely chopped green peppers. Spread the upper slice with mustard butter and press on. Cut into desired shapes and serve on leaves of lettuce.

Hamburger Sandwich I

Ground raw beef, onions, bread, pickle

Make thin, round cakes of finely chopped or ground raw beef. Remove sinews and work in a few finely minced onions. Season well and either fry on griddle or broil cakes. Serve between two slices of untrimmed bread. These sandwiches are generally served without garnish of any kind unless it be a slice of onion or pickle. Knives or food chopper should be sharp or all the juice of beef will be pressed out, making cake extremely dry. A quick, fast broiler or griddle is the thing for cooking hamburger.

One-third pound of finely chopped, cooked potatoes and two-thirds pound of finely chopped raw beef or veal with one egg yolk, salt, pepper and one finely minced onion make an ideal mixture to press into thin cakes to grill or fry. Add one-half cup of bread crumbs to hold mixture together and take up surplus moisture.

Hamburger Sandwich II

See Broiled Hamburger

Hard-Boiled Egg Sandwich I

Bread, anchovy butter, hard-boiled eggs, lettuce

On a very thin slice of white bread spread with anchovy butter or mayonnaise, place thin slices of hard-boiled eggs, seasoned. Press on tightly top slice and cut in squares, diamonds or finger slices. Serve on flattened out leaves of lettuce.

Bread can be toasted, then cut into squares and a Thousand Island dressing poured over squares. Garnish with a round of cold slaw or small hollowed out tomato filled with slaw.

Hard-Boiled Egg Sandwich II

Toast, mayonnaise, hard-boiled egg, lettuce, pickles

Spread a thin piece of toast with butter and mayonnaise, cover with slices of hard-boiled egg. Season, press on upper slice and trim. Cut into desired shapes. Mayonnaise may be sprinkled with finely ground broiled bacon or cooked liver for added flavor.

Chopped cress worked into mayonnaise adds zest to sandwich also. Serve on leaves of lettuce and garnish with small pickles, or quartered tomato.

Harlequin Sandwich (Open)

Beef tongue, truffles, parsley, cream, toast, bread crumbs, eggs

Grind and pound in mortar one ounce of boiled, smoked beef tongue. Add a teaspoon of chopped parsley and one tablespoon of finely chopped truffle. Heat two ounces 40% cream and parsley, tongue and truffle and cook for a minute. Fry two eggs and trim to shape with a round cutter so that they are uniform. Place eggs on rounds of toast, pour over cream, etc., sprinkle with bread crumbs and paprika, brown quickly and serve.

Hash Sandwich

See also

Chicken	Lamb
Corned Beef	Southern

Hash De Lux Sandwich
Hysitium

Cabbage, corned beef hash, tomato, beets, cress, egg, bread crumbs

Parboil leaves of cabbage for four minutes and allow to cool. Take as many leaves as you desire and roll a small ball of cold corned beef hash in each one of them. Place balls in roast pan with a little stock, sprinkle with butter then place in oven and braise and baste until brown. Remove from oven and allow to cool. Cut balls in half and flatten out. Dip them in egg and plenty of bread crumbs, then fry brown in butter. Insert a slice of peeled ripe tomato between two half slices of fried corned beef hash and place two of the sandwiches on a hot plate. Garnish with chopped pickled beets and cress. This makes an unusual, tasty item.

Hawaiian Sandwich

Raisin bran bread, mayonnaise, pineapple, lettuce

Toast thin slices of raisin bran bread and spread either with butter or mayonnaise. Place a thin slice of freshly fried pineapple on toast; press on upper slice. Trim and serve as soon as made. A leaf of lettuce may be placed on pineapple if desired. Plain bread may be used in place of toast, or pineapple can be placed between two slices of buttered raisin bran bread and toasted in a patent toaster. This makes a very tasty, economical item.

Pineapple can be chopped very fine and the surplus moisture drained off, then mixed with mayonnaise and finely chopped lettuce if desired.

Head-Cheese Sandwich

Rye bread, mustard butter, head-cheese, Mexican slaw, lettuce

On thin slices of rye bread spread with mustard butter press on thin slice of head-cheese. Cover cheese with a very thin layer of Mexican slaw. Press on upper slice and cut in two diagonally. Serve on leaves of lettuce.

Health Sandwich—I

Whole wheat bread, mayonnaise, lettuce, carrots, cabbage, tomato

On a thin slice of whole wheat bread, spread with mayonnaise and butter, place a thin layer of julienned lettuce. Sprinkle lettuce with finely ground raw carrots and cabbage. Season, then place a slice of red ripe tomato, peeled, on top of cabbage and press on upper slice. Cut into desired shape and serve on leaves of lettuce. The sandwich should not be over one inch high. Julienned lettuce, ground carrots and cabbage can be bound together with a lemon mayonnaise and then used as a spread if desired.

This is really a health giving item and when eaten for lunch with a glass of milk and a few shelled nuts will furnish the sedentary worker with enough health giving minerals, as well as proteins, to carry him or her thru until night. This is the kind of food that clears the brain, brings sparkle to the eye and pep to the step. For elderly people, office girls, boys and school teachers it is ideal.

This sandwich cut into squares and masked with a Thousand Island dressing makes a real salad sandwich.

One-half cup of cole slaw ground fine and then

mixed with an equal amount of raw ground carrots and bound together with a lemon mayonnaise makes a good combination.

Health Sandwich—II

Cucumber, onion, cress, celery, whipped cream, salt, buttermilk, lemon juice, whole wheat bread, lettuce

Peel half a cucumber and slice very thinly, then soak in a bowl of salted water for twenty minutes with one slice of onion. Remove the onion and squeeze the cucumber in a towel until very nearly dry, chop the cucumber, one small bunch of cress, and one small stalk of celery very finely, mix one-half cup of whipped cream, one-third teaspoon salt, four teaspoons buttermilk and one teaspoon lemon juice. Spread this mixture on thin slices of whole wheat bread, cut to shape. Serve on leaves of lettuce.

NOTE: In case the mixture is too thin, add more cucumber. The ingredients can be spread on white bread, graham bread, in fact any kind of bread, but the whole wheat bread gives it the best flavor. This mixture spread on very thin finger sandwiches made of white bread and served with the fish course is delicious.

Health Sandwich—III

Cabbage, green peppers, carrots, mayonnaise, salt, brown bread, white bread, butter, cress, tomatoes

Mix one-half cup each of finely chopped cabbage, green peppers, carrots and bind together with three tablespoons of lemon mayonnaise; add one-half teaspoon salt and mix well. Cut thin slices of white and graham bread and spread with butter. Cover the lower slices of white bread with the vegetable mixture and press on upper graham slices. Trim the sandwiches and cut them in half, then in half again. Place two quarters of the graham and two of the white sandwich on a cold salad plate in shape of a cross, leaving center open. Arrange a pompom of cress in center hole and place a quarter of a ripe, peeled tomato at each intersection of sandwich, using four quarters. Garnish with lettuce.

Health Sandwich—IV

Bread, sauerkraut, spinach, Thousand Island dressing

Press out juice of sauerkraut and chop fine. Chop an equal amount of raw spinach. Mix together and add enough Thousand Island dressing to bind.

Spread on thin slices of bread and press on upper
slice. These slices can be cut in any shape you desire. This makes a delicious, healthful sandwich.

Henri Sandwich

*Roquefort cheese, cream, white bread, lettuce, ripe
olives, celery hearts*

Rub two ounces of Roquefort cheese thru a fine
sieve and reduce to spreading consistency with a
little raw cream. Spread on thin slices of white
bread, press on leaf of lettuce and upper slice. Cut
into desired shapes. Garnish with lettuce, ripe
olives and celery hearts.

Equal quantities of white meat of chicken and
Roquefort cheese make a good combination. Serve
on leaves of lettuce.

Herb Sandwich—I

*Bread, mint, chervil or cress butter, mayonnaise,
lettuce, cress*

Spread slices of whole wheat bread with mint,
chervil or cress butter, or chop fine equal portions
of these and mix with enough mayonnaise base
No. 3 to bind, then spread on bread. Press on leaf
of lettuce and upper slice. Cut into small, fancy
shapes and serve on bed of cress.

AUTHOR'S NOTE: This is a basic sandwich and
one which may be used to advantage when mingled
with an assortment of meat sandwiches. Human
blood should be slightly alkaline; this sandwich
leaves an alkaline ash and will help to neutralize
the acids which are generated in the body.

Herb Sandwich—II

Whole wheat bread, mayonnaise, endive, cress

On a thin slice of whole wheat or white bread,
spread some finely julienned pieces of French endive bound together with a lemon mayonnaise.
Sprinkle with a little salt. Press on upper slice
and cut in fancy shapes. Serve on bed of watercress.

Chicory, cos, lamb lettuce, sorrel, cress, pepper
grass, Boston lettuce, borage, fennel, chervil, and
mint can be chopped and mixed with mayonnaise
and spread on thin slices of white bread and rolled
or cut in fancy shapes. All these herbs give an
alkaline reaction and can be mixed in with the
more substantial sandwiches. They are not only
decorative and tasty but are essential to health,
supplying minerals which are necessary to the main-

tenance of health. In serving sandwiches of this
kind you help to keep your family or your guests
healthy.

Herb Sandwich III
See Fine Herbs

Herb and Egg Sandwich
Toast, herb butter, egg, veal gravy

Spread a thin slice of trimmed toast with herb
butter. Arrange toast on a platter and cover with
a fried egg turned over. Press on upper slice of
trimmed and buttered toast. Cut in four pieces and
Serve hot and at once. Veal gravy may be poured
over sandwich.

Herb and Egg Combination Sandwich
*Tarragon, chervil, sweet basil, chives, eggs, cream,
toast, butter, lettuce*

Chop fine one teaspoon each of tarragon, chervil,
sweet basil and chives. Whip up two eggs with
one tablespoon cream, add chopped herbs and season. Divide mixture into two parts and fry quickly
in two small egg pans. Turn mixture over and
fry on both sides as you would "eggs over." Butter
a thin slice of toast and place one-half of the fried
mixture on it. Press on a second slice of thin toast,
then place the second half of mixture on it; lastly,
press on a third thin slice of toast. Trim and cut in
half diagonally. Serve on bed of lettuce.

This sandwich cut into four squares and served
with a little well flavored tomato sauce poured over
it will be very much appreciated by those who
try it.

Herbs and Flower Sandwiches
*Bread, nasturtiums, violets, sorrel, chervil, sour
grass, tarragon, cress, dandelion, chives, onion tops*

Any of the above herbs or flowers can be used in
sandwiches to an advantage. The flowers as well
as the small leaves of nasturtiums, chopped fine
and mixed with sweet butter or mayonnaise and
served on thin, trimmed slices of bread are ideal.
Chervil, tarragon, pepper grass, cress, chives and
the small, new leaves of the dandelion, chopped and
mixed with butter, then spread on thin slices of
bread are basic in composition and are real health
items. They are tasty and economical and will be
relished by all who try them. Mixed in with meat
and cheese sandwiches they constitute the balancing
items.

Herkimer Cheese Sandwich—I

Herkimer cheese, gherkins, hard-boiled eggs,
mayonnaise, toast

Mix equal parts of finely chopped gherkins, hard-boiled eggs and aged Herkimer cheese. Bind together with mayonnaise base No. 3. Spread on thin slices of plain break or toast. Press on upper slice. Trim and cut into desired shapes. This is a very nippy item if cheese is genuine.

Herkimer Cheese Sandwich—II

Herkimer cheese, cucumber, rye bread, bacon, lettuce

Mash to a paste two ounces of Herkimer cheese. Mix into paste one ounce of finely chopped pickled cucumber. Spread mixture on a thin slice of rye bread. Press on a strip of broiled bacon, leaf of lettuce and upper slice. Cut in two diagonally and serve. This is a likable combination.

If cheese mixture is too stiff add a little French dressing base No. 5.

HERKIMER CHEESE: Cheese should be at least one year old in order to get that mellow tang and flavor, the flavor that all epicures and men who know seek. Cheddar and Stilton cheese are not considered good until two years old.

Herring Sandwich

See Kippered Herring

Hickory Nut Sandwich

Nuts, mayonnaise or cream cheese, bread, lettuce

Mix chopped hickory nuts in mayonnaise base No. 3, or with a cream cheese thinned down with French dressing base No. 5. Spread on thin slices of bread, press on leaf of lettuce and upper slice. Cut in desired shapes and serve on bed of lettuce. This makes an ideal sandwich filling. Almonds, filberts, pistachios, walnuts, or pecans mixed with butter and lemon juice, mayonnaise or cream cheese make ideal fillings also. Use only enough mayonnaise to bind nuts together.

AUTHOR'S NOTE: Nuts are entitled to one of the foremost places in the diet of man because they are rich in proteins and fats, two of the most important nutrients in the chemistry of food. Most proteins and fats drawn from the soil and ripened under the rays of the sun are undoubtedly superior to those we get from animal flesh, which are in a state of decay as quickly as killed; and carry toxic poisons in the form of uric acid, crenitin, etc., as

well as many other poisons carried thru disease of
the animal when slaughtered.

Hoi Toi Sandwich

*Pork tenderloin, toast, butter, apple, Long Branch
potatoes*

On a round of buttered toast place a very thin
slice of fried apple.   On apple place a thin slice
of Frenched pork tenderloin, broiled or fried. Press
on upper slice and serve.   Garnish with Long
Branch potatoes.   Toast may be spread with butter
and then with apple sauce, instead of using fried
apple, if desired.   Tenderloin should be cut thin
and pressed to hold shape while frying or broiling.
Two rounds of toast should be served to an a la
carte order.

Horseradish Sandwich

White bread, horseradish butter, lettuce

On a thin slice of plain white bread spread with
horseradish butter press a second slice buttered on
both sides.   On upper side of second slice place an
inner leaf of head lettuce, then press on a third
slice of thin white bread.   Trim and cut into diamonds, squares or fingers.   Be sure to cut bread
thin so that sandwiches are not too high.   If too
high and very small they will topple over and be
hard to manage.

Horseradish sandwiches should be made as late
as possible as the horseradish quickly loses its pungent characteristic.

Horseradish Butter Sandwich

Butter, horseradish, bread, lettuce, aromatic vinegar

Mix sweet butter and finely grated horseradish
flavored with a little aromatic vinegar.   Add just
as much vinegar as the butter will take up.   Use
one-fifth horseradish to four-fifths butter if horseradish is fresh, or mix to suit taste.   Spread mixture on thin slices of white bread, lettuced.   Cut
into strips and serve on leaves of lettuce in accompaniment with other sandwiches.

Butter should be partially melted in order to take
up the additional moisture in the form of vinegar.
(See orange butter.)

Horseshoe Sandwich (Open)

*Ham, toast, egg, cheese, butter, paprika, Long
Branch potatoes*

Place a horseshoe cut of ham, broiled, on a piece
of toast cut in horseshoe shape.   Set toast and ham

in a dish and crack an egg on top of ham. Sprinkle with ground American cheese, melted butter, paprika, and finish cooking in the oven. Arrange on platter and garnish with Long Branch potatoes.

Hot Roast Beef Sandwich—I
Beef, bread, potatoes

Place two slices of untrimmed bread on a silver platter, lengthwise. Cut a slice of prime roast beef, about one-fourth of an inch thick, from the top part of a five- or seven-rib roast. Lay it on bread. Pour over the beef just a little of the natural juice (no thick gravy) and garnish side of beef or sandwich with a small spoon of well seasoned, snow white, mashed potatoes. Beef roasted, either chuck, round, rump, rib or loin should all be cut against the grain and served medium to medium rare. However, many people like well done beef and the top part of the ribs can be cut off and laid aside for this class of patronage. When a round, rump or chuck is used it is best to serve a thin slice of the fatty and well done and a thin slice of the medium on the bread at one time, unless your guest or customer requests a specific kind. A certain kernel or part of the butt of the loin furnishes one of the most luscious steaks or roasts in the entire beef carcass.

Hot Roast Beef Sandwich—II (Open)
Bread, butter, roast beef, mashed potatoes, gravy, cress

On two slices of whole wheat or plain bread place a slice of hot roast beef. Garnish with mashed potatoes. Pour over a little hot roast beef gravy, slightly thickened, and serve.

When roasting a rib roast if you will tie a piece of the short ribs to the light end on fat side, and place the roast in pan fat side down in the roasting you will get a more evenly roasted item. In doing this the small end is raised off of the bottom of pan and heat does not penetrate so quickly. A fast oven should be used for the first fifteen minutes to seal the pores, and then heat should be reduced.

Hot Roast Ham Sandwich
Corn bread, roast ham, raisin sauce, sweet potatoes

On square slice of well baked corn bread, cut in half, place a horseshoe cut of roast ham on bottom piece. Pour over ham a piquant raisin sauce. Press on upper slice and garnish with candied sweet potatoes. Serve a salad with this sandwich.

Corn bread should not be too short, but very thin and baked well done.

Hungarian Sandwich (Open)
Hungarian goulash, toast, cheese, tomato

Grind warm Hungarian goulash very fine and drain off surplus moisture. Spread thick on a freshly made slice of toast, sprinkle with old American cheese and brown under hot broiler. Garnish with slices of fried tomato and serve at once. This is an excellent outlet for left-over stews. The goulash can be ground and surplus moisture reduced or evaporated in oven and residue then mixed with ground hash as a binder.

Hunter Sandwich
See Ye Olden Hunter

Hysitium Sandwich
See Hash De Luxe

Ice Cream Sandwich
Sponge cake, ice cream, strawberries

Line the bottom of a quart mold with a thin slice of sponge cake. Cover cake with a layer of partially frozen vanilla ice cream, one inch thick. Place a second slice of cake on top of cream and then a layer of pistachio cream. Now place a third slice of cake on top. Set in cooler or freezer to harden; then cut into one inch slices. Serve crushed strawberries on the side and pour over sandwich at the table.

This makes an excellent sandwich dessert. Ice cream should be spread on top of cake evenly and cake pressed down so that sandwich, when completed, looks uniform. Sandwich should not be over three and one-half inches square. It may be made with two layers of cake if desired.

Indian Sandwich—I
Eggs, cream, curry powder, butter, toast, bacon butter, tomato

Whip up the whites of two eggs with one tablespoon of cream; whip up two yolks with one tablespoon of cream and one-fifth teaspoon of curry powder. Fry whites and yolks separately in butter and turn them over. Have ready two thin slices of toast spread with bacon butter. Arrange fried egg whites on lower slice. Press on upper slice and cut in two diagonally. Garnish top slice with the fried yolks and the sides with slices of fried tomato. Curry powder may be whipped into the entire egg with cream and then turned over.

Indian Sandwich—II

India relish, mayonnaise, bread, cress, celery

Grind one-half cup of sweet India relish and drain thoroly, then bind together with mayonnaise. This makes an excellent spread for rolled sandwiches or as an item for small, fancy assorted ones. Garnish with cress and small inner hearts of celery.

One-half cup of warm butter mixed with one-half cup of mayonnaise worked together in a porcelain bowl over chopped ice and then two cups of well ground and drained India relish worked in makes a real filling.

Italienne Sandwich (Open)—I

Green pepper, onion, canned tomatoes, toast, eggs, cheese

Chop fine one small green pepper and one small onion. Dust in flour and saute in butter until brown. Place one cup of canned tomatoes in a chafing dish and add onion and pepper. Reduce to one-half and season. Arrange two slices of thin toast on a platter and place two fried eggs on toast. Pour tomato mixture over the eggs. Cover top of sauce with grated Gorgonzola or Parmesan cheese and place under a hot broiler. Brown quickly and serve at once, very hot. This is a real, honest to goodness treat.

Italienne Sandwich (Open) II

Spaghetti, bacon, shrimp, cheese, toast, catsup, lettuce, Worcestershire sauce

Chop very fine one cup of boiled, well drained spaghetti, two strips of broiled bacon and one-half cup of cooked shrimps, mix together and add two tablespoons of tomato catsup and one of Worcestershire sauce. Season. Spread on toast, sprinkle with grated cheese and brown under a hot broiler. Garnish with lettuce and serve at once.

Jack Wright Sandwich (Open)

Toast, tomato, eggs, Buerre Noir sauce

On two rounds of toast place two slices of fried tomato; on tomato place a poached egg. Pour Buerre Noir sauce over eggs and serve at once.

Jam Sandwich
See Strawberry Jam

Jap Sandwich
Cream dressing, cucumbers, onion, bread, butter

Make a dressing of one-fourth cup of fresh sweet cream (thick), one-fourth cup of whipped cream, one teaspoon of lemon juice, one-fifth teaspoon of freshly ground black pepper, one-fourth teaspoon of salt, one tablespoon chopped chives. Whip cream and the whipped cream together, add salt, pepper, chives and then whip in the lemon juice. The cream must be fresh. Peel, sear and slice thinly a large hot house cucumber and marinate in a little salt water with a few slices of onion for an hour and then squeeze cucumbers in a towel. Add cucumber to sauce and allow to stand in ice box twenty-five minutes.

Arrange cucumber on thin slices of buttered bread. Press on leaf of lettuce and upper slice, cut in fancy shapes and serve on folded napkin. This sandwich served as an accompaniment to fish is always acceptable.

Cucumbers can be marinated with onions in French dressing, squeezed and then mixed with a little cream cheese to bind. Squeezed cucumbers, chives and shredded lettuce make a good combination. The sauce poured over the cucumbers and served as a hors d'oeuvre makes an ideal item.

Jean Sandwich (Open)
Toast, butter, eggs, shallots, mushrooms, cream sauce, parsley

On two rounds of toast, spread with butter, place two well drained poached eggs. In a half-cup of good cream sauce mix a tablespoon of chopped shallots and one of mushrooms which have been previously sauted in butter. Pour sauce over eggs and sprinkle with parsley. Serve at once.

Jefferson Sandwich (Open)
Chicken, mushrooms, green pepper, cream, toast, Herkimer cheese, cole slaw, cress

Put thru a grinder one cup of cooked white meat of chicken. Saute in butter two finely chopped large mushrooms and one green pepper. Add mushrooms and pepper to chicken and place in a chafing dish. Moisten with one cup of cream, season and simmer until reduced and thick. Spread mixture on thin slices of toast, sprinkle with ground Herkimer cheese and brown quickly under a hot broiler. Garnish with cole slaw and cress.

AUTHOR'S NOTE: Dr. Coogan in 1612 wrote regarding chicken sandwiches or chicken on sops of bread, "As for chicken upon sops, they are no meat for poor scholars, unless they can get them." This open sandwich must have been soaked with the broth. It was also in the days before they used forks in England, so the sops and chicken must have been eaten with a spoon or just "au natural."

Jewish Sandwich

Smoked beef, mayonnaise, toast, lettuce

Cut thin slices of smoked beef and place on thin slice of toast spread with mayonnaise, press on leaf of lettuce and upper slice. Cut into desired shapes to serve.

Kewanee Sandwich

Toast, prairie hen, butter, mayonnaise, lettuce

Butter thin slices of toast and spread with a paste made of legs of any cooked game, grouse, prairie hen, duck, etc. Remove sinews, pound meat to a paste in a mortar, season with salt, pepper; add shredded lettuce. Add enough mayonnaise to bind. Cut into desired shapes and serve. Kewanee is the Indian word for prairie hen.

Guinea hens' legs, pounded to a paste and seasoned, makes an ideal meat to use in a wild rice cake sandwich, spread with currant jelly.

Wild rice cakes should be made very thin, then fried, allowed to cool and then split.

The breast of any roast wild fowl cut in thin slices and made up like a club sandwich makes a rare treat; in fact, this type of sandwich belongs to the "Rara Avis" type.

Kiddies' Sandwich

Bread, butter, shredded lettuce, carrots, mayonnaise

Cut thin slices of whole wheat or white bread and spread with butter. Mix equal quantities of chopped lettuce and carrots together and bind with a lemon mayonnaise base No. 3. Spread mixture on bread and cut into fancy shapes. Serve on picture plates.

For the children who refuse to drink milk or eat carrots, try a sipper with the former, and cut the sandwich in a peculiar shape for the latter; and both will forget their prejudices.

Kippered Herring Sandwich I (Open)

*Toast, butter, herring, tomato, eggs, tomato sauce,
parsley*

On two slices of buttered toast, arranged length-wise on a platter, place four fillets of hot kippered herring. Over top of herring at one end place a slice of fried tomato, then next to tomato place a small mound of scrambled eggs, next another slice of fried tomato, and last another small mound of scrambled eggs. Pour a little tomato sauce around the base and serve at once. Garnish with parsley. Tomato and eggs are alternately placed the length of the toast. This makes a pretty breakfast dish. Two eggs are ample and should be mixed with a little cream before scrambling.

Kippered Herring Sandwich II (Open)

Toast, eggs, butter, kippered herring, parsley

Fry two eggs in butter and while eggs are cooking add two or three fillets of kippered herring. When eggs are nearly set put them in oven to finish. Serve on toast on a hot platter. Garnish with parsley. Eggs may be turned over and a little good tomato sauce poured over them just before serving, for sake of variety.

Kippered Herring Sandwich III

Kippered herring, eggs, chives, butter, toast, parsley

Whip up two eggs with two fillets of boned kippered herring and one teaspoon of chopped chives. Scramble in egg-pan with butter. Turn out on slice of trimmed and buttered toast, press on upper slice and cut in two diagonally. Garnish with parsley and serve at once. An excellent Friday or Lenten item.

Kraut Sandwich Cooked

*Kraut, onion, carrot, garlic, chicken stock, toast,
butter*

Simmer one pound of kraut (after pressing out juice) with one small onion, one carrot, one-fourth clove garlic in one quart of chicken or veal stock for about two hours. Chop up all ingredients and press out surplus moisture. Brown in a little bacon grease. Spread kraut on buttered slices of toast, press on upper slice, trim, cut and serve at once. Spread kraut evenly over the toast.

A few thin slices of Thuringer sausage (cooked) mixed into kraut while browning adds to flavor of sandwich.

Kugel Sandwich
Veal, peas, beans, egg, toast

Put five ounces of raw veal, two ounces of canned or new peas and two ounces of stringless beans thru a fine grinder. Add one-half teaspoon of salt, one-half teaspoon of pepper and one-half raw egg. Mix thoroly and make into thin cakes and broil or fry. Serve on thin slice of toast, press on upper slice and trim. Garnish with quartered tomato and lettuce.

A thin tomato or cream sauce (hot) can be poured over at last minute if desired.

Lady Finger Salad Sandwich
Chicken salad, lady fingers, lettuce, lemon

Make a chicken salad and then put it thru a fine meat grinder. Split lady fingers and spread paste on one-half. Press on upper half and arrange three or four on bed of lettuce. Garnish with lemon.

This makes a very fine afternoon tea sandwich item.

Lamb Sandwich
Lamb, white bread, lettuce, mint butter

On thin slices of white bread, lettuced and spread with mint butter or mint jelly and butter, place thin slices of cold roast lamb. Press on upper slice, trim and cut in fancy shapes. Serve on bed of lettuce.

Lamb Sandwich
See also

Lamb Tongue   Pickled Lamb
Mutton   Roast Leg of Lamb

Lamb Hash Sandwich (Brown)
See Beef Hash

Lamb's Kidneys Sandwich I (Open)
Lamb's kidneys, onions, toast, butter, bacon, cress, lemon

Split three lamb's kidneys in half and soak in cold water for fifteen minutes. Wipe dry and dredge with a little salt, pepper and flour. Fry in bacon grease until brown on both sides with a few minced onions and then cover, allowing them to smother for about ten minutes on the back of the range. Place kidneys on buttered toast, cut diagonally. Sprinkle with butter and strip with bacon. Serve at once. Garnish with cress and lemon.

Lamb kidney stew strained and then put thru a

food chopper makes a real filling for a sandwich. Spread the ground lamb's kidney stew on toast, press on upper slice, cut in two and serve hot.

Lamb's Kidneys Sandwich II
Lamb's kidneys, bacon, chicken, mayonnaise, chervil, toast, butter, lettuce

Grind finely two grilled lamb's kidneys (cold), three strips of broiled bacon (cold) and three ounces of boiled chicken (cold). Mix with enough mayonnaise to bind, then work in one tablespoon of chopped chervil or cress. Spread on thin slices of buttered toast, press on upper slice and cut in finger shapes. Serve on bed of lettuce. This is an excellent midnight item.

These tiny sandwiches, dipped in beaten egg and cream mixture, then fried, make real tid-bits.

Lambake Sandwich
White milk bread, lamb, bacon, mayonnaise, mint butter

On thin slices of plain white milk bread, spread with mint butter, place thin slices of cold roast lamb. Press on second slice, spread with mayonnaise, and cover with three strips of bacon. Press on third slice. Trim and cut diagonally. Serve on leaves of lettuce. Garnish with mint jellied croutons.

Mint Jelly Croutons: Cut thin slices of toast in heart shape and spread with jelly. Make two hearts out of one slice of bread.

Laparose Sandwich (Open)
Butter, anchovy paste, sardines, chervil, gherkins, toast, radishes, lettuce

Mix three ounces of butter with one-fourth ounce of anchovy paste. Chop up separately six small French oil sardines (boned and skinned), one teaspoon of chervil, one-half ounce of gherkins and mix in butter. (Chop all ingredients very fine.) Spread mixture on small fanciful cuts of white or rye bread, toasted or plain. See that the mixture is put on evenly and then pressed with fork tongs to give a criss-crossed effect to the top. Garnish top of sandwich with very thinly sliced hot-house radishes; using at least three slices on each open sandwich. Arrange on a bed of lettuce.

This may be used either as a hors d'oeuvre or sandwich.

Laperouse Sandwich (Appetizer Combination)

Smoked or canned salmon, anchovies, wine herring, sardines, caviar, tomato, olives

Cut four pieces of thin toast three inches long by one and one-half inches wide and one piece (round) the size of an American dollar. Spread first slice with minced salmon mixed with mayonnaise and garnish top with chopped pickles; the second slice spread with butter and then garnish top with fillets of anchovies cut to shape; the third slice with caviar and the edges garnished with tiny pearl onions, the top with various colored butters; the fourth slice spread with butter and then garnish with fillets of sardines (boned and skinned). Place these four slices on a salad or sandwich plate around the round slice of toast. Garnish center slice with a thick slice of peeled ripe tomato with center removed and in center place a rolled fillet of wine herring nicely trimmed and rolled to shape; the toast to be under-lined with lettuce and garnished with lilied radishes and green olives.

This sandwich if handled correctly will make a beautiful picture.

AUTHOR'S NOTE: Heraclides in his treatise en-titled "The Banquet," says "It is good to take a moderate quantity of food before drinking, and especially to eat such food as one is accustomed to; such as cockles, solens, sea mussels, chemae, peri-winkles, perfect pickles, salt fish (void of smell), and many kinds of juicy fishes. And it is good that, before the main dinner, there should be served up what is called salad, and beet root, and salt fish, in order that by having the edge of our appetite taken off we may go with less eagerness to what is not equally nutritious."

Lenten Sandwich (Open)

Toast, codfish cakes, eggs, cream sauce

On thin rounds of toasted bread place thin, well rounded codfish cakes, browned and well done. On top of fish cakes place two well-drained and trimmed poached eggs. Pour over eggs a thin, well made cream sauce, highly seasoned. Serve a green vege-table or a spring salad with this sandwich. Serve hot and at once.

Lettuce Sandwich

White bread, butter, lettuce, mayonnaise, radishes, gherkins

On a slice of buttered white bread, plain or

toasted, spread a mixture of chopped lettuce and mayonnaise base No. 3 (just enough mayonnaise added to bind). Press on upper slice, trim and cut in finger shapes. Serve on leaf of lettuce. Garnish with lilied radishes and fanned gherkins.

An excellent item to be used as one on a platter of assorted sandwiches. As a filler for a whole wheat sandwich it is par excellent. The filling should be rather heavy and the bread cut rather thin.

Lettuce and Bacon Sandwich
Toast, mayonnaise, bacon, lettuce, tomato

On a thin slice of toast, spread with mayonnaise, lay three strips of broiled bacon covered with finely julienned heart of lettuce. Press on upper slice, trim and cut in two diagonally. Place on leaf of lettuce and garnish with quartered tomato. Serve warm.

In place of using the julienned lettuce, lettuce can be finely chopped, then add mayonnaise to bind.

Lettuce Combination Sandwich
Lettuce, cucumbers, mayonnaise, chives

Mix equal amounts of finely chopped, well drained cucumbers and lettuce (season). Bind together with mayonnaise and add enough chopped chives to flavor. This makes an excellent filling for rolled sandwiches or for the small fancy types.

This class of sandwich should be served as quickly as possible, as the vinegar breaks down the connective tissues of the lettuce and the salt absorbs the water, reducing the lettuce to a pulpy mass. Finely chopped nuts may be added for flavor.

Lettuce, Cress and Tomato Sandwich
See Cress, Lettuce and Tomato

Liederkranz Sandwich I
Brown bread, mayonnaise, Liederkranz cheese, strawberry preserves, lettuce

On a thin slice of steamed brown bread, spread with mayonnaise, place a thin slice of Liederkranz cheese. Over this spread a little conserve of strawberry. Press on upper slice and cut in plain or fancy shapes. Serve on leaves of lettuce.

LIEDERKRANZ: A soft cheese of excellent flavor, somewhat on the camembert type; put up in rectangular packages of about four ounces each and sold in all high class delicatessen stores.

Liederkranz Sandwich II

French rye bread, mustard butter, Liederkranz cheese, lettuce, dill pickle

Spread six thin slices of French rye bread with mustard butter. Press a thin slice of Liederkranz cheese (cut to shape) between each two slices, serving three small tid-bit sandwiches to the order. Garnish with lettuce and a dill pickle cut in shape of an octopus.

French rye bread is made much like the French white bread in shape, only it is very much smaller in circumference.

Limburger Sandwich

(At which my nose is in great indignation)
Limburger cheese, lettuce, rye bread, mustard butter, dill pickle

Slice Limburger cheese and seal it between two leaves of lettuce (hermetically if possible). Spread two thin slices of rye bread with mustard butter. Enclose the wrapped cheese between the rye slices, cut sandwich in two diagonally and serve with slices of dill pickle on leaves of lettuce.

The lettuce helps to hold back from the olfactory nerves the fumes of this malicious and premeditated outrage. The odor never forsakes this item, and sticks closer than a brother to all who touch it.

Lindbergh Sandwich
See Aeroplane

Little German Band Sandwich

Pigs' feet, rye bread, mustard, onions, radishes, lettuce

Split a pickled pig's foot in half and remove all moisture. Place it in center of platter on bed of lettuce. Spread two pieces of rye bread with German mustard, press together and cut in half. Place one-half of sandwich at either side of platter with flat sides out. Garnish ends of pig's foot with small red radishes and young green onions. Serve with near beer and a simple salad.

Liver Sandwich
See Chicken Liver
See Mushroom and Liver

Liver and Onion Sandwich (Smothered)
Toast, liver, onions, bacon

Trim and spread with butter two pieces of toast. Place two or three slices of freshly sliced and fried calves liver on lower slice of toast. Press on upper slice and cut in two diagonally. Garnish with French fried onions and strip top of sandwich with two pieces of broiled bacon, criss-crossed.

This sandwich may be made open style by placing the liver on toast and smothering liver with a thin layer of fried onions.

Lobster Sandwich I
Lobster, chicken, lettuce, mayonnaise, toast, hard-boiled eggs, olives

Cut in fine dice, proportionately, three-fifths boiled lobster, one-fifth cold chicken and one-fifth heart of lettuce, and bind together with mayonnaise. Spread mixture on thin slices of toast, press on upper slice, cut into desired shapes and serve. Garnish with quartered hard-boiled eggs and green olives. Serve on leaves of lettuce.

Lobster Sandwich II
Lobster, turkey, celery, mayonnaise, toast, lettuce, bacon, hard-boiled egg, lemon

Mix equal amounts of finely diced lobster, turkey and inner hearts of celery. Bind together with mayonnaise. Spread mixture on thin slices of toast, press on leaf of lettuce and upper slice. Trim, cut in two diagonally and serve on leaf of lettuce. Garnish with two strips of broiled bacon, a slice of hard-boiled egg and lemon.

Lobster Sandwich III (Open)
Lobster, toast, egg, mayonnaise, celery, capers, lettuce

On a slice of toast, cut square and trimmed, place thin slices of boiled lobster. Arrange neatly and mask with a creamy mayonnaise. Garnish mayonnaise with a tri-color butter. Place this slice of toast in center of cold platter; cut a second slice of toast in half and place a piece at either end of center slice. Garnish these two halves with an inner leaf of lettuce and on one piece place hard boiled egg, quartered, and arranged in form of circle with a mound of mayonnaise in center. White parts of egg should be up, and center of mayonnaise should be decorated with a little lobster coral. On opposite half make a mound of a mixture of chopped celery, shredded lettuce and mayonnaise and sprinkle with a few chopped capers.

Lobster Cardinal Sandwich (Open)

Lobster, mushrooms, butter, cream sauce, toast, Herkimer cheese

Cut in fine dice a one-pound boiled lobster and add an equal amount of finely diced mushrooms, which have been previously sauted in butter. Bind the mushrooms and lobster together with a highly seasoned, thick cream sauce. Spread the mixture on thin finger slices of buttered toast. Sprinkle with grated Herkimer cheese, butter and brown under a hot broiler. Add just enough cream sauce to bind or mixture will run off toast.

Lobster Newburg

Lobster, butter, sherry, cream, eggs

Dice a 1½-pound baby lobster (boiled) and place in an enamel sauce pan with a little butter. Season and fry lightly. Moisten with two tablespoons of sherry wine and reduce one-half. Add one-half cup of double cream and reduce one-third. Whip up one egg yolk with two tablespoons of cream and one of sherry wine. Add this to the lobster and toss to incorporate and thicken, but do not boil.

Or—Cut up into one-fourth inch slices a two-pound lobster, boiled. Heat lightly in two ounces of butter, add one cup of 40 per cent cream and bring to a boil. Season with salt and paprika. Whip up three yolks of eggs with two tablespoons of cream and add to lobster to thicken. Do not boil. Add one-half gill of sherry last. Place in chafing-dish and serve. Serve on sippets of toast.

Lobster Newburg can be served as in Chicken a la King.

Lobster Salad Sandwich

Lobster, celery, mayonnaise, toast, lettuce, Russian dressing, lemon

Cut in fine dice equal amounts of cold boiled lobster and hearts of celery. Bind together with mayonnaise base No. 3 or marinate lobster in French dressing for one hour, drain and bind with mayonnaise. Spread mixture on thin slices of toast; cover with leaf of lettuce and press on upper slice. Trim and cut into four squares. Serve on leaf of lettuce and pour a little Russian dressing over squares. Garnish with fanciful cut pieces of lemon and lobster claws or feelers.

Lobster Thermidor Sandwich
Toast, butter, lobster mixture, Herkimer cheese, cress, lemon, potatoes

Spread thin finger-shaped pieces of buttered toast with a mixture used in Lobster Thermidor. Sprinkle with grated Herkimer cheese, butter, and brown under a hot broiler. Serve on doilies or hot plates. Garnish with cress, slices of lemon, lobster claws and julienned potatoes.

Lobster Thermidor

Cut in fine dice a one-pound boiled lobster and two fresh mushrooms. Saute mushrooms in one ounce of butter until done (do not brown); add the diced lobster, season with salt, cayenne and paprika. Add three tablespoons of raw cream or cream sauce and one of tomato paste, simmer a few minutes, then add one-third cup of fresh bread crumbs to take up moisture. Spread on toast and proceed as directed. See that toast is entirely covered with mixture and that mixture is neither too thin nor too stiff. If too thin, add a little more bread crumbs; if too thick, add a little more cream sauce. If you have a little sherry wine add one tablespoon just before adding the crumbs.

Loin of Pork Sandwich
See Smoked Loin of Pork

Love Potion Sandwich
See Philters

Luncheon Sandwich
See also

Bridge   Fancy   Friday   Sunday

Lyons Sandwich
Rye bread, mustard butter, Lyons sausage, dill pickles, lettuce

On thin slices of rye bread, spread with mustard butter, place thin slices of Lyons sausage. Sprinkle with finely chopped dill pickles, press on upper slice and cut in two diagonally. Serve on leaves of lettuce. Pickle may be omitted.

Lyons sausage is made exclusively of pork, four parts lean to two parts of fat, spices and garlic, stuffed in hog casings and air dried. It makes a delicious sausage.

Two parts sausage, one part cole slaw and one

part cold chicken (boiled) bound together with mayonnaise makes a fine filling.

Mango Sandwich
See Melon Mango

Manhattan Sandwich
Toast, ham, turkey, butter, tomato, mayonnaise, pickle, slaw

On one of two slices of buttered toast place a leaf of lettuce and on top of lettuce a slice of ham. On other slice of toast arrange slices of white meat of roast or boiled turkey. On top center place a slice of tomato covered with mayonnaise. Garnish with fanned pickle and slaw.

Maple Fruit Sandwich (Open)
Toast, butter, mayonnaise, orange, maple sugar, lettuce

On very thin slice of toast cut diagonally and spread with butter and mayonnaise, place very thin slices of sectioned oranges. Sprinkle orange with grated maple sugar and serve on lettuce leaves. After connective tissue from orange section has been removed cut section in two or three very thin slices lengthwise.

Thin slices of raw or cooked peaches or pears can be substituted for oranges. Fruit can be served between two thin slices of toasted pound cake.

Marine Sandwich (Open)
Toast, butter, lettuce, lobster salad, tomato, green pepper, crawfish, Russian dressing

On two rounds of toast, buttered and lettuced, arrange a little finely cut lobster salad. On salad place a slice of ripe, peeled tomato. Around tomato arrange a thick ring of green pepper. Over top of tomato pour a Russian dressing. Garnish base of sandwich with trussed crawfish.

Mariner Sandwich
Toast, mayonnaise, cucumber, smoked whitefish, lettuce, cold slaw

On thin slices of toast, spread with mayonnaise, place a layer of very thin sliced and squeezed out cucumber. On cucumbers place a fillet of smoked bloater, whitefish or herring (skinned and boned). Press on second thin slice of toast, cut diagonally and serve on leaves of lettuce. Garnish with cold slaw or dill pickles, quartered. Fillets should be cut from small fish.

Marmalade Sandwich

Marmalade, cream cheese, toast, lettuce

Chop very fine two ounces of orange or lemon marmalade. Incorporate it with enough cream cheese to make it the right consistency to spread. Spread on thin trimmed slices of plain or toasted bread. Cut into desired shapes and serve on leaves of lettuce. A few chopped Thompson seedless raisins give the sandwich an added zest.

Sandwich can be spread with sweet butter and then with marmalade if desired.

Melon Mango Sandwich

Bread, melon mangoes, chicken, ham, mayonnaise

On very thin slices of white bread, plain or toasted and buttered, arrange a layer of thinly sliced melon mangoes. Press on upper slice and cut into desired shapes. Serve on leaves of lettuce.

Equal amounts of chopped melon mangoes added to minced chicken and minced ham, bound together with mayonnaise base No. 5, make a very tasty item.

Mangoes can be chopped finely, the surplus moisture drained off and then added to enough sweet butter to bind.

Mexican Novelty Sandwich

Mexican slaw, bacon, curry powder, corn meal, egg, tomato, toast

Press out moisture from one-half cup of Mexican or plain slaw, add one strip of broiled bacon, chopped, one-fifth teaspoon of curry powder, three tablespoons of corn meal and one small egg. Dust hands with dry corn meal and make into thin cakes. Fry in round cakes the size of trimmed slice of bread. Place one cake in center of slice of toast, and place a second slice of toast, cut in half, at either end of center slice. Garnish top of each cut half with slice of tomato.

If mixture is too thin add more cornmeal. Fry in shallow hot bacon grease. Sauerkraut, fried or raw, can be handled in the same manner. A teaspoon of finely chopped onions added to slaw adds to the flavor of the sandwich. Sandwich can be garnished with French fried onions or Long Branch potatoes.

Midnight Festival Sandwich

White bread, Roquefort cheese, butter, lettuce, olives, cress

Spread a thin slice of white bread with Roquefort cheese mixed with a little butter. Press on upper slice and toast between a fine wire broiler. Cut in three strips and serve on leaves of lettuce. Garnish with green olives and cress.

Minced Tenderloin Sandwich (Open)

Tenderloin, onion, mushroom, butter, sauce, toast, tomato, cress

Saute one large mushroom, sliced, and one small onion, minced, slowly in two tablespoons of butter until done. Add two ounces of thinly sliced ends of tenderloin and saute two minutes. Season, add three tablespoons good brown sauce, toss and place on toast. Garnish with two slices of fried tomato and cress. Serve at once.

This is a good way to use up the ends of tenderloins.

Mirabeau Sandwich (Open)

Green olives, anchovy butter, toast, eggs, julienned potatoes, cress

Grind fine four stoned jumbo green olives and bind together with anchovy butter. Spread butter on two thin round slices of toast and arrange two well trimmed poached eggs on top. Garnish with julienned potatoes and cress. Serve hot.

Monk Sandwich

Cress, lettuce, mayonnaise, black bread, mint, hard-boiled eggs

On thin slices of white or black bread spread a mixture of equal amounts of chopped cress and lettuce bound together with a little mayonnaise base No. 3. Garnish with mint leaves and slices of hard-boiled eggs.

AUTHOR'S NOTE: A few chopped anchovies added to cress and lettuce gives an added zest, a flavor loved by the monk of the middle ages.

Morning Sandwich
See Sunday Morning

Muffin Sandwich
See Toasted Muffin

Mushroom Sandwich
See Chicken and Mushroom

Mushroom and Liver Combination Sandwich
(Open)

Mushrooms, chicken livers, tomato sauce, tomato, toast, parsley

Saute in butter one large mushroom (finely sliced) and six fresh chicken livers cut in thirds. When done add four tablespoons of well seasoned tomato sauce and cook for two minutes longer. Arrange mushrooms and livers on two slices of freshly made toast and pour sauce over. Garnish ends of toast with two slices of fried tomato. Sprinkle with parsley and serve at once.

Mustard Sandwich

Bread, mustard butter, lettuce

Mustard butter spread on plain white bread, then covered with a little chopped lettuce, and the upper slice pressed on makes a delicious simple sandwich. Trim and cut into desired shapes.

Mutton or Lamb Sandwich

White bread, butter, currant jelly, capers, lettuce, mutton or lamb

Spread a slice of white or whole wheat bread with sweet butter, currant jelly, and sprinkle with finely chopped capers. Press on leaf of lettuce and cover with a slice of cold roast mutton or lamb. Salt and press on upper slice. Trim to desired shape.

A hot slice of roast lamb or mutton placed on buttered toast, garnished with a crouton of currant jelly and cress makes a really tasty hot sandwich. Serve a light sauce over the sandwich at the last minute, or on the side, as desired.

Newburg Sandwich

See Lobster Newburg

New Orleans Sandwich (Open)

Toast, tomato, egg, cream, Herkimer cheese, bacon

On two rounds of thin fresh toast place two slices of fried tomato. On tomato place one egg which has been seasoned, mixed with one tablespoon cream and scrambled. Sprinkle two ounces of freshly grated Herkimer cheese over the egg. Brown under a hot broiler and serve hot and at once. Garnish with two strips of broiled bacon.

Norge Sandwich

Eggs, anchovies, lemon juice, butter, bread

Rub thru a fine sieve three yolks of hard-boiled eggs and six anchovies, skinned and boned. Add a

few drops of lemon juice and work into mixture
two ounces of creamed butter. Spread on thin
slices of bread and cut in fancy shapes.

This is an excellent item for rolled sandwiches or
small, fancy tidbits. Smoked sardines may be used
in place of anchovies.

Nut and Olive Combination Sandwich
Almonds, green olives, cream cheese, vinegar, bread,
lettuce

Chop and pound one-third cup of blanched almonds, mix in one-third cup of stoned green olives
(chopped fine), then work in one package of Philadelphia cream cheese. Add a few drops of aromatic vinegar or lemon juice. Spread on thin
slices of plain white or toasted bread. Press on leaf
of lettuce and upper slice. Trim and then cut into
desired shapes. Serve on leaves of lettuce. Cheese
may be omitted and olives and nuts mixed with
mayonnaise. Pecans, filberts or walnuts may be
used.

Nut Sandwiches
See also

Hickory Nut   Walnut

Olive Sandwich
See also

Perfumed   Salted Spanish

Omelet Sandwich
Eggs, toast, seasoning, cream

Make a plain omelet out of one or two eggs, well
beaten and seasoned. Turn out on one or two
pieces of trimmed toast and serve either with Creole
or Spanish sauce; or incorporate in omelet ham,
bacon, cheese, oysters, brains, kidneys, asparagus
tips, mushrooms, onions, herbs, tomatoes or any other
garnish used with fried or scrambled egg recipes.
An omelet sandwich is a fine addition to the menu
of sandwich shops. Omelets should be made in a
clean pan, used for no other purpose. Eggs should
not be stirred in the pan but rolled; rolled quickly
and served still quicker if you would have a dish
worth while. One egg rolled into an omelet, then
placed between two slices of freshly made trimmed
toast, with a little tomato sauce poured over, makes
a real item. A tablespoon of cream may be added
to each egg in the making of omelets.

To make an omelet, eggs should be whipped
well, so that they are aërated, full of bubbles, light.

Have the frying pan that you are going to make the omelet in clean, hot and well greased. *(Do not use butter or any other frying material containing salt or water if you expect to keep your pans in condition and to roll a real omelet.)* As quickly as your omelet mixture is whipped up pour it into your hot pan and start rolling at once.

Do not allow the mixture to stand a minute after it is whipped up if you would have a light omelet. Roll the omelet quickly over a hot fire.

Onion Sandwich—I

Onions, cress, bread, butter

Cream three ounces of butter and add two tablespoons of chopped onion tops (green) and two of chopped cress. Spread on thin slices of bread, press on upper slice and trim. Cut into desired shapes and serve.

Onion Sandwich—II

Onions, eggs, cream, toast, bacon, cress

Slice six cooked glazed boiling onions and heat in butter in small frying pan. Whip up two eggs with one tablespoon of cream and add to onions. Season, scramble quickly and arrange on a thin slice of trimmed toast. Press on upper slice. Garnish with two strips of bacon, cress and serve at once.

Onion Sandwich III

See Raw Onion

Onion Combination Sandwich

Bermuda onion, whole wheat bread, mayonnaise, lettuce, tomato, cucumbers, Mexican slaw

Peel and slice very thin a Bermuda onion and lay the slices in a little water or fresh milk for at least an hour. Spread slices of whole wheat bread with mayonnaise mixed with finely chopped lettuce. Place sliced onion on top and press on upper slice. Trim and serve on leaves of lettuce. Garnish with a small, ripe, hollowed out tomato filled with chopped cucumber and Mexican slaw mixed with mayonnaise.

Onion and Liver Sandwich

See Liver and Onion

Onion Unique Sandwich

Whole wheat bread, butter, onions, cheese, paprika, bacon, cress

On two slices of buttered whole wheat bread

place three slices of boiled onion which have been breaded and then fried. On top of onion place enough thin slices of good Herkimer cheese to cover. Sprinkle with paprika. Place onions, cheese and bread on plate under a hot broiler. Melt and brown cheese. Strip with broiled bacon, garnish with cress and serve at once.

Onions should not be boiled too much so that they can be cut in uniform slices, one-half inch thick. After they are browned with cheese one cannot tell in the eating that they are onions. This makes a real tasty tidbit.

Ox Tongue Sandwich
See Smoked Ox Tongue

Oyster Sandwich—I (Open)
Green pepper, butter, tomato, eggs, cream, oysters,
toast

Dice one green pepper and simmer in butter in white enamel sauce pan until tender, then add one diced and peeled tomato (without seeds) and simmer for three to five minutes. Whip up two eggs with two tablespoons of cream, season, then whip into pepper and tomato. Stir until nearly thickened, then add six chopped oysters previously poached in butter. Pour mixture on toast and serve at once.

Mixture can be sprinkled with cheese and browned under hot broiler if desired.

Oyster Sandwich—II (Open)
Butter, oysters, seasoning, toast, watercress, celery,
lemon

Place two tablespoons of butter in a chafing dish or frying pan and melt. Dry six New York counts and dredge with salt and pepper. Lay them in the butter and heat on both sides. When thoroly heated thru and set (not brown), arrange on rounds of toast and pour the melted butter over them. Garnish with watercress, small curled hearts of celery and lemon. Serve at once, hot.

This is an excellent way to eat oysters.

Oyster Sandwich—III
Oysters, bacon, toast, anchovy butter, lettuce, Long
Branch potatoes

Dry six New York counts and dredge with salt, pepper and flour. Roll oysters in a very thin strip of bacon and secure strip with a toothpick. Fry in French fryer or brown in oven. Remove and serve on thin, freshly made toast spread with anchovy

butter. Garnish with lettuce and Long Branch potatoes. Remove toothpicks before serving.

Bacon can be partially cooked and then wrapped
around oyster, and afterwards sprinkled with cheese
and browned. This latter item can be used as a
hot hors d'oeurve.

Oyster Tenderloin Sandwich (Open)

Oysters, toast, butter, cream, pickles, cress, eggs

Remove the hard part of twelve New York counts
and saute the tenderloin or soft part in a little butter until oyster stiffens up or until albumen sets.
Whip one tablespoon of oyster liquor and one of
40 per cent cream into two eggs and season.
Scramble eggs in butter, adding oysters to eggs
while scrambling. Have ready on a hot platter two
rounds of toast spread very lightly with butter; and
place eggs and oysters on top of toast. Garnish
with fancy slices of pickle and sprigs of cress.

Pancake Sandwich

Sausage, pancakes, maple syrup, fried apples

Broil three links of farm sausage and place between two freshly made pancakes. Garnish sandwich with slices of fried apple and serve maple
syrup on side; this makes an excellent breakfast
sandwich, an unusual sandwich, one that sells on
sight. Sausage may be split and broiled, if desired.

Pancakes can be made out of buckwheat, plain
white wheat flour or corn meal.

Parmesan Cheese Sandwich

Lettuce, Parmesan cheese, mayonnaise, bread

Chop fine one small head of lettuce and mix with
three ounces of grated Parmesan cheese. Add
enough mayonnaise base No. 3 to bind and spread
on thin slices of bread. Press on upper slice and
cut in fancy shapes.

Use as one in an assortment of fancy sandwiches.

Pate a Chou Sandwich

*Pate a Chou shells, chicken, asparagus tips, cheese,
butter, cress*

Fill finger Pate a Chou shells with Chicken a la
Ritz mixture. Garnish top with asparagus tips and
sprinkle with ground American cheese and butter.
Brown and serve on paper doilies. Garnish with
cress.

Any meat mixture or puree of vegetable can be

served au gratin in Pate a Chou shells. Shells should
be cut one-eighth inch from top the entire length
of the shell and then filled.

Pate a Chou Shells

Place over the fire one cup of butter and a scant
one and one-fourth cups of milk. Bring to a boil,
then work in one and one-fourth cups of flour with
a spatula until dough breaks from the side of the
pan. Remove to the back of range and work in
five eggs, adding one at a time until all are thoroly
worked into paste, then add a few drops of vanilla
and one teaspoon of sugar if desired (but sugar
is not necessary), also a pinch of salt. Drop in
finger shapes on buttered paper in baking sheets
with large spoon drawing out paste to desired
length and shape.

One-half cup butter, one cup flour, one cup water
and four eggs, will also make a good Chou Paste
handled as above.

Pate de Foie Gras Sandwich—I (Open)
Pate de fois gras, butter, toast, lettuce

Puree a small jar of liver pate and chop or cut
truffles artistically. Spread puree on buttered toast
and cut into fancy shapes. Dot the top with truffles. Serve on leaves of lettuce. Use only the
truffles that are taken out of jar. This sandwich
should have no garniture; it is enough in itself and
anything added to it would be like painting a lily.

Liver can be sliced very thinly in place of being
pureed if desired.

Pate de Foie Gras Sandwich II
Pate de foie gras, lettuce, sweet butter, toast truffles

Slice the goose liver very carefully and work the
liquid from jar into a little sweet butter and spread
it on thin slices of toasted bread.

Arrange an inner slice of lettuce on bottom slice
of toast, place the thin slices of liver on lettuce and
press on top slice. Trim to shape. This is an extremely dainty concoction. Garnish with fanned
gherkins, green olives and lilied radishes. Serve on
lettuce leaves.

* * *

Foies gras signifies fat livers and applies especially
to the livers of geese, so-called because they were
first put up in pie or pate form and sold in jars,
tins and boxes. The most famous come from Strass-
burg and Toulouse, France. In the best grades
the livers are whole, the inferior grades are of cut

pieces. Pate de foie gras should be served cold, as it is only in this condition that it is possible to get the full, fine flavor of the liver. If placed in the ice-box for several hours, right on the ice and then served, it will give you an ideal item. Puree de foie gras is made of whole livers and liver trimmings with a little pork added, seasoned and cooked, then pressed thru a fine sieve and small pieces of truffles added and canned.

FOIE GRAS SAUSAGE

Foie gras sausage consists of very fine pieces of goose livers, nuts, trimmings of pork and truffles, highly seasoned and then cased and canned. Either of the last two items make ideal sandwiches; served with a few branches of celery and salted olives they make real appetizing canapes or sandwiches.

Peanut Butter Sandwich—I
Peanut butter, white bread, lettuce, gherkins

Spread peanut butter on thin slices of white bread and cover with finely chopped lettuce. Sprinkle with a little salt, press on upper slice and cut into desired shapes. Serve on bed of lettuce, garnish with fanned gherkins.

Peanut Butter Sandwich—II
Peanut butter, green olives, sweet gherkins, bread, lettuce

Chop (fine) one ounce green olives (without stones) and one ounce sweet gherkins. Press out surplus moisture and whip into two ounces of peanut butter. Use as a spread on thinly cut slices of plain or toasted white bread. Serve in conjunction with other assorted sandwiches on leaves of lettuce.

Peanut Rolls
Peanuts, mayonnaise, rolls, lettuce, olives, radishes, gherkins

Put some freshly roasted peanuts thru a fine grinding machine two or three times, then pound to a paste in a wooden bowl or mortar. Season with a little salt and add butter to bind. Split a finger roll, made in the shape of a small peanut. Spread roll with nut mixture, place a thin strip of lettuce between roll and serve on lettuced plates or platters. Garnish with fluted olives cut in rings, lilied radishes and fanned gherkins.

Pear Sandwich
See Fresh Pears
See Sliced Pears

Pepper Sandwich
Sweet red and green peppers, butter, bread, lettuce

Chop fine equal amounts of sweet red and green peppers. Drain off surplus moisture and bind to-gether with creamed butter. Spread on thin slices of plain white or whole wheat bread. Insert lettuce leaf, press on upper slice and cut into desired shapes. A few chopped olives or pickles added to mixture adds zest to filling. This is an excellent health giving item and one to be used in an assort-ment of sandwiches. Bread can be first spread with mayonnaise for variety.

AUTHOR'S NOTE: Sweet peppers help to promote health by their stimulating action upon the kidneys, liver and lymphatics.

Perfumed Olive Sandwich
Ripe olives, garlic, olive oil, lettuce, mayonnaise, bread

Crush well two cloves of garlic in the bottom of a bowl. Place eighteen large ripe olives on top of gar-lic and cover them with pure olive oil. Stir and set in ice-box until chilled. Remove olives from oil, take out stones, chop up fine and mix with an equal amount of finely julienned lettuce. Bind together with a little mayonnaise base No. 3. Spread on thin slices of bread, press on upper slice and cut into finger shapes. Serve in conjunction with other sandwiches.

The perfumed olive (whole) is an excellent item and can be served as a relish. Serve them in the oil when used as a relish or as a hors d'oeuvre.

AUTHOR'S NOTE. These morsels call for no gar-nish other than the bowl they are served in. They are complete in themselves and to add to them would be like putting mustard on Virginia ham or a strong flavored sauce on a delicious steak.

Philadelphia Scrapple Sandwich
Philadelphia scrapple, toast, sauce, slaw

Bread and fry a thin slice of Philadelphia scrap-ple. Place on a slice of toasted plain white or whole wheat bread, untrimmed, toast to be cut in half and placed on platter in diamond shape. Pour over scrapple a light veal gravy or tomato sauce. Garnish with hot slaw. Serve at once.

The under slice of toast spread with mayonnaise, then covered with a slice of fried scrapple, a strip of broiled bacon and a slice of tomato, and the up-per slice makes a real tasty item. Sandwich should be trimmed and served warm.

Philters (Love Potion) Sandwich (Open)
Toast, anchovy paste, tomato, egg, cream,
tomato sauce

On a round of toast, spread with anchovy butter, place a slice of fried tomato. Whip up one egg with one tablespoon of cream, scramble and place on top of tomato. Pour a rich tomato sauce around base of toast. This may be served as an open sandwich or without tomato sauce as a hot hors d'oeuvre. Serve at once.

Pichi Sandwich
Chicken, pineapple, toast, mayonnaise, butter,
lettuce, olives

Mix equal quantities of finely diced white meat of chicken and finely chopped pineapple with enough creamy mayonnaise to bind. Spread mixture on buttered toast or plain bread, press on upper slice, trim and cut into desired shapes. Garnish with lettuce and mixed olives. This is a very nice item to be included in an assorted sandwich platter.

Pickled Lamb's Tongue Sandwich
Pickled lamb's tongue, toast, mayonnaise, lettuce

Peel tongue and slice very thin. Arrange slices on whole wheat or white bread, toasted and spread with mayonnaise, press on upper slice and cut in two diagonally. Arrange sandwich on leaves of lettuce and serve on cold plate.

Chopped lamb's tongue mixed with an equal amount of white meat of chicken and bound together with mayonnaise makes a good combination.

Pickled lamb's tongues can be purchased at any first class grocery house. They are put up in glass containers.

Pickled Walnut Sandwich
Bread, butter, pickled walnuts, lettuce

On very thin slices of white bread, plain or toasted and buttered, arrange a layer of thinly sliced pickled walnuts (well drained). Press on leaf of lettuce and upper slice and cut into desired shapes. This sandwich should be served on a platter of assorted ones. Walnuts drained, chopped and mixed with chopped endive and enough mayonnaise to bind or equal amounts of chopped pickled walnuts and lettuce, drained and mixed with mayonnaise, adds to the variety.

Picnic Sandwich—I
Meat loaf, bread, butter, lettuce

Mix eight ounces cooked meat, ground; eight ounces raw veal or pork, ground; two ounces raw bacon, ground; one ounce raw ham, ground; one teaspoon salt, one-half teaspoon pepper, one egg yolk, one-half teaspoon ground sage, one-half cup bread crumbs together, make into a loaf and bake in moderate oven three-quarters hour. Allow to cool, slice thin and place on slices of buttered bread. Trim and cut diagonally. Serve on leaves of lettuce. Bread crumbs can be omitted if a more meaty slice is desired.

Picnic Sandwich—II
See Simple Picnic Sandwich

Pie Crust Sandwich—I
Pie crust, chicken, cheese, onions

On a round of fresh made pie crust, place three slices of boiled fowl. Over fowl pour a well seasoned fricassee sauce (not too thin), and then sprinkle liberally with grated Herkimer cheese. Brown quickly under hot broiler and garnish border of crust with glazed, small boiling onions. Serve hot and at once. This is an excellent sandwich and a real money-maker. The crust should be as large as a slice of Pullman bread and at least one-fourth of an inch thick; it should also be rich and flaky.

Pie Crust Sandwich—II
Pie crust, chicken fricasse, sauce, potatoes, parsley

Make a crust like you would for an individual chicken pie and bake it. The crust should not be over four inches wide. After it is baked place it on a dinner plate and cover it with three or four thin slices of white and dark meat of chicken. Pour over the chicken a little fricasse sauce made out of chicken stock, cream, butter, flour and seasoning and garnish sandwich with a small spoonful of mashed potatoes, and a sprig of parsley. The pie crust should be warm and sauce hot. Serve at once. This open sandwich has a very pleasing appearance and is a sandwich that when once tried will be called for many times in the future. For a little noon-day luncheon, I know of nothing that will give better satisfaction or that can be more quickly prepared. A few new green peas and a small canned carrot added to the sauce makes it especially attractive.

Pigs Feet (Boiled) Sandwich (Open)

Rye bread, pigs feet, mustard butter, sauerkraut

On two slices of rye bread spread with mustard butter, placed lengthwise on a platter, arrange a boiled pig's foot split in half. Garnish with fried sauerkraut, cole slaw, dill pickle or mashed turnips.

Pigs feet should be drained well. They also can be split, breaded and fried.

Pimento Sandwich

Pimento cheese, toast, lettuce

Spread thin slices of toast or plain bread with pimento cheese, plain or thinned down with a little aromatic vinegar, French dressing, lemon juice or prepared horseradish. Press on upper slice, trim and cut into desired shapes. This is an excellent cheese item.

Three ounces of pimento cheese, one ounce of finely chopped blanched almonds and one ounce of finely chopped green olives, thinned down with raw cream, makes a tasty combination.

Three ounces of pimento cheese, one ounce of crushed pineapple and a little finely chopped lettuce, seasoned with salt, is a good combination.

One ounce of broiled bacon, ground, three ounces of pimento cheese, thinned down with cream or a heavy No. 5 French dressing, makes an acceptable combination.

Pineapple Sandwich

*Pineapple, almonds, mayonnaise, bread, butter,
lettuce, olives, pickle*

Mix equal amounts of finely chopped pineapple and blanched almonds with just enough mayonnaise to bind. (Drain all surplus moisture out of pineapple before mayonnaise is added.) Spread mixture on thin slices of buttered bread. Trim and cut into desired shapes. Decorate with almonds, sliced olives and octopus pickle. A nice afternoon tea item.

One-half cup of finely chopped and drained pineapple, one-half cup of chopped almonds and one-fourth cup of spiced cantaloupe, mixed with enough cream cheese to bind, is an excellent combination.

Pineapple Combination Sandwich

Pineapple, cream cheese, toast, turkey

Mix finely chopped pineapple with Philadelphia cream cheese, using moisture of pineapple to reduce cheese to proper consistency. Spread on plain or toasted bread; arrange thin slices of white meat of turkey on top of cheese. Press on upper slice, trim and cut into desired shapes. Season turkey with a little salt.

Pineapple (well drained) may be mixed with mayonnaise in place of cream cheese if desired.

AUTHOR'S NOTE: Pineapple contains a ferment called bromelin capable of digesting proteins in an acid media, and is a good source for vitamins A and B.

Pineapple and Ham Sandwich
See Ham and Pineapple

Pinta Sandwich
Anchovies, butter, egg, cream, toast, cress, julienned potatoes

Cut up one-half ounce of boneless anchovies and heat in a little melted butter. Whip up one egg with two tablespoons of cream and cook in a small frying pan just like you would fry eggs. When the egg is set on one side add anchovies and turn over quickly Have two slices of trimmed toast ready. Place egg and anchovies on one slice of toast and cover with second. Cut in two and arrange in diamond shape on plate. Garnish with cress and julienned potatoes. Serve hot.

AUTHOR'S NOTE: Hors d'oeuvres or those eatables more or less salt, were in the early times sold as incitements to drink, and went by the cant term of shoeing horns, gloves or pullers-on. These pullers-on are often referred to by ancient writers. "There comes me up a service of shoeing-horns of all sorts, salt-cakes, red-herrings, anchovies, gammon of bacon and abundance of such pullers-on." *Mundus alter et idem.*

Poha Sandwich
Hawaiian pohaberry jam, bread

Spread on thin slices of bread and roll, or spread with tangy Herkimer cheese and then pohaberry jam and roll. This gives a unique flavor. (See rolled sandwiches.)

Pohaberry grows on low bushes near the rim of the volcano. The berry is about the size of a white cherry containing seeds, but the seeds are very soft and the skin most tender.

Guava jam or jelly combined with cream cheese makes a delicious sandwich filling.

Pork Sandwiches
See also Roast Pork
See also Salt Pork
See also Smoked Pork

Pork Tenderloin Sandwich
Pork tenderloin, butter, toast, baked apple

Cut pork tenderloin down the center lengthwise or in three pieces crosswise. After it has been trimmed, flatten out and season. Either fry or broil them; baste with butter if broiled. If fried use butter and smother slowly after browning until thoroughly cooked. Lay these slabs of delicious tenderness on toasted and buttered bread, press on top slice, trim and cut into desired shapes. A small glazed and baked tart apple may garnish this delectable dish, or a spiced seckel pear and cress.

Tenderloins cut lengthwise should be scored to keep them from curling. Dusting in a seasoned flour helps retain juices and adds to the flavor.

Port Du Salut Sandwich
*Port du Salut cheese, rye bread, mustard butter,
lettuce, dill pickles*

On thin slices of rye bread, spread with a mild mustard butter, place thin slices of Port du Salut cheese. Add a leaf of lettuce, press on upper slice and cut into desired shapes. Serve on cold plates garnished with pin money or dill pickles cut in rings.

Port du Salut is a mild cheese of the Limburger type without the fumes. It was originated by the Trappist Monks or Fathers of Quebec.

Bread can be spread with a gooseberry relish or currant jelly in place of mustard butter for variety.

Portuguese Sandwich, Hot (Open)
*Toast, butter, tomato, egg, tomato sauce with
Bermuda onions*

On a round of buttered toast place a slice of fried tomato of equal size. On tomato place a poached egg. Around toast pour a tomato sauce to which has been added some finely minced and sauted Bermuda onions. Serve at once.

Potato Cake Sandwich—I
*Potato, onion, bacon, egg, cornmeal, flour, baking
powder, salt, apple, parsley*

Grind together one medium sized raw potato and one-half small raw onion, and mix with one strip of chopped broiled bacon, one-half egg, one-fourth teaspoon salt, one teaspoon chopped parsley, two tablespoons of flour, two tablespoons of cornmeal and one-half teaspoon baking powder. Mix thoroly. If too thin add a little more cornmeal; if too thick add a little melted butter or cream. Fry in thin cakes as large as a slice of bread. Place one cake in center of plate and two strips of bacon on it. Place a second cake on top. Garnish side of sandwich with a small baked apple and a little parsley. Serve at once.

A dish of apple sauce could replace baked apples if desired. This makes a real tasty luncheon dish.

Center of cakes may be spread with apple sauce and garnished with lettuce. If desired, and for quicker service, bacon may be dispensed with and the cakes fried in bacon grease, which will give them a real flavor. Use just a little grease when frying.

Potato Cake Sandwich—II
Potato cakes, spinach

Make thin cakes of cold, mashed potatoes and fry in butter until brown. Place one cake on a hot plate and cover it with finely chopped and seasoned fresh spinach, cooked. Press on upper cake and serve hot.

This is an excellent way to teach children to eat spinach and is a real health item. Nearly all children rebel at eating spinach, but in this disguise they will like it.

A little good cream sauce poured over cake sandwich or a bright tomato sauce will sell this item to man or child.

Cakes should be made thin.

Potato Combination Sandwich
Bread, potato salad, cucumbers, egg, shallot,
mayonnaise, onion

Chop finely one cup of potato salad, one-half cup of squeezed cucumbers, one hard-boiled egg, and one very small onion, or shallot, and mix all together. Season with salt. Spread mixture on thin slices of bread, press on upper slice, trim and cut into desired shapes. Two slices of broiled bacon chopped finely can be added to mixture if desired.

Preacher Sandwich
Chicken, toast, butter, mayonnaise, lettuce

Slice the white meat of cold, boiled chicken, season, dust in flour, dip in beaten egg and then in bread crumbs. Fry in hot bacon grease quickly, browning on both sides. Spread a thin slice of toast with butter and then with mayonnaise; place chicken on toast, press on a leaf of lettuce and upper slice. Trim and cut in two diagonally. Serve on leaf of lettuce.

Slice of chicken should be cut large enough to cover toast, or use two slices. A strip of broiled bacon added to center of sandwich adds to the flavor.

Provincial Sandwich, Hot (Open)

Toast, egg, tomato sauce, chervil, bacon grease

On a round of toast, fried in bacon grease, place a fried or poached egg. Mask egg with a garlic flavored tomato sauce. Sprinkle with chopped chervil. Serve hot and at once.

Prune Sandwich—I

Prunes, lemon juice, lettuce, mayonnaise, bread

Mix together six large prunes, chopped, two teaspoons lemon juice and one-third head lettuce, chopped fine. Spread with butter and mayonnaise on slices of plain bread. Press on upper slice and cut in desired shapes. Prunes should not be cooked; soak over night and handle as in Prune Sandwich II, then stone and chop. Chopped figs or dates may be handled the same way.

Prune Sandwich—II

Prunes, whole wheat bread, lemon butter, brown sugar, lettuce

Soak one dozen large Oregon prunes over night. Drain, add fresh water and bring them to a boil. Allow to cool and remove stones. Put prunes thru a fine grinder. Spread whole wheat bread or plain white, toasted, with lemon butter and then with the prune puree. Sprinkle with a little brown sugar. Press on leaf of lettuce and upper slice. Cut into desired shapes and serve.

Prunes should not be boiled. Oregon prunes are rather tart and the finest of all prunes in the opinion of the author.

Pyrog Sandwich (Russian Combination)

Rice, cabbage, fish, parsley, onions, mayonnaise, lettuce, rye bread

Mix one-half cup of cooked rice (well drained) and the same amounts of chopped raw cabbage and flaked boiled halibut (cold), one teaspoon of minced parsley, the same of minced raw onions, one-half teaspoon of salt, one-fourth teaspoon of pepper and enough mayonnaise to bind all together. Spread on thin slices of rye or pumpernickel bread and cut into desired shapes. Serve with red cabbage slaw to which has been added a little chopped summer sausage.

Queen Ann Sandwich

Queen Ann cherries, artichoke tubers, spiced canta-
loupe, mayonnaise, toast, lettuce

Chop one-half cup of Queen Ann cherries, one-
half cup of artichoke tubers, peeled, and one-third
cup of spiced cantaloupe. Bind together with mayonnaise base No. 3. Spread on toast or plain bread,
trim, press on leaf of lettuce and upper slice. Cut in
rounds or finger shapes. This makes an excellent
sandwich.

Artichoke tubers can be replaced with blanched
almonds.

Surplus moisture should be drained off before mixing with mayonnaise.

Sweet sandwiches should be served as one of a
variety on a platter of assorted sandwiches.

Rabbit Sandwich

Rabbit, bread, butter, lettuce, bacon

Saute the leg or loin of rabbit, then smother
until tender. Allow to cool, then cut in thin slices.
Arrange them on thin slices of buttered bread.
Season, press on leaf of lettuce, a strip of grilled
bacon and upper slice. Trim and cut in two
diagonally. Serve on leaves of lettuce.

A fried leg of rabbit or whole saddle can be
arranged on two slices of toast (open fashion) and
creamed gravy poured over it. Garnish with fried
onions. Rabbit may also be ground and mixed with
chicken and boiled ham, equal parts, then bound
together with mayonnaise and used as a spread.

Radish Sandwich

Radishes, mayonnaise, cream cheese or creamed
butter, white bread, lettuce

Chop small, round hot-house radishes finely, skin
and all. Bind with enough mayonnaise, cream
cheese or creamed butter to make a good spreading
mixture. To cheese add a little raw cream or
French dressing. Spread on thin slices of white
bread. Press on leaf of lettuce and upper slice.
Cut into desired shapes and serve.

Rarebit Sandwich
See Welsh Rarebit

Rarebit with Eggs Sandwich

Butter, cheese, beer, eggs, seasoning

Melt an ounce of butter in a small skillet and
add one cup of grated American cheese, also add

one tablespoon of beer, stir well and mix in one-third spoon of English mustard (dry). When cheese is completely melted whip up one egg and add it to mixture. As soon as egg is cooked remove rarebit from fire and place on hot toast on a hot plate and serve at once. Do not cook egg but a minute and add a little salt as egg is poured into skillet.

Raw Beef Sandwich—I
Beef, bread, butter, lettuce, seasoning

Scrape or grind the pulp from strips of lean beef. Season with salt and pepper; spread on thin slices of buttered bread. Press on leaf of lettuce and upper slice. Trim and cut into halves or finger shapes. Sandwiches may be placed in patented toaster to toast or between a wire broiler and toasted over a hot broiler. If toasting, omit the lettuce and cut bread thicker.

Raw Beef Sandwich—II
Cannibal Sandwich

Spread thin slices of bread with finely ground or chopped raw beef, without tissues and sinews, mixed with a little finely chopped onion, and seasoned. This is an open sandwich and the layer of meat should be about the same thickness as the bread. Sprinkle with chopped chives and criss-cross with fork tines to give a decorated appearance. This is called tartar or cannibal sandwich at times.

Raw Onion Sandwich
Bermuda onion, butter, lettuce, bread, dill pickle

Peel a white Bermuda onion and cut into one-fourth inch slices. Place in porcelain dish and cover with boiling water; allow to stand five minutes. Drain, allow to cool, then cover with ice water and allow to stand ten or fifteen minutes. This makes them crisp and very delicate. Place one or two slices between rye or plain white bread, buttered and lettuced. Garnish with lettuce and slices of dill pickle.

Raw Vegetable Sandwich
Cabbage, carrots, green peppers, mayonnaise, bread, lettuce, tomato, Thousand Island dressing

Grind one-third cup of raw cabbage (green leaves), one-third cup of young, short, stubby carrots and one-fifth cup of green peppers. Drain off surplus juice, mix and add enough mayonnaise to bind. Spread on slices of whole wheat or white bread, plain or toasted. Press on upper slice and serve on leaf of lettuce, garnished with quartered tomato. Serve a little Thousand Island dressing on the side, or cut sandwich into four equal parts, place on salad plate, garnish with lettuce and then pour a little Thousand Island dressing over the four parts.

The short carrots are sweeter, have more flavor and less fiber than the long type carrots.

Razorback Sandwich

Rye bread, mustard greens, pork, pickles

On thin slices of rye bread, spread with well-drained, chopped and cooked mustard greens, place thin slices of roast loin or boiled leg of pork. Season and press on upper slice; cut in two diagonally and serve. Garnish with slices of dill pickle.

AUTHOR's NOTE: Most every family in the South has its herd of razorbacks, who roam thru the woods in search of roots, worms and nuts. The native razorback is successful in picking up a woodland living but never succeeds in filling out its lean sides.

Red Devil Combinations

Bread, butter, Paoli tomato paste, ham, lettuce

1. Spread a thin slice of plain or toasted bread with butter, then with a very thin layer of Paoli tomato paste. On top of paste place a thin slice of ham or tongue, press on leaf of lettuce and upper slice, trim and cut into desired shapes. Serve on leaves of lettuce.

2. Sardines, turkey, chicken, veal, shrimp, etc., can be handled as above. Two thirds creamed butter and one-third tomato paste makes an excellent tomato butter; add a dash of tabasco sauce for tang.

3. Equal amounts of creamed butter and Paoli tomato paste mixed together and spread on thin slices of whole wheat or plain white bread, then covered with grated Herkimer cheese and browned under a hot broiler makes a real appetizing rarebit.

4. Trimmed bread spread with tomato and butter as in rarebit, then covered with a slice of turkey, ham, tongue or chicken and sprinkled with cheese and browned makes another real treat.

Red Head Sandwich

Beets, cabbage, cream cheese, bread, lettuce, radishes

Mix one-third cup of marinated red beets and one-third cup of red cabbage, finely ground (with all surplus moisture removed) with one cake of cream cheese or a like amount of pimento cheese. In case mixture is too thick, thin with a little French dressing base No. 5. Spread mixture on rounds of white bread. Press on a leaf of lettuce, press on upper slice and cut in round shapes. Arrange on bed of lettuce and surround with small red radishes with curious faces carved into skins. This makes an excellent Hallowe'en party item. One of these sandwiches served on a bed of chicory, the chicory dusted with paprika representing the locks of a Red Head, and the sandwich representing the head, makes a real novelty. Top of sandwich to be dotted with cheese and pimentoes for eyes, nose, and mouth completing the picture.

Chopped connective tissue of red ripe tomato and chopped red beets mixed with enough mayonnaise to bind makes a good combination. All surplus tomato juice must be drained off before adding mayonnaise.

Red Hot Butter Sandwich

Radish skins, butter, white bread, lettuce, cress

Peel small hot-house strawberry radishes and chop the skins. Cream one-fourth cup of butter and work in the chopped skins of radishes. A little chopped cress may be added for color. Use one-fourth butter to three-fourths radishes. Season with salt and spread on thin slices of white bread. Cover with leaf of lettuce, press on upper slice and trim to desired shape.

A little cayenne or tabasco sauce can be added to butter for additional heat.

Red, White and Blue Sandwich (Open)

Bread, rubyettes, green pepper, almonds, mayonnaise

Chop separately one ounce of rubyettes and drain, one small blue-green pepper or a small bunch of cress, and one ounce of blanched almonds. Mix separately with just enough mayonnaise to bind. Spread in separate rows on thin slices of white bread.

Spread the rubyettes on one side, the peppers on the other and almonds down the center, trim and serve on leaves of lettuce, garnish with small American flags.

A Fourth of July item. Lettuce can be used in place of peppers. The spreading of these colors should be done with care.

After sandwich has been trimmed it can be cut into finger slices.

Red, White and Brown Sandwich

Whole wheat or white bread, liver butter, broiled bacon, tomato, lettuce

Spread thin slices of white or whole wheat bread with liver butter. Press on three thin slices of broiled bacon, a slice of ripe tomato, peeled, then the upper slice of bread. Cut into squares and serve on bed of lettuce. This is an excellent economical and tasty luncheon sandwich.

Rehm Sandwich

French sardines, salted peanuts, mayonnaise, lemon juice, salt, lettuce, whole wheat bread

Skin and bone one small can of French sardines and mash. Put one-half cup of shelled salted peanuts thru a fine grinder and add to the sardines. Mix in three tablespoons mayonnaise, one-third teaspoon salt, and one teaspoon of lemon juice, and spread on thin slices of whole wheat bread. Press on a leaf of lettuce and then upper slice of bread and trim in any desired shape. This is an excellent sandwich, highly protein in content. Should be eaten with a simple salad.

Ribbon Sandwich

Bread, butter, tomato paste, Swiss cheese, cress, mayonnaise

Spread on one side only with creamed butter, four long, thin slices of Pullman bread cut the length or half-length of the loaf. On the buttered side of the first slice spread a highly seasoned tomato-paste or pulp. Place the second slice on top, buttered side up, spread it with grated Swiss cheese which has been reduced to a paste by the addition of cream. Place the third slice, buttered side up, and spread with finely chopped watercress mixed with just enough lemon mayonnaise to bind. Place the fourth slice, buttered side down, and press together tightly. This long sandwich should be placed in a cold place under pressure for at least one hour, then cut into finger strips or sandwiches.

This gives a red, white and blue combination and is very effective.

These sandwiches placed around a mound of candy firecrackers with the border of platter garnished with cress make a real effective item. The red of the crackers in center, the white of the platter and the blue green cress add to the red, white and blue idea carried out in the filler of the sandwich. Red currant jelly, cream cheese and finely chopped green peppers, mixed with enough mayonnaise to bind, is another good combination. The sandwiches may be tied with red, white and blue baby ribbon. The height of all four slices, plus the filling should not be over three-fourths to one inch. If made thicker the effect is lost.

Ripe Banana Sandwich

Banana, white or whole wheat bread, butter, lettuce

Mash a ripe banana to a paste. Spread a thin slice of white or whole wheat bread with sweet butter, cover butter with banana paste and then with finely chopped lettuce. Press on upper slice, trim and cut in finger style sandwiches. Serve on bed of lettuce. Banana should be bathed or marinated in lemon juice to keep it from turning black. Mash banana with a wooden potato masher in a porcelain dish. Bananas may be sprinkled with finely ground carrots and seasoned with a little mayonnaise for sake of variety.

AUTHOR'S NOTE: "From observations made on patients at the Infants' Hospital and the Children's Hospital in Boston conclusions are drawn that ripe bananas can be fed with safety to very young babies and that it constitutes a valuable addition to the diet of children, particularly of those whose appetite must be stimulated during recovery from protracted illness."

Roast Beef Sandwich
See Hot Roast Beef
See Cold Roast Beef

Roast Ham and Fried Banana Sandwich (Open)

*Ham (roasted), sweet potatoes, toast, butter,
bananas*

Make a puree of sweet potatoes and season. Spread two slices of toast with butter, then spread with puree. Place two slices of roasted sugar-cured ham on top of puree. Garnish side of sandwich with quartered fried bananas.

PUREE: Boil sweet potatoes and drain. Press thru a Chinese sieve, season with salt, pepper and butter. Add a little raw cream to reduce to proper consistency for spreading. Serve hot and at once.

A little hot raisin sauce poured over ham gives sandwiches an additional zest.

Roast Ham and Raisin Sandwich

Toast, mustard butter, seedless raisins, roast ham

Toast two slices of white bread and trim. Spread

with a little mustard butter to which has been added
some finely chopped seedless raisins. Place a thin
slice of hot roast ham on toast, press on upper slice
and cut into desired shapes. Ham may be placed
between thin slices of buttered raisin bran bread
and toasted in a patent toaster for variety. A little
hot raisin sauce may be poured over sandwich just
before serving. Plain butter may be substituted for
mustard butter, if desired.

Roast Leg of Lamb Sandwich (Open)

Lamb, white bread, butter, sauce, peas, mint

Place three thin slices of roast leg of lamb on two
trimmed slices of white bread spread with butter.
Pour over lamb a little well seasoned hot lamb sauce.
Garnish sides of sandwich with seasoned new green
peas. Place a few sprigs of mint on top of lamb and
serve.

Roast Pork Sandwich

Roast pork, bread, butter, apple salad, lettuce

Cut cold roast loin of pork in thin slices and trim
off the fat. On thin slices of buttered white or rye
bread place the pork slices and press on upper
slice. Cut in desired shapes and garnish with a little finely chopped apple salad. (Jonathan apples
minced and mixed with an equal amount of celery,
bound together with mayonnaise.) Serve salad at
side of sandwich on leaf of lettuce. Bread spread
with apple sauce or pork sprinkled with finely
chopped broiled bacon, and apple sauce served on
the side, make desirable combinations. Grilled pork
chop sandwich with glazed onions is always a good
seller, a real shoeing horn.

Roe Sandwich
See Shad Roe

Rognon Sandwich (Open)

*Toast, butter, egg, lamb's kidney, tomato sauce,
parsley, tomato*

On a round of buttered toast place a poached
egg. At either end of egg place a crescent of buttered toast and on each crescent place a broiled
half of lamb's kidney, points out. Mask egg with
tomato sauce and in center of crescent place sprigs
of parsley. At opposite two sides of egg place a
small slice of ripe tomato fried. Serve quickly.
This is a very tasty and delicious item.

Roll Sandwich
See also

Celery Roll   Peanut Roll
Cream Cheese Roll   Salmon Roll
Finger Roll

Roquefort Sandwich
Roquefort cheese, cream, crackers, pimola

Mash one-fourth pound of Roquefort cheese and add enough 40% cream to reduce to proper consistency for spreading. Spread mixture on toasted round butter wafers. Mark outer edge of cheese with fine lines using a small pronged fork for this purpose. Garnish top center of cracker with a slice of pimola. Serve on folded napkin. Reduced Roquefort cheese can be forced thru a pastry sack and small tube on the crackers, giving the top a more fanciful appearance. The cheese reduced in the same way can be used to stuff the inner branches of celery. This makes an ideal appetizer.

Roquefort cheese can be used in very thin finger sandwiches made of white bread plain with a leaf of lettuce pressed in center.

Roquefort Combination Sandwich
White bread, Roquefort cheese, mustard, mushroom catsup, lettuce

Spread a thin slice of white bread with a mixture of Roquefort cheese, to which has been added a little made mustard and a few drops of mushroom catsup. Press on upper slice and toast between a fine wire broiler. Cut into finger pieces. Serve on leaf of lettuce.

ROQUEFORT: "Roquefort—a famous cheese named after the French village of Roquefort, where great herds of the sheep that supply the milk are pastured on an immune plain of rich velvet-like herbage which is stringently protected by both law and custom. "The herbage is supplemented by a diet of prepared food, and the water supplied to them is whitened with barley flour. The yield of milk is, indeed, the best in every possible way.

"The moldy bread process which produces the special characteristic of Roquefort is the crumb of the finest wheat bread leavened with a large quantity of brewer's yeast kneaded to excess and thoroly baked. The crust is removed and the crumb is pounded in a mortar and put away in a damp place till it is covered with the blue-green mold, Pencillium glaucum. When it is ripe enough the new cheeses are rubbed thoroly with the moldy bread and layers of it are placed between the layers of curd in order that they may absorb still more of the mold.   After several days of pressing the cheeses are wrapped in linen and dried and then sold to owners of vaults or caves, natural clefts or artificial excavations in limestone rocks near by the town. The cheeses are piled up and salted in these caves, being frequently rehandled and rubbed to make sure that the salt thoroly impregnates them. They are next scraped and pricked with long needles so that the mold may run entirely thru them, thus producing the mottled appearance of Roquefort. They are then again piled up to dry more thoroly, in this process developing a long white mold, which is scraped off from time to time.   Goats milk and cows milk have been used whole and in part, but the true Roquefort remaining thru sheep milk only."

Roquefort De Lux Sandwich

White bread, Roquefort cheese, butter, turkey, lettuce

Mix Roquefort cheese with a little butter and spread on thin slice of white bread. On this place a slice of white meat of chicken or turkey. Press on upper slice and toast between a fine wire broiler. Cut in three strips and serve on leaves of lettuce.

Cheese can be mixed with a little raw cream in place of butter.

Rossini Sandwich

Toast, liver paste, egg, tomato sauce, chicken livers

Spread two thin slices of toast with highly seasoned liver paste. Fry one egg in butter on both sides and place between toast. Cut in two diagonally. Pour a light tomato sauce, garnished with chicken livers, over sandwich and serve hot. Chicken livers should be sauted lightly in butter and diced before being placed in tomato sauce.

Do not fry livers until over done or hard; for, if you do, they will not be fit to eat. Poach or fry lightly in butter, and as quickly as they are set remove. The albumen in the liver gets hard just like the albumen in the egg when it is cooked too long. You know that it is easier to find the hard boiled egg than it is to find a stomach to digest one.

Round Bar Sandwich

Ham, tongue, German mustard, rye bread, dill pickles

Grind and reduce to paste scraps of roast ham

or boiled tongue or both, and mix with enough mayonnaise to bind. Spread on thin slices of rye bread and sprinkle with chopped dill pickles. Press on upper slice, cut in rounds or diagonally and serve. Scraps of ham and chicken, or tongue and chicken, handled the same way add to the sandwich possibilities. Remove all sinews. A few caraway or cardomen seeds added to mayonnaise adds flavor to the rye sandwich.

Some twenty-five years ago The Round Bar on Clark street, Chicago, served many varieties of delectable sandwiches; the above was one of the Round Bar specialties. In place of mayonnaise they used German mustard to bind ingredients together.

Another Round Bar specialty was a Swiss combination made by grinding equal amounts of Swiss cheese, smoked and boiled tongue, ham and cole slaw and binding together with a mild German mustard. This mixture was spread on rye bread and topped with a slice of dill pickle.

Rubyette Sandwich

Rubyettes, pineapple, cream cheese, white bread, mayonnaise, lettuce

Mix three tablespoons of rubyettes and two of ground pineapple with enough cream cheese to bind. Spread thin slices of white bread with mayonnaise and then with the rubyette mixture. Press on leaf of lettuce, upper slice and cut into desired shapes.

Rubyettes are seedless Thompson grapes put up in jars in red and various colored syrups. They are excellent for garnishing sandwiches and beverages.

Rubyettes and pickles (chopped) or spiced cantaloupe, marmalade, spiced figs make good combinations. Cream cheese or butter should be used as a binder and the bread should be spread previously with mayonnaise. When rubyettes are mixed with a more assertive item such as spiced cantaloupe the proportion should be three of the former to one of the latter.

Rump Steak Sandwich
See Broiled Rump

Russian Combination Sandwich
See Pyrog

St. Patrick Sandwich

Cress, mayonnaise, potato bread, clover leaves,
potato chips

Clean and chop one bunch of watercress. Mix
with enough mayonnaise to bind. Spread on thin
slices of potato bread. Trim and cut into shamrock shapes. Serve on folded napkin. Garnish with
thin potato chips and clover leaves.

This makes an execellent novelty item.

Salami Sandwich—I

Salami, celery (or tuber artichokes), olives,
mayonnaise, rye bread, lettuce

Chop fine equal amounts of salami, raw celery
or tuber artichokes and green olives and bind together with mayonnaise. Spread on buttered rye
or white bread. Press on upper slice and cut into
fanciful shapes. Serve on leaves of lettuce.

Salami, pickles and hard-boiled eggs, with a few
chopped chives added, bound together with mayonnaise make an appetizing sandwich.

Ground salami and cooked chicken or veal when
mixed with enough mayonnaise to bind makes an
excellent mixture.

Salami Sandwich—II

Rye bread, mustard butter, salami, lettuce, cole slaw

Spread thin slices of rye bread with a mustard
butter and lay on thin slices of salami. Press on
leaf of lettuce, then upper slice. Cut in two diagonally and garnish with cole slaw or piccalilli
placed in a small basket-shaped lettuce leaf. Drain
slaw well so that it does not make sandwich wet.

Salami placed in center of a split rye or plain
roll makes an excellent item.

Salami and Swiss Cheese Sandwich (Open)

Salami, Swiss cheese, rye bread, potato salad

Cut equal size strips of salami and cheese and
place them alternately on buttered white or rye
bread, so that salami nestles and cheese makes dis-
tinct lines. Garnish with a little German potato
salad. This makes a very fine looking sandwich
and a very tasty one also; and is quickly prepared.

Sally in Our Alley Sandwich
See Frankfurter

Salmon Roll
Salmon, capers, mayonnaise, bread, ribbon

Rub one cup of salmon thru a sieve and mix with one tablespoon of finely chopped or ground capers, bind together with just enough mayonnaise so that mixture spreads nicely. Spread on very thin slices of bread. (See note on celery roll.) Roll, cut and press; then tie each individual sandwich with baby ribbon. Arrange on doily or on bed of lettuce. (Have the lettuce perfectly dry so that ribbons do not run.)

Salmon Sandwich I
Salmon, eggs, butter, chili sauce, toast, gherkins, parsley

Whip up two eggs with two ounces of canned salmon, and scramble them in butter. Turn out in a hot bowl and whip in one tablespoon of hot chili sauce. Place mixture on toasted slices of white bread and serve at once. Garnish with fanned gherkins and parsley. Pour a little additional chili sauce over sandwich before serving.

Cooked shrimp, cod, trout, crabmeat can be handled in the same way.

Salmon Sandwich II
See Smoked Salmon

Salmon Salad Sandwich
Salmon, cucumber, mayonnaise, toast, lettuce

Chop fine one cup of salmon and add one-third cup of finely chopped and squeezed marinated cucumber. Bind together with mayonnaise base No. 3. Spread on freshly made toast. Trim and cut in two diagonally. Serve on leaves of lettuce.

One tablespoon of chopped capers added gives additional zest to mixture.

Salon Sandwich
Raw beef, onions, parsley, toast, Bermuda onion, dill pickle

Press finely chopped and seasoned raw beef into thin flat rounds, sprinkle with finely chopped onions and parsley and serve on rounds of toast, or press between plain slices of bread and toast in patent toaster or between a fine wire broiler. Garnish with slice of Bermuda onion and dill pickles or with French fried onions. Raw beef can be spread on squares of bread and pressed with a fork giving a better appearance; then sprinkled with chopped chives. Beef may also be spread on toast or plain bread and then placed under hot broiler for a few minutes to brown. Great platters of this chopped raw beef seared with a fork and sprinkled with chopped chives were found on the free lunch bar in the days gone by.

Salt Pork Sandwich

Salt pork, buttermilk, bread crumbs, butter, lettuce, cornbread, preserved figs

Soak very thin slices of salt pork in buttermilk over night to freshen, then parboil, bread and fry. Serve on buttered and lettuced slices of corn, white or graham bread. Garnish with two or three preserved figs.

Salted Spanish Olive Sandwich

Salted Spanish olive, mayonnaise, lettuce, bread

Stone and chop salted Spanish olives. Mix with enough mayonnaise base No. 3 to bind, or mix with Neufchatel cheese and French dressing base No. 5. Spread on thin slices of bread, press on lettuce leaf and upper slice, cut into desired shapes. This makes a real appetizing sandwich.

Sam Ward Sandwich (Open)

Lamb, mushrooms, green pepper, cream sauce, toast, cheese, butter, paprika, bananas, cress

Saute in butter three fresh mushrooms, and one green pepper (diced) until done; then add one cup of diced scraps of roast lamb and heat. Add enough cream sauce to bind and season with salt. Spread mixture on two slices of trimmed toast. Sprinkle top with grated Cheddar or Herkimer cheese, butter and paprika. Brown quickly under a hot broiler. Garnish with two slices of fried banana and a little cress.

ATHOR'S NOTE: Cheddar. This is the richest and best of all English cheeses and is made of whole milk and with veins generally marked by green or bluish green mold. It is of a pale yellowish color tender and tangy. It should not be sold until aged for two years.

Sandwich Bon Bouchees
See Bon Bouchees

Sandwich Rolls

Pullman bread, cream cheese, green olives, chicken paste, lettuce, baby ribbon

Take freshly baked Pullman bread, wrap with a towel or cloth wrung out in ice cold water, wrap a second and a third cloth around same and set in a cool place for at least five hours; trim and cut loaf in half and then cut slices the length of half loaf with a very thin, sharp knife. Spread with a thin layer of cream cheese and finely ground green olives, Chicken paste as in Chicken Almondine or with pimento cheese, horseradish and French dressing or any other tasty and fine filling. Roll carefully and closely and trim. Tie with colored baby ribbons and pile in log shape on shredded lettuce or napkin. Serve on plates or platter. Garnish with cress and cucumber rings, with a lilied radish set in center of each ring.

Do not make or roll sandwiches too thick. A slice cut across the loaf if cut thin enough will make a very attractive roll sandwich.

Sardelle Sandwich

Toast, sardelles, mayonnaise

Spread thin slices of toast very lightly with a paste of sardelles which have been cleaned, washed, pounded and rubbed thru a sieve, then mixed with enough mayonnaise to spread. Press on upper slice and cut into desired shapes. Hard-boiled egg yolks and a little lemon juice may be added for variety.

SARDELLES: Should be freshened in plenty of cold water. After they have remained in water at least three hours place them in olive oil until needed.

Sardelles generally come in small kegs and are dry and very salty. They are used as appetizers.

Sardine Sandwich—I, Hot

Sardines, butter, eggs, cream, lemon juice, toast, parsley

Skin and bone six small French sardines. Place a teaspoon of butter in a small egg pan and lay fillets in butter until heated thru. Whip up two eggs with a tablespoon of cream and one-sixth teaspoon of salt. Add them to sardines and scramble lightly. When eggs are nearly coagulated squeeze in a few drops of lemon juice. Serve on diagonal cuts of toast spread with butter. Garnish with parsley.

Anchovies may be prepared the same way only omit salt. Do not allow butter to brown and toss

eggs lightly. Do not break fillets too much. This
sandwich may be served open style or with upper
slice. Trim and cut to any desired shape. Eggs
may be omitted and sardines served plain.

If anchovies are too salty or strong they can be
blanched for a few minutes and freshened up.

Sardine Sandwich—II (Open)

Sardines, toast, butter, lemon, lettuce, paprika

Broil on an oiled, fine wire broiler fillets of large
French oil sardines, skinned and boned. Serve on
ovals of toast spread with sweet or anchovy butter.
Fillets should be laid on toast with boned side down
and the edges of toast piped or decorated with a
well flavored lemon butter.

The whole sardine can be broiled and served on a
salad plate underlined with lettuce and garnished
with crescents of toast placed on either side, crescent points out and toast spread with lemon butter
and tips dipped in a little paprika or lobster coral.

Sardine and Virginia Ham Sandwich

*Sardines, Virginia ham, lemon juice, toast, mustard
butter, lettuce, cress*

Rub one small box of boneless and skinless sardines thru a fine sieve and mix with an equal
amount of finely ground boiled Virginia ham and
one tablespoon of lemon juice. Spread thin slices
of toast or plain bread with sweet or mustard butter and then the sardine mixture. Press on leaf
of lettuce and upper slice. Cut into desired shapes
and serve on leaves of lettuce and cress.

Toast, spread with sardine paste, then a thin slice
of Virginia ham, a leaf of lettuce and upper slice
pressed on makes a desirable combination.

Sauerkraut Sandwich

Kraut, onion, rye bread, mustard

Fry one cup of sauerkraut (drained) with one
small minced onion. On a thin slice of rye bread,
spread lightly with German mustard, place enough
kraut to cover. Press on upper slice, cut in half
diagonally and serve. A few slices of frankfurter
mixed with kraut while frying and placed in sandwiches enhances flavor of the kraut.

SAUERKRAUT: Shred very fine two or three heads
of cabbage. Use a three-gallon crock. Place a little
salt on bottom of the crock, then a layer of finely
shredded cabbage and alternate layers of salt and
cabbage until crock is three-fourths full, salt being

the last layer. Press a plate on top and hold it down with a brick. Put in a moderately cool place for ten or fifteen days to macerate and slightly ferment.

A few caraway seeds added to kraut when frying adds a peculiar but desirable flavor to it.

Sausage Sandwich
See Farm Sausage

Sausage and Bean Sandwich
Baked beans, tomato catsup, toast, butter, sausage, tomatoes, lettuce

Rub one-half cup of warm baked beans thru a fine sieve and mix with one tablespoon of tomato catsup. Spread mixture on thin slices of buttered toast. Arrange very thin slices of broiled sausage on top of beans. Press on upper slice and cut in two diagonally. Serve garnished with quartered tomatoes and lettuce.

Do not spread toast too thickly with beans.

This mixture spread on plain bread garnished with either salt pork, cooked sausage or broiled bacon and finished in a patent toaster is delicious. Serve with tomato catsup.

Savory Sandwich
Cheese, egg, bacon, pickles, French dressing, bread

One ounce cream cheese, one egg, three ounces grated Herkimer cheese, three strips broiled bacon chopped finely, one ounce sweet pickles, one tablespoon French dressing.

Method: Grind Herkimer cheese and chop bacon and pickles and add cream cheese and French dressing. Mix this into a paste. Cut and trim four thin slices of white bread. Spread mixture on the two lower slices and press on the two upper. Cut the sandwiches in two diagonally or into four squares. Whip up the cream and egg together. Dip the sandwiches in the egg mixture and fry brown on both sides.

Savory August Sandwich
See August Savory

Savory Combination Sandwich I (Open)
Toast, butter, turkey, salami, veal, potato salad, beets, lettuce

On a thin slice of buttered toast place ribbon slices of white meat of turkey and salami alternately, all of uniform size. Arrange the slices so that the

white ones tip the brownish red of the salami. Cut
a second slice of toast in four diagonally, and place
a piece at either end and sides of center slice.
Garnish the side pieces of toast with a thin slice of
roast veal or lamb. Garnish one of the opposite
ends with potato salad and lettuce, the other with
sliced pickled beets and mayonnaise.

Savory Combination Sandwich II

*Pork, beef, egg, bread crumbs, onion, sage, corn-
meal, rye bread, mustard, butter,
Long Branch potatoes*

Mix one-fourth pound of ground raw pork with a
like amount of ground raw beef. Add one egg,
one cup of bread crumbs, one small onion (chopped
fine), one teaspoon powdered sage, and seasoning.
Mix all well, flatten out in thin cakes, bread in cornmeal and fry brown on both sides. Spread slice
of rye or white bread with a little made mustard
and butter. Garnish top of bread with a cake,
press on upper slice, cut in two diagonally and
serve with Long Branch potatoes. This cake served
on toast with slices of dill pickle makes a tasty
combination.

AUTHOR'S NOTE: A simple salad should be served
with this type of sandwich to help neutralize the
acids generated in this bread and meat combination.

Scallop Sandwich

*Scallops, butter, toast, Tartar sauce, lettuce,
julienned potatoes, cress*

Saute in butter scallops, cut thin, and arrange
on thinly cut toast spread with butter and Tartar
sauce. Press on upper slice and trim. Cut in two
diagonally and arrange on leaves of lettuce. Garnish with julienned potatoes and cress.

Scallops can be cooked, chopped very fine then
mixed with Tartar sauce or mayonnaise and chopped
pickles and used as a sandwich filling.

Slices of cooked scallops and broiled bacon finished in a patent toaster between two slices of buttered bread makes a real feast.

Shad Roe Sandwich—I

*Shad roe, anchovy butter, butter, bacon, lemon juice,
toast, celery, lettuce*

Pound to a paste in a mortar a freshly broiled
shad roe. Add one teaspoon of anchovy butter, one
ounce of fresh butter, creamed, two slices of finely
ground broiled bacon, a few drops of lemon juice

and cayenne. Spread mixture on very thin slices of freshly made toast. Press on upper slice, trim and cut in finger shapes. Serve with curled hearts of celery and slices of lemon on leaves of lettuce. Anchovy butter as well as fresh butter can be dispensed with and mayonnaise used if desired.

Shad Roe Sandwich—II

Shad roe, toast, bacon butter, tomato, green olives, lettuce

Broil slowly one shad roe in an oiled paper bag until done. Spread two thin slices of toast with bacon butter and trim. Split shad roe and place between the two pieces of toast. Cut in two diagonally. Serve on plate garnished with a slice of grilled tomato, two green olives and a leaf of lettuce. Do not cook too much; roe should be moist when done, not hard like so many small bullets. (See note on Rossini sandwich.)

Shad Roe Combination Sandwich—I

Cooked shad roe, bacon, Tartar sauce, toast

Put one-half of a cooked shad roe and two strips of broiled bacon thru a fine grinder, add enough Tartar sauce to bind, spread on thin slices of toast. Press on upper slice and cut into desired shapes.

Shad Roe Combination Sandwich—II

Toast, mayonnaise, turkey, shad roe, bacon, lettuce, tomato

Toast two thin slices of trimmed plain white bread and spread lower slice with mayonnaise. On it place a thin slice of white meat of turkey and on top of turkey a split half of a freshly broiled shad roe (not a pair). Place a strip of broiled bacon along the side of roe and press on upper slice. Cut in two diagonally and serve on leaves of lettuce. Garnish with quartered tomato. After the half of roe is broiled, split it with a sharp knife. Broil roe in oiled paper bag.

Shrimp Sandwich—I (Open)

Toast, butter, shrimp, capers, green pepper, tomatoes, Thousand Island dressing, lettuce

On a slice of trimmed, toasted and buttered Pullman bread place nine halves of shrimp (shrimp should be cut thru length of body and laid flat on toast, white side up). Place them in three rows of three and garnish with a caper in center of each one right where the two ends come together. Arrange a strip of green pepper around each shrimp

to form sort of a horse-shoe. Place a second slice
of trimmed, toasted and buttered Pullman bread
next to first slice and arrange a whole slice of
tomato in center with four half slices around the
center one. Fill center slice with a stiff Thousand
Island dressing and serve on bed of lettuce.

Shrimp Sandwich—II

Shrimp, lemon juice, butter, toast, lettuce

Cook and clean one pound of fresh shrimp. Allow
to cool, then cut in very fine pieces; mash to a
paste and rub thru a fine sieve. Season with salt,
cayenne and lemon juice and work into it enough
mayonnaise or creamed butter to bind. Spread on
thin, well trimmed slices of toast or plain bread.
Press on a leaf of lettuce and upper slice. Cut into
desired shapes.

Lobster may be handled in the same manner,
using a two-pound fresh lobster.

Shrimp Sandwich—III

Toast, butter, shrimp, mayonnaise, tomato, lettuce

On thin slices of buttered toast or plain white
bread trimmed, arrange cold cooked shrimp, cleaned
and split in half thru the center lengthwise. Mask
shrimp with mayonnaise base No. 3 and serve. A
second slice of trimmed and buttered bread can be
placed on top and the sandwich cut in two diagonally, or second slice may be placed at side of the
first one and garnished with a thick slice of peeled
ripe tomato set in a leaf of lettuce.

Shrimp Club Sandwich

Shrimp, celery, lemon juice, mayonnaise, toast,
cucumber, lettuce

Chop fine one cup of boiled shrimp and mix in
one-half cup of finely chopped white stalks of celery.
Season with salt, paprika and add two teaspoons of
lemon juice. Bind together with mayonnaise base
No. 3. Spread mixture on thin slices of freshly made
toast and press on second slice, spread with mayonnaise on the upper side. Garnish the second slice
with thin slices of squeezed and marinated cucumber. Press on third slice of toast, trim and cut in
half diagonally. Serve on leaves of lettuce.

Lobster, crabmeat and boiled and flaked fish can
be handled the same way. Finely chopped lettuce
may be used in place of celery.

In place of marinated cucumbers two or three slices

of red ripe tomatoes (peeled) and a strip of broiled
bacon can be used.

Shrimp Salad Sandwich I

Shrimp, celery, spiced sauce, toast, watercress

Dice finely cooked and cleaned shrimp and add
one-fifth the amount of finely chopped celery hearts.
Add enough spiced sauce to bind. Place on toasted
slice of bread. Press on upper slice, cut diagonally
and garnish with watercress and a few whole
shrimps. Serve a little shrimp spiced sauce on
the side.

Shrimp spiced sauce: Mix three parts chili sauce
to two parts catsup and one part prepared horseradish.

Shrimp Salad Sandwich—II

*Toast, butter, lettuce, shrimp salad, green pepper,
tomato, Russian dressing, cress*

On a round of toast, buttered and lettuced, place
a finely cut shrimp salad. On salad place a thick
slice of peeled, ripe tomato. Around tomato arrange a thick ring of green pepper. Over top of
tomato pour a Russian dressing. Garnish with
cress. Serve at once.

Simple Sandwich

Bread, butter, lettuce, mayonnaise, cheese

Spread two thin slices of white bread with
creamed butter and place an inner leaf of Boston
lettuce, which has been dipped in lemon mayonnaise, on the lower slice. Sprinkle lettuce with
freshly grated Swiss or Herkimer cheese. Press on
upper slice, trim and cut in two diagonally. Serve
on leaf of lettuce and garnish with lillied round
radishes. This is an excellent item.

Simple Picnic Sandwich

*Lettuce, watercress, horseradish, mayonnaise,
bread, butter*

Chop one-half head of lettuce and one small
bunch of cress very finely and mix, then add one
teaspoonful horseradish, one-fourth teaspoon salt,
and two teaspoons mayonnaise. Spread thin slices
of white bread with butter, then with the above
mixture. Cut into finger shapes and serve. This
class of sandwich should be served as one of a
variety in a platter of meat sandwiches. It is tasty,
healthful and well-balanced. The three ingredients
that enter into this mixture blend so well that it is
almost impossible to tell what is in the sandwich.

The blandness of the lettuce cuts down the assertive-ness of the peppery grass and the tangy horseradish so that all three are mellowed into a wholesome tidbit.

Singapore Sandwich
Vegetable Hamburger Sandwich

Mexican slaw, green peppers, red beets, chutney sauce, Thousand Island dressing, rye bread

Chop fine one cup of Mexican slaw, one-half cup of green peppers, one-half cup of red beets and one-fourth cup of Major Grey's chutney. Mix with enough Thousand Island dressing to bind. Spread on rye bread, press on upper slice, cut diag-onally and serve.

Surplus moisture should be drained off of ingre-dients before adding Thousand Island dressing.

Sirloin of Beef Sandwich

Sirloin of beef, toast, horseradish butter, lettuce

Cut thin slices of cold roast sirloin of beef and place between thin slices of toast or plain bread; spread with horseradish butter. Cut in squares or fingers and serve on leaves of lettuce.

All rough unsightly edges should be trimmed away.

A thin strip of Virginia ham placed on top of beef gives an added zest to sandwich.

This class of sandwich served with a simple salad and a glass of milk makes an ideal well bal-anced luncheon.

Gruiod de la Reyineri holds that the roast should be served without entrees or entremets, flanked merely by four different salads. "On the table spread the cloth. Let the forks be bright and clean. Vegetables get and salad both, Let them each be fresh and green, With sweet milk or water fine; O Ye Gods! How I shall dine."

Sleepy Eye Sandwich

Spanish onion, butter, cream, toast

Julienne a large Spanish onion and place it in a good, heavy saute pan with one ounce of butter, one cup of water and seasoning. Smother onion until it is thoroly cooked and all the water evapo-rated. When nearly dry add one-half cup of cream and simmer a few minutes (do not boil). Place a piece of trimmed toast on a platter and place onion on it with a pierced spoon. Press on upper slice and pour cream over. Serve at once. If you wish to go to sleep this sandwich, eaten at night, will undoubtedly help to produce results.

Sliced Apple Sandwich
Sliced Pear Sandwich
Apple (or pear), lemon juice, cream cheese, almonds, lettuce

Core and peel a Jonathan, Russet or Snow apple. Slice very thin and marinate in lemon juice for one hour in ice-box. Dry thoroly and spread one slice of apple with cream cheese mixed with chopped blanched almonds. Press on upper slice of apple and serve on bed of lettuce. Serve two or three of these apple sandwiches to an order. Cheese should not be thinned down.

Apple sandwiches may be dipped in powdered sugar, then in egg and cream beaten together and fried in hot grease. Brown on both sides and serve at once. Do not cook apples until they are soft.

Thin slices of peeled raw pear, spread with cream cheese and ground nuts, then dipped or rolled in non-caking sugar and served at once make very tasty fruit sandwiches. Serve finger bowls with this class of sandwich. Pear and apple sandwiches may be served in combination with an assortment of fancy sandwiches. A little Herkimer cheese may be grated on top slice of apple or pear then browned under a hot broiler. This makes a tasty tidbit.

Sliced Curried Chicken Sandwich (Open)
Toast, chicken, butter, curry flavored sauce, bread crumbs, cheese

On two toasted slices of trimmed white bread, buttered, place enough boiled and sliced white meat of chicken to cover. Pour over a rich, well seasoned sauce made of chicken stock, cream and flavored with curry; then thickened with a roux made of butter and flour. The sauce should be rather heavy. Sprinkle top of sauce with bread crumbs and grated Cheddar or Herkimer cheese. Brown under broiler and serve at once. The two trimmed slices of toast should be laid lengthwise on platter.

Smelt Sandwich—I
Smelts, toast, butter, parsley, tomato, tartar sauce, lettuce

Add a little salt and white pepper to two tablespoons of flour. Clean and wipe dry two or three smelts; dredge them with the seasoned flour and fry in shallow grease until done. Remove from pan and bone carefully. Place the boned fillets on two slices of trimmed and buttered toast. Pour over a little melted butter and reheat under broiler for one minute. Garnish with fried parsley and a small hollowed out tomato or pickled beet filled with tartar sauce. Serve at once on leaf of lettuce.

"A smelt in Latin is called Eperlauus, a pearlâ, a pearl, because of its color. They call it also Viola marina because it smells like a violet."

Smelt Sandwich—II
Smelts, toast, butter, lettuce, dill pickle

Handle as in Smelt Sandwich I, only fillet out the smelts before cooking. Bread fillets, then fry lightly and quickly. Place boned fillets on buttered slice of toast. Press on upper slice, cut in two diagonally and arrange cut sandwich in shape of a diamond. Garnish with lettuce and slices of dill pickle.

The entire smelt may be fried and placed in center of platter with four half slices of buttered toast surrounding it. The top of smelt should be decorated with fried parsley and a little tartar sauce served on the side.

Smoked Loin of Pork Sandwich
Rye bread, pork, red cabbage (cooked), butter

Spread thin slices of rye bread with butter and cover with thin slices of smoked loin of pork, press on leaf of lettuce and upper slice and cut into desired shapes. Garnish with a liberal spoonful of cooked red cabbage on leaf of lettuce.

A little vinegar to be added to cabbage while cooking. Cabbage cooked with a ham hock, an onion and a few carrots gives it additional flavor.

Smoked beef as well as smoked pork can be purchased at any first class delicatessen store. Both these items lend themselves to excellent sandwich combinations and fillers.

Smoked Ox Tongue Sandwich—I
Tongue, butter, lettuce, bread, dill pickles, cress

Butter and lettuce thin slices of white, rye or whole wheat bread. Place on under slice thin slices of trimmed tongue. Press on upper slice, trim and cut in finger shapes, rounds, triangles, diamonds, crescents or diagonally. Serve on lettuced plates or platters. Garnish with slaw or dill pickles thinly sliced and small rosettes of cress.

Smoked Ox Tongue Sandwich (Hot)—II

Rye bread, mustard butter, tongue with sharp sauce, spinach cakes, piquante sauce

On a slice of rye bread spread with mustard butter place two slices of hot boiled ox tongue. Press on upper slice, cut in two diagonally and place on a hot plate. Garnish sides of sandwich with two fried cakes of spinach and mashed potatoes. Pour a little piquante sauce over sandwich and serve at once, hot.

SPINACH AND POTATO CAKE: Chop and squeeze out thoroly one cup of freshly cooked spinach; mix with an equal amount of freshly riced potatoes, season and bind together with one egg yolk and make into flat cakes. Fry brown in butter.

Smoked Salmon Sandwich

Rye bread, butter, mayonnaise, lettuce, smoked salmon, gherkins

On a thin slice of rye bread, spread with butter, mayonnaise and lettuced, place a thin slice of cold smoked salmon. Press on upper slice and cut in two diagonally. Garnish top of sandwich with fanned gherkins. Place on leaves of lettuce and serve on cold dish.

Smoked Sturgeon Sandwich (Open)

Toast, butter, sturgeon, Russian dressing, cress

On toasted white bread, spread with sweet butter, place thin slices of smoked sturgeon. Trim and cut into squares and pour over them a little Russian dressing. Garnish with cress.

Smoked Whitefish Sandwich (Open)

Toast, butter, smoked whitefish, tomatoes, parsley

On two squares of buttered toast place two boned fillets of smoked whitefish (small). Garnish with fried tomatoes and parsley and serve on silver platter.

Bloater or herring can be handled in the same manner. Fillets of smoked whitefish boned and mixed with scrambled eggs, then used as a sandwish filling makes a good Friday item.

Soldier Sandwich (Open)
Toast, fried onions, bacon, American cheese

Toast two slices of white or whole wheat bread, and spread liberally with fried onions. Place two strips of broiled bacon on top and cover onions and bacon entirely with grated American cheese. Place open sandwich under a hot broiler and when cheese is melted and browned remove. Serve at once on a hot plate.

Sole Cakes
See Codfish Cakes

Sole Sandwich
See Fried Filet

Soubrette Sandwich
Onions, green peppers, butter, tomatoes, eggs, toast, chervil

Saute in butter until brown one tablespoon of finely diced onions and one of green peppers; then place them in a small stew pan with one cup of canned tomatoes, cook until reduced to half and season. Place two fried eggs on slice of toast. Cut a second slice of toast diagonally and place triangles at either end of square. Pour over eggs and toast the above sauce, sprinkle with chopped chervil and serve at once. This is an excellent Lenten open sandwich, a real treat.

Sour Sweet Sandwich
See Sweet Sour

Soused Tripe Sandwich
Tripe, spiced vinegar, rye bread, mayonnaise, lettuce

Boil tripe until very tender and pickle for a few days in a light spiced vinegar. Dry carefully and cut in squares or in julienne. Serve on rye bread spread with mayonnaise and butter. Press on upper slice, cut into desired shapes and serve on leaves of lettuce. If tripe is too sour freshen in clear, cold water.

Tripe can be put thru a grinder, then mixed with mayonnaise and shredded lettuce and used as a sandwich filler.

Southern Hash Sandwich
Hash, toast, string beans, cress

Arrange hash in center of toast and garnish both ends of hash with French fried string beans and

opposite sides of sandwich with cress. This is an
excellent sandwich if hash is made well.

SOUTHERN HASH: Dice and saute slowly until
brown one small onion, one green pepper and one
small mushroom; then add three or four ounces of
diced roast beef (trimmings will do), one ounce of
diced raw potatoes and five ounces of canned tomatoes. Season and cook until potatoes are done.

Hash cooked down until dry, allowed to cool and
then put thru a meat grinder makes an ideal sandwich filling. A sandwich made out of the above
filling and finished in an electric toaster will surprise you; it is delicious.

Spaghetti Sandwich (Open)

*Tomato catsup butter, Herkimer cheese, bacon,
spaghetti, toast, paprika*

Use enough tomato catsup butter to bind the following: two tablespoons of Herkimer cheese, two
strips of broiled bacon, and two tablespoons of
boiled spaghetti, all chopped. Spread mixture rather
thick on thin slices of toast. Sprinkle with paprika
and brown quickly. Serve hot. This makes an excellent hors d'oeuvre.

Spanish Sandwich

Toast, butter, egg, Creole sauce, hard-boiled egg

Toast two slices of whole wheat bread and spread
with butter. Fry one egg over, place between toast
and trim. Cut toast in four, place squares on platter and pour a well made Creole sauce over them.
Garnish top of sandwich with slices of hard-boiled
egg. Serve hot.

Yolk should be broken while egg is frying to make
the egg large enough to cover toast.

Spanish Olive Sandwich
See Salted Spanish Olive

Special Sandwich—I

*Chicken, Roquefort cheese, egg, cream, ham, bread
crumbs, toast, cole slaw, tomato*

Put two ounces white meat of chicken thru a fine
grinder and mash two ounces Roquefort cheese to a
paste. Whip up one egg and one ounce of cream
and add to the cheese and chicken. Season with salt.
Pass two thin slices of ham thru flour or bread
crumbs and then thru the above mixture and then
bread crumbs again. Shake off surplus crumbs. Fry
in very shallow grease in a hot pan. Place ham on

slice of toast, press on upper slice and cut in two diagonally. Garnish with cole slaw and quartered tomato. Serve as quickly as possible.

Special Sandwich II
Bread, ham, chicken, egg, butter, lettuce, cole slaw

Place two thin slices of boiled ham on two thin slices of trimmed and buttered bread, and four thin slices of cold boiled chicken on top of the ham. Press on the two upper slices of bread and cut the two sandwiches in half. Whip one egg and one ounce of cream together and dip the four half sandwiches well in the egg and cream mixture and fry in hot grease as you would French toast, turning the sandwich over to brown on both sides.

AUTHOR'S NOTE: Be sure the grease is hot so that as quickly as the sandwich is placed in it the egg and cream mixture will immediately seal the pores of the bread, otherwise the bread will be greasy and soggy. This sandwich should be soaked lightly in egg mixture so that it takes up only certain amount of moisture.

Bacon can be substituted for ham if desired, or cream cheese and bar le duc spread can be used in place of the ham and chicken; in fact, any combination can be used.

This sandwich should be served as quickly as it is made and garnished with lettuce and a little cole slaw.

Special Combination Salad-Sandwich
Celery, Thousand Island dressing, ham, chicken, Swiss cheese, lettuce, bread

Mix one cup julienned celery, three-quarters cup Thousand Island dressing, one-half cup julienned boiled ham, one-half cup julienned boiled white meat of chicken, one-half cup finely julienned Swiss cheese and one head lettuce and mound out on beds of lettuce. Serve with French dressing.

This mixture is an excellent item to be used in a toasted sandwich. Spread the mixture without lettuce on slices of whole wheat or plain white bread, then trim and place in either a patent toaster or on a thin steel plate, plate to be placed upon the range and then sandwich placed upon plate when hot. Then place a silver platter on top of sandwich to hold sandwich in place. Turn over when toasted and toast on the opposite side. This sandwich served with a glass of buttermilk will make an excellent item. After sandwich is toasted it can be

cut in four blocks and a little Thousand Island
or Russian dressing poured over the top. Garnish
with cole slaw and lettuce.

Spiced Fruit Sandwich

Spiced cantaloupe, cream cheese, bread, lettuce

Chop 2 ounces of spiced cantaloupe very fine and
work enough cream cheese into it to bind. Spread
on thin slices of white bread, press on leaves of
lettuce and upper slice. Trim and cut into desired
shapes. Serve on leaves of lettuce. Any spiced fruit
may be used. Excess moisture should be drained
off before mixing cheese.

Butter may be used in place of cheese.

Spinach Sandwich—I

Raw spinach, bread, butter, lettuce, mayonnaise

Chop equal amount of roots of raw spinach and
green leaves. Mix with enough mayonnaise base
green leaves. Drain off surplus moisture. Mix with
enough mayonnaise base No. 3 to bind and spread
on thin slices of buttered and lettuced white bread.
Cut into desired shapes and serve as one variety
with a mixture of assorted sandwiches.

Roots and leaves must be carefully cleaned and
wiped thoroly dry before chopping.

Spinach Sandwich—II

Raw spinach, radishes, mayonnaise, bread,
butter, lettuce

Chop equal parts of raw spinach and small red
radishes and bind together with mayonnaise. Spread
on thin slices of buttered and lettuced white bread.
Cut into desired shapes and serve as one of a
variety of sandwiches.

A few chopped dandelions added to the spinach
gives it a delicious bitterness and makes a real
health-giving sandwich if spread on whole wheat
bread.

Chopped raw dandelions and sorrel, or sorrel and
spinach mixed with mayonnaise make healthful combinations.

SORREL: A perennial herb whose large, tender,
fleshy root leaves when young makes an excellent
salad or a fine green to cook. It is especially good
mixed with spinach, giving the spinach a pleasing
acid taste.

Spinach Sandwich III

See Fresh Spinach

Spinach Combination Sandwich I

Toast, raw spinach, hard-boiled eggs, cole slaw, mayonnaise, butter, lettuce

On thin slices of toast, spread with butter, place a mixture composed of two heaping tablespoons chopped raw spinach, one tablespoon of chopped hard-boiled eggs, one of chopped cole slaw and one tablespoon of mayonnaise. Press on a leaf of lettuce and then upper slice. Trim, cut diagonally and serve on leaf of lettuce.

Spinach Combination Sandwich II (Open)

Toast, raw spinach, lettuce, celery, mayonnaise, gherkins

On thin slices of toast spread a mixture made of two heaping tablespoons of chopped raw spinach, two heaping tablespoons of chopped raw lettuce, one tablespoon, heaping, of chopped raw celery added to enough mayonnaise to bind. Trim and serve on bed of lettuce. Garnish with gherkins.

Spinach and Egg Sandwich (Open)

Spinach, toast, butter, eggs, veal gravy

Form two pats of well squeezed out spinach. Place these round pats of spinach on rounds of thin, buttered toast. In center of spinach place a trimmed poached egg and over egg pour a light veal gravy. Serve at once. Spinach should be cooked in a very little water, pressed out and seasoned with salt, pepper, butter and nutmeg.

Spokane Sandwich

Bacon, apple, bread, mayonnaise, lettuce

Dice two strips of bacon and one small sweet apple. Saute bacon, then add apple and cook until it is soft. Spread slice of white bread with mayonnaise or butter and above mixture. Press on upper slice, trim and cut into desired shapes. Serve on leaves of lettuce. An unusual and tasty sandwich.— F. S. Fair.

Squeezed Cucumber Sandwich

Cucumber, bread, butter, sour cream, chives, lettuce

Sear with a fork one peeled hot-house cucumber and slice finely. Place in a porcelain bowl, sprinkle lightly with salt and add enough clear water to cover. Allow to marinate for ten minutes, then drain and place cukes in a towel and squeeze. Spread thin slices of bread with creamed butter to which has been added a little sour cream. Cover lower slice with a thin layer of squeezed cucumber and sprinkle with finely chopped chives. Press on upper slice and cut into any desired shape. Serve in napkin on bed of shredded lettuce. This sandwich is a fine accompaniment of any fish course. Chives may be left out if desired.

Squirrel Sandwich
Handle the same as Rabbit Sandwich.

Stale Bread Sandwich
Stale bread, milk wash, stewed tomatoes, Herkimer cheese

Dip two slices of bread in a special milk wash and fry brown on both sides. Cover lower slice with strained stewed tomatoes and grated Herkimer cheese. Press on upper slice, sprinkle with cheese, and brown under a quick broiler. Serve at once. To three ounces of pulp of stewed tomatoes add one ounce of grated cheese.

SPECIAL MILK WASH: Beat one egg up in one cup of milk seasoned with salt and paprika.

AUTHOR'S' NOTE: A bowl of stewed tomatoes (hot), to which has been added two ounces of diced Herkimer cheese while heating and then seasoned with salt, pepper and a little sugar makes a real feast. The author recommends this simple fare as a tasty, economical luncheon dish and when served with a slice of rye or whole wheat bread spread with butter makes a well balanced meal. "Enough is as good as a feast."

Steak Sandwich
See Broiled Rump
See Ham Steak

Sterham Sandwich
Rye bread, ham, roast sirloin, mustard butter, cress butter

On a thin slice of rye bread, spread with German mustard butter, place a thin slice of cold boiled ham. Press on second slice spread with chopped cress butter. On cress butter place a thin slice of cold roast sirloin of beef. Sprinkle with salt and cover with third slice of rye bread. Cut diagonally and serve on leaves of lettuce. This makes an excellent noon-day sandwich.

Strawberry Sandwich

*Bread, mayonnaise, strawberries, lettuce, galax
leaves*

On thin slices of toast or white bread buttered
and spread lightly with mayonnaise base No. 3
place sliced strawberries. Cover with a leaf of lettuce and press on upper slice. Cut in fancy shapes
and garnish with large berries and galax leaves.

Currant jelly may be used in place of mayonnaise.
Use large ripe berries to garnish with and do not
remove green stems.

Strawberry Jam Sandwich

Toast, butter, strawberry jam, bacon, lettuce

On a thin slice of buttered toast, spread with
strawberry jam, place three strips of broiled bacon.
Press on upper slice, trim and cut into desired shape.
Serve on leaf of lettuce. This makes a real treat
for an afternoon tea.

Sturgeon Sandwich

See Smoked Sturgeon

Sudoise Sandwich (Open)

Toast, eggs, onion puree, parsley

On rounds of toast place well trimmed fried or
poached eggs. Pour over them a rich puree of
onions. Sprinkle with chopped parsley. Serve hot.

Sugar-Cured Ham Combination Sandwich

*Bread, mustard butter, ham, gherkins, mayonnaise,
lettuce*

On thin slices of white bread, spread with mustard butter, place a thin layer of finely ground
boiled ham and sweet gherkins mixed in equal proportion and bound together with mayonnaise base
No. 3. Press on a leaf of lettuce and upper slice.
Cut into desired shape and serve.

Summer Sandwich (Open)

*Toast, mayonnaise, ham, tomato, peppers, slaw,
lettuce*

On a slice of trimmed toast or plain bread spread
with butter and then mayonnaise place a thin slice
of boiled ham; on top of ham place several very-
thin slices of peeled ripe tomato; sprinkle tomato
with chopped green peppers. Place this slice in
center of plate and garnish either end with a half
slice of toast, the toast to be spread with mayonnaise

and top spread with a very finely chopped and squeezed Mexican slaw. Underline with lettuce and serve immediately.

Sunday Luncheon Sandwich

Rye bread, Roquefort cheese, cream, lettuce, cucumber

Spread thin slices of rye bread with Roquefort cheese which has been thinned down to the proper consistency to spread with raw cream. Cover cheese with thin slices of chopped and well squeezed cucumber. Press on upper slice and cut into desired shape. Serve on bed of lettuce.

Sunday Morning Sandwich (Open)

Toast, eggs, butter, eggplant, bacon, parsley, tomato sauce

On two rounds of buttered toast place two scrambled eggs. Eggs should be scrambled with a little cream, seasoned and moulded up artistically on the rounds of toast. Garnish center sides of egg with two small rounds of fried eggplant (same size as toast). Criss-cross top center with two strips of bacon. Garnish ends with parsley. Serve hot. A little tomato sauce may be poured around the base, adding color and flavor to sandwich. This is an excellent combination.

Sweetbreads Sandwich I (Open)

Sweetbreads, butter, cream sauce, bread crumbs, toast, Swiss cheese

Blanch and skin one-half veal sweetbread. Heat one-half cup of cream. Melt one teaspoon of butter and stir in one teaspoon of flour. Whip in cream, season to taste and allow to cook for a few minutes. Cut sweetbread in slices and place on toast (toast to be cut diagonally). Pour sauce over sweetbreads and sprinkle with bread crumbs (Polonaise) and finely chopped Swiss cheese. Place under a hot broiler and brown, or serve without cheese and crumbs by just sprinkling sauce and sweetbreads with finely chopped parsley or chervil.

The finest of veal sweetbreads are sold in pairs and wrapped in paper. They are white and extremely tender. One-fourth of a pair is sufficient for a sandwich.

SWEETBREAD: The soft, milky thymus gland of a young calf or lamb, the former more highly esteemed and considered a great delicacy. The glands are divided into two classes, throat and heart or breast sweetbreads; the latter are generally preferred on account of their size, color and tenderness. They are most delicate when obtained from the suckling calf, as they gradually shrink and finally disappear when the calf is turned out to grass. The pancreas of the older animal, frequently, but incorrectly styled "sweetbread" (also known as the stomach sweetbread) is an entirely different gland. The beef gland, while not as choice as the true sweetbread, can be worked up into a very palatable and profitable dish by a competent cook.—*Encyclopedia of Food.*

The beef pancreas is darker, flabbier, tougher and can never be mistaken for the veal sweetbread.

Sweetbread Sandwich II
Veal sweetbread, egg, toast, tomato sauce

Dice one-fourth of a pair of blanched veal sweetbreads and heat in butter. Simmer lightly until cooked. Whip up one egg with a little cream and scramble, add sweetbread, remove and place on slice of trimmed buttered toast, press on upper slice and pour a little hot tomato sauce over sandwich. Serve at once. Tomato sauce should be thick so that it does not soak toast too much.

Sweetbread En Brochette Sandwich (Open)
Sweetbread brochette, toast, lamb's kidneys, lettuce, cress, tomato sauce

Arrange two small brochettes of broiled sweetbreads on two slices of thin, trimmed toast. Place sweetbreads in center, garnish ends with two half lamb's kidney, grilled, and leaves of lettuce. Garnish the sides with cress. Pour a little light tomato sauce over sweetbreads just before serving. Serve hot and at once.

Cooked sweetbreads ground and mixed with ground white meat of chicken seasoned and then bound together with mayonnaise, makes a fine filling. Chopped pickles or capers can be added for flavor.

SWEETBREADS EN BROCHETTE: Blanch two veal sweetbreads in salted water for five minutes. Remove and cool. Trim off surplus connective tissue and cut into one and one-half inch square pieces, one-half inch in thickness. Run on a four-inch skewer alternately pieces of sweetbread and pieces of underdone broiled bacon cut one and one-half inches long. After skewer is filled season and roll in bread crumbs. Place on a wire broiler, baste with melted butter and finish.   Arrange on toast, remove skewers and serve as directed.

● Sweetbreads can be browned in the oven without blanching, with a few herbs and butter.   They can also be sauted and browned, then smothered in a little rich Creole sauce, until done, allowed to cool and then sliced and sauce poured over them on slices of toast.

Sweet Sour Sandwich (Open)
Eggs, toast, brown butter sauce, currant jelly

On rounds of toast place two poached or fried eggs.   Pour over them a Buerre Noir sauce to which has been added a little currant jelly.

Swiss Cheese Sandwich
See Club Swiss
See Salami and Swiss Cheese

Tartar Sandwich
Tartar sauce, bread, lettuce

Spread a well garnished Tartar sauce on thin slices of bread.   Press on leaf of lettuce and upper slice.   Trim and cut into desired shapes and serve.

Tavern Sandwich
Pork, bread, gravy, seasoning

On a slice of bread moistened with gravy fresh from the roast, whether it be pork, beef or mutton, place a generous slice of any of the named items, season, moisten the upper slice with gravy, press on the upper slice and eat au natural.   If the meat has been roasted on the spit and the gravy has oozed from the roast on the bread you have a feast fit for a duke, nabob, king or whatnot.

AUTHOR'S NOTE: In early Colonial days the Tavern was the public gathering place.   It was the center of activities; it was the stopping and starting point of all travel; it was the place where man and beast were fed and lodged; it was the place where news was created, enlarged upon and dispensed; it was the election place, the auction shop, the theatre, the museum, etc.   At meal times, while the spit turned round, juicy slices of joints fresh from the spit were dispensed to the hungry traveler and were washed down with copious draughts of cooling beverages.

Ten P. M. Sandwich (Open)

Butter, onion, flour, tomatoes, eggs, toast, Gorgonzola cheese

Melt a level tablespoon of butter in a small enamel stewpan and add one teaspoon of finely minced onion. Cook slowly for a few minutes, then add one level teaspoon of flour; stir and cook flour, then add one-half cup of canned tomatoes (hot). Season well, stir and cook for five minutes. Whip up two eggs and add to mixture; stir until all thickens and remove from fire. Have ready two slices of trimmed toast and spread with the mixture. Sprinkle top liberally with grated Gorgonzola or old American cheese, butter and paprika. Place under a hot broiler and brown.

GORGONZOLA CHEESE is hard to cut in slices, but especially fine to mix with mayonnaise or French dressing and spread on crackers, whole wheat or rye bread. Gorgonzola lends itself excellently to dressing for salads. It is rich, pungent and made of whole milk (cows'); it comes from the mountain villages of Northern Italy, and is mottled like Roquefort.

Tenderloin Sandwich

See Minced Tenderloin

See Oyster Tenderloin

See Pork Tenderloin

Thanksgiving Sandwich—I

White or brown bread, butter, cranberry sauce, turkey, lettuce, celery, cress, olives, radishes

On thin slices of white bread spread with sweet butter and strained cranberry sauce, or cranberry jelly, place very thin slices of cold roast turkey, sprinkled with salt. Press on an inner leaf of lettuce and then a thin slice of brown bread. Trim into fancy shapes and garnish with small white inner branches of curled celery and cress. Celery should be placed leafy ends up in center of platter, cress piled around it to hold it in shape and sandwiches be placed around cress. Lilied radishes and fluted olives can be arranged around outer edge of sandwiches for pleasing effect.

AUTHOR'S NOTE: The first Thanksgiving week (not day) was celebrated in Plymouth in December, 1621. The following is a copy of letter written by Edward Winslow to a friend in England: "Our harvest being gotten in our govener sent four men on fowling that so we might after a special manner rejoice together after we had gathered the fruits of our labours. They four killed as much fowl as with a little help besides served the company for a week. At which times among other recreations we exercised our arms, many of the Indians coming amongst us, and among the rest their greatest king Massasoyt, with some ninty men, whom for three days we feasted and entertained and they went out and killed five deer which they brought and bestowe'd on our govener, and upon the captains and others." Govener Bradford writes "besides waterfowl there was a great store of wild turkies," we can have the satisfaction of feeling sure that at that first Pilgrim Thanksgiving our fore-fathers and fore-mothers had turkey. In 1630, on February 22, the first public Thanksgiving was held in Boston by the Bay Colony, in gratitude for the safe arrival of food-bearing and friend-bringing ships. From 1631 to 1684 there were at least twenty-two public Thanksgiving Days appointed in Massachusetts—about one in every two years. The early Thanksgivings were not always held on Thursday.

Thanksgiving Sandwich—II

White bread, turkey dressing, cranberry sauce,
turkey, lettuce, celery

Spread a slice of toast or white bread with a little cold turkey dressing thinned down with turkey gravy or strained cranberry sauce. On dressing arrange thin slices of cold roast turkey. Season, press on upper slice and cut in fancy shapes. Serve on leaves of lettuce and garnish with curled celery.

AUTHOR'S NOTE: A fast often preceded a Thanksgiving feast in the early Colonial days, an excellent plan but a super-excellent plan if they had had a fast after the feast also.

Thanksgiving Sandwich—III

Cold turkey, dressing, toast, butter, cranberry sauce,
gravy

Grind up scraps of cold turkey and mix into cold turkey dressing. Make into small thin cakes, fry and serve on toast spread with butter and cranberry sauce. Cut in two diagonally or in finger shapes. Serve plain or pour a little hot turkey gravy over sandwich and serve at once.

AUTHOR'S NOTE: The following is a copy of the First Fast Day broadside Proclamation known to be issued in America:

"At a Council held at Boston September 8, 1670. The Council taking into their serious consideration the low estate of the Churches of God throughout the World, and the increase of sin and evil amongst ourselves, God's hand following us for the same; Do therefore Appoint the Two and twentieth of this instant September to be a Day of Publick Humiliation throughout this Jurisdiction, and do commend the same to the several Churches, Elders, Ministers and People, solemnly to keep it accordingly: Hereby prohibiting all Serville work on that day.

By the Council,
Edward Rawson Secret."

Thanksgiving Sandwich—IV

Turkey liver, heart, gizzard, turkey dressing, white or whole wheat bread, cranberry jelly

Grind or chop up cooked turkey liver, gizzard and heart and mix in cold turkey dressing. Spread on plain white or whole wheat bread and press on upper slice. Place sandwich in a wire broiler or patent toaster and toast. Cut in half or in four and garnish with a small mound of cranberry jelly or serve with a hot turkey gravy poured over sandwich and a spoon of snow potatoes, browned.

Thermidor Sandwich

See Lobster, Thermidor

Thuringer Combination Sandwich

Thuringer sausage, red cabbage, horse radish, dill pickle, rye bread, lettuce

Put thru a grinder one cooked Thuringer sausage, one cup of cooked red cabbage and mix well, adding one tablespoon of prepared horseradish. Spread on thin slices of rye bread, press on upper slice and garnish with lettuce and slices of dill pickles.

This is an excellent combination and an excellent way to use up any left overs.

Thuringer Sausage Sandwich

Rye bread, German mustard, butter, Thuringer sausage, red cabbage

On a slice of rye bread spread lightly with German mustard and sweet butter place a split link of Thuringer sausage which has been cooked, skinned and browned. Press on upper slice and cut in two diagonally. Garnish with a little fried red cabbage which has been previously boiled. A little tarragon vinegar added to red cabbage while boiling adds to its flavor and heightens color of cabbage.

Three Yells Sandwich

White bread, Roquefort cheese, sardines, lemon juice, lettuce

Spread a thin slice of white bread or toast with a paste of Roquefort cheese made by adding raw cream to cheese. Skin and bone three French sardines. Place the six fillets or halves on the cheese and squeeze over them a little lemon juice. Press on leaf of lettuce and upper slice. Cut in two diagonally and place on leaf of lettuce. Garnish with slice of lemon.

AUTHOR'S NOTE: Roquefort cheese is as loud as the sardine and the lemon is as assertive as either; so while all three are yelling their loudest you eat, and in the eating you will find that the yells are blended into a delicious whole.

Toast
See French Toast

Toasted Cheese Sandwich (Open)

Toast, American cheese, butter

On a slice of toasted and buttered white bread place a slice of old American cheese, one-eighth of an inch thick. Toast or melt and brown cheese in hot oven or under hot broiler. Serve at once on hot plate. Paprika sprinkled over the cheese will give it a better appearance, but detracts from the flavor.

Toasted Chicken Sandwich

Chicken, cream, toast, American cheese, cress, julienned potatoes

Grind very fine one-fourth cup of white meat of chicken and moisten with a little raw cream. Season and heat. Spread mixture on a thin slice of trimmed toast. Sprinkle with finely chopped American cheese and paprika. Place under broiler or in oven to melt cheese, then press on upper slice, trim and cut in two. Garnish with cress and julienned potatoes. Serve at once.

This is truly a delectable item. This mixture may be spread on plain bread, sprinkled with finely chopped cheese and then toasted in a patent toaster.

Toasted Muffin

Muffin, ham, egg, Hollandaise sauce, butter

On a half of a toasted English muffin (buttered) place a thin slice of broiled or fried ham. Place one poached egg on top of ham and mask with Hollandaise sauce.

Toasted Ritzie Roll Sandwich

*Rolls, chicken, asparagus tips, cheese, butter, celery,
green olives, cress*

Cut off the top of a three-inch French roll about
one-fourth of an inch down. Remove the crumb and
fill with a Chicken a la Ritz mixture. Arrange
four asparagus tips around edge of roll. Sprinkle
the top with chopped American cheese (old), paprika and butter. Place under a hot broiler or in
oven and brown. Serve at once. Garnish roll with
hearts of celery, green olives and cress. Two rolls
should be served to an a la carte order. This is a
real aristocrat in the sandwich family. The chicken
mixture must not be too dry. A small sauce boat
of hot cream sauce can be served on the side.

Toasted Veal Ham Sandwich

White bread, veal, ham, curry, cress, lettuce

On a thin slice of toasted white bread, spread with
light flavored curry butter, place a thin slice of cold
roast veal. Press on second slice, spread with butter and a leaf of lettuce. On this place a slice of
cold boiled ham. Cover with third slice of toast and
trim. Cut diagonally or in fingers and serve on bed
of cress or lettuce. This class of sandwich should be
served as soon as made.

Tomato Sandwich—I

Tomato, toast, mayonnaise, bacon, lettuce, egg

On rounds of toast, spread with mayonnaise, place
thin slices of peeled tomato. Cut a piece of broiled
bacon in half and place on top of tomato. Press on
upper round of toast and serve on small salad plates.
Garnish with lettuce and decorate top of sandwich
with slices of hard-boiled egg.

Sandwich may be cut square and cut into four
and a little Thousand Island dressing poured over
the entire sandwich.

Tomato Sandwich—II

*Tomato, lettuce, bacon, chives, mayonnaise, toast,
butter*

Chop up connective tissue of ripe, peeled tomato
and mix with an equal amount of chopped lettuce.
Add one chopped, broiled strip of bacon and one-
fifth teaspoon of chopped chives. Mix with enough
mayonnaise to bind and spread on buttered pieces
of toast. Press on upper slice and cut in any desired
shape. This is a very tasty combination. The
above mixture mixed with Lorenzo dressing instead

of mayonnaise and a little diced white meat of
chicken added makes a desirable combination.

Tomato Sandwich—III

Tomatoes, sardines, mayonnaise, toast, lettuce

Chop up equal amounts of connective tissue of raw,
peeled, ripe tomatoes and sardines, boned and
skinned. Bind with a little mayonnaise and spread
on toasted white bread. Press on upper slice and
cut in desired shapes. Serve on leaves of lettuce.

Tomato Sandwich—IV

*Tomatoes, cress, lettuce, mayonnaise, butter, toast,
bacon*

Chop equal amounts of connective tissue of ripe,
peeled tomatoes, watercress and lettuce. Mix and
bind with mayonnaise. Spread on plain bread or
thin buttered toast. Press on upper slice and cut
into desired shapes. Garnish with lettuce and strip
with broiled bacon.

Tomato Sandwich—V

*Tomato, bread, lettuce, chives, cress, radishes, bacon,
mayonnaise*

Peel a ripe chilled tomato and slice about one-
fourth of an inch thick. Butter whole wheat, white
or graham bread, cover with a thin layer of shredded
lettuce, then lay on slice of tomato. Season with
salt and pepper and sprinkle with chopped chives.
Press on top slice and trim, or cut round with a plain
cutter. A good sized doughnut cutter makes an attractive looking sandwich. These slices can be arranged on a lettuce-leaved platter and garnished
with cress, lilied radishes and thin strips of broiled
bacon. If the doughnut cutter is used, make the
sandwiches thin and press right thru the tomato and
all. Fill all the holes with rosettes of cress. Chives
may be omitted and a little mayonnaise spread on
tomato, if desired.

Tomato Sandwich—VI (Open)

Bread, eggwash, tomatoes, cheese, bacon

Trim two stale slices of bread and dip in beaten
egg mixed with milk. Fry slices in hot grease,
brown on both sides. Place them on platter and
cover with well strained, stewed tomatoes. Season
tomatoes, sprinkle with paprika and a liberal amount
of chopped Herkimer cheese. Place in oven to
brown. Serve hot. Garnish with a strip of broiled
bacon. Cut one slice of fried bread in half and ar-

range a half slice at either end of whole one, turning flat ends in.

A tomato paste can be substituted for stewed tomatoes.

Tongue Sandwich—I

White or rye bread, tongue, lettuce, tomato, cole slaw

On thin slices of white or rye bread, buttered, place very thin slices of boiled smoked ox tongue. Lettuce and press on upper slice. Trim and cut diagonally or in finger shapes. Garnish with a small red ripe tomato hollowed out and filled with cole slaw.

This vegetable garniture gives an alkaline reaction which helps neutralize the acids formed thru the eating of the meat and bread portion of diet.

Tongue Sandwich—II

Tongue, ham, capers, mayonnaise, toast

Mix one-third cup of ground, boiled, smoked ox tongue, one-third cup of boiled sugar cured ham and one tablespoon of chopped capers. Bind together with mayonnaise base No. 3. Spread on thin slices of toast, trim and cut in two diagonally. Serve toast warm and fresh. This is an excellent item; one that talks for itself.

Tongue Sandwich III

See Pickled Lamb Tongue

Tri Color Sandwich—I (Open)

Toast, tongue, eggs, parsley, cream sauce

On two rounds of toast place two poached eggs. Pour over them a rich cream sauce garnished with chopped boiled ox tongue and parsley. Serve at once on hot platter.

Tri Color Sandwich—II (Open)

Plain bread or toast, cabbage, carrots, green peppers, mayonnaise, radishes, cheese, hard-boiled eggs, lettuce, gherkins, olives, lilied radishes

On a full single slice of plain or freshly toasted graham or white bread, buttered, spread a thin layer of finely ground and seasoned raw cabbage, carrots and sweet peppers. The vegetables are to be mixed separately and with enough mayonnaise to bind; then spread on bread in alternate parallel strips about 1½ inches wide. Cut bread in opposite direction from strips about 1½ inches wide so that colors show up well. Pipe a little thinned-down cream cheese around border of sandwich and an extremely thin line of stiff, chilled mayonnaise between the vegetables, showing the line of demarcation.

This sandwich can be made up quickly, if a number are desired, by cutting a slice of bread the entire length of the loaf and toasting this large slice. Then place the ground cabbage on one side lengthwise, the green peppers on the opposite side and the carrots in the center. Pipe the mayonnaise down both sides of carrots, then cut bread in two-inch strips across and afterwards pipe on the border of cream cheese. This sandwich is just an open, one-pieced affair and is extremely attractive and tasty. The plate or platter should be garnished with rounds of hard-boiled eggs, lettuce, small sweet gherkins, olives and lilied radishes. This is a real vegetarian sandwich. Any ground raw vegetables can be used. Pickled or baked beets make an attractive center. Vegetables should be pressed out before mayonnaise is added and the sandwich made nearly to order to get best results.

Trio Sandwich

Rye bread, mustard, cole slaw, Virginia ham, mayonnaise, turkey, Swiss cheese, cress, tomato

On a thin slice of rye bread, cut on a slant and spread with butter place a thin layer of cole slaw. On slaw place a thin slice of boiled Virginia ham. Cover with second slice of thin rye and spread top of slice with mayonnaise and cover with a thin slice of white meat of turkey. On turkey place a thin slice of Swiss cheese or Gouda. Press on third slice. Cut sandwich in two diagonally. Garnish with cress and tomatoes.

Replace ham with smoked tongue when Gouda cheese is used.

AUTHOR'S NOTE: Gouda Kosher cheese is made for the Jewish trade. It is a Holland cheese bearing a special stamp for identification. It can be made into sandwiches by grating and pounding into a paste and adding cream or mayonnaise to thin paste to the proper consistency. Chopped chives or bar le duc may be added to it. Serve on rye bread and cut into finger shapes, round or diagonally.

Tripe Sandwich I (Hot Boiled)

Tripe, toast, butter, Creole sauce, mushrooms

Scrub and clean tripe thoroly. Boil until tender with a few slices of onion, a carrot, a clove of garlic, a slice of lemon, salt and a few coriander seeds. Allow to cool and then cut into fine julienne. Heat the julienned tripe in a little butter and add enough Creole sauce to bind. Pour heated mixture over a slice of trimmed, buttered toast. Place the second slice of toast either on top of tripe or at end of first piece of toast as in Hot Roast Beef Sandwich. Garnish with grilled mushrooms.

Mixture should not be too thin or too thick and should be seasoned well.

AUTHOR'S NOTE: Should you ever make a stew of Tripe a la Creole and have any left over, put it thru a meat grinder, then spread mixture on slices of whole wheat or white bread, and toast in a wire broiler. Serve hot.

Tripe Sandwich II
See Soused Tripe

Triple "V" Sandwich—I (Open)
Bacon, lamb kidneys, toast, butter, onions, cress, tomatoes

Fry four strips of bacon until medium crisp. Have ready two or three lamb kidneys split and soaked in cold water for ten minutes. Dry, dust with flour, season and fry them in bacon grease slowly until done. Arrange kidneys round side up and alternate with strips of bacon on two pieces of toast, cut diagonally. Pour over them a little melted butter or a hot tomato sauce. Garnish with French fried onions or fried tomatoes and cress. Serve at once.

This makes an ideal breakfast dish. Kidneys, liver and tomatoes contain vitamins A, B, and C.

Triple "V" Sandwich—II (Open)
Whole wheat bread, sweetbreads, butter, tomato, chicken livers, cress

On two slices of toasted and buttered whole wheat bread place one calf's sweetbread which has been parboiled, split, breaded and fried brown in butter. Garnish sides of sweetbread with two slices of fried tomato, placing one on either side. Chop up three chicken livers (raw) or one ounce of calf's liver, shake in a little flour and fry in butter until done (3 minutes), add one-third cup of hot tomato sauce to livers and pour livers over sweetbreads. Serve at once. Decorate with cress. This is an excellent item for the anemic.

A La Turc Sandwich (Open)

Toast, eggplant, tomato sauce, anchovy butter, egg

On rounds of toast, spread lightly with anchovy butter, place a round of fried eggplant. On eggplant place a poached egg. Over the top pour a rich tomato or Creole sauce. Serve at once. Eggplant should be cut thin, the same as toast and then fried.

Turkey Sandwich

Bread, butter, turkey, lettuce

On thin slices of white or brown bread, buttered, plain or toasted, place thin slices of roasted or boiled turkey. Lettuce bread and press on upper slice. Cut into hearts, fingers, rounds, diamonds, squares, ovals, clubs or leaves. Serve on leaves of lettuce and garnish with any of the following: pimolas, olives, gherkins, hard-boiled eggs, stuffed or curled celery, potato chips, lilied radishes, etc. Sandwiches may be spread with mayonnaise, nut, sweet, lemon, cranberry, apple or aromatic butter.

Turkey Combination Sandwich

White bread, mayonnaise, cream cheese, turkey

Spread a thin slice of white bread with mayonnaise and thinned-down cream cheese. Arrange a thin slice of white meat of turkey on cheese, season and press on upper slice. Trim and cut into desired shapes.

Turkey and Cranberry Sandwich

Toast, turkey, cranberry sauce, cheese, cress

On a slice of trimmed toast place two or three thin slices of cold roast turkey. Cover turkey with hot cranberry sauce and sprinkle grated old American cheese over it. Place open sandwich under hot broiler to melt cheese. Serve at once. Garnish with cress or lettuce.

Turkey and Roquefort Sandwich

Toast, Roquefort cheese, lettuce, turkey, French dressing

Toast two thin slices of bread and spread one slice with a paste made of Roquefort cheese thinned down with French dressing. Press on a leaf of lettuce and then two or three slices of cold roast turkey. Cover with upper slice, trim and serve on leaves of lettuce.

Turkey and Tomato Sandwich

*Toast, turkey, Swiss cheese, tomato, mustard, mayon-
naise, lettuce, butter*

Place a thin slice of Swiss cheese on a thin piece
of toast, spread with butter and prepared mustard.
On top place a second slice of toast spread with mayonnaise. On this place a lettuce leaf and a thin
slice of white meat of turkey. Over turkey lay a
thin slice of cold, ripe tomato. Press on third slice
of toast. Trim and cut diagonally and place on lettuce leaves on platter in shape of a diamond.

Unique Sandwich—I (Open)

*Bacon, chicken livers, egg, toast, French fried
onions, Pullman bread*

Fry three strips of bacon crisp. Remove bacon
and saute three chicken livers slowly in the bacon
grease until done. Drain grease, place bacon back
in pan with livers and break one egg on top. Finish cooking egg in hot oven. Baste while cooking.
Serve as an open sandwich on slice of toasted Pullman bread. Garnish with French fried onions.

A little tomato sauce poured over sandwich when
finished gives color, life and flavor.

Unique Sandwich—II

Toast, butter, currant jelly, mustard, lamb

In a small frying pan heat a tablespoon of butter,
two tablespoons currant jelly and one-sixth of a teaspoon of dry mustard. In this mixture place two
thin slices of cold roast leg of lamb. Heat thoroly.
Arrange meat on a trimmed slice of buttered toast.
Press on upper trimmed slice an serve at once.

Veal Sandwich

Veal, white bread, lettuce, mayonnaise, prunes

On thin slices of toasted or plain white, rye or
whole wheat bread lettuced and spread with mayonnaise or butter, place thin slices of cold roast veal.
Press on upper slice. Cut in desired shapes and
serve on bed of lettuce. Garnish with lettuce and
two or three large stewed prunes, without juice.

Veal Combination Sandwich—I

*Veal, gherkins, pimentoes, mayonnaise, white bread,
butter, lettuce*

Grind one cup of cooked veal, one-third cup of
gherkins and one-fifth cup pimentoes. Mix together
and add enough mayonnaise to bind. Spread on
thin slices of buttered white bread. Press on leaf

of lettuce and upper slice, cut into desired shapes. Serve on cold plates garnished with lettuce.

This makes a very tasty hot weather item. Pork or chicken may be handled the same way.

Veal Combination Sandwich—II

Veal kidney, beef tongue, gherkins, bacon, mayonnaise, rye bread, Swiss cheese, lettuce

Grind and bind together with mayonnaise three ounces of veal kidney (cooked), three ounces of cooked beef tongue, two ounces of gherkins and two ounces of broiled bacon. Spread mixture on thin slices of rye bread. Press on a very thin slice of Swiss cheese and upper slice; cut into desired shapes. Serve on bed of lettuce.

Veal Ham Sandwich
See Toasted Veal Ham

Veal Loaf Sandwich

Toast, butter, veal loaf, lettuce, cole slaw

On thin slices of toast or plain bread, spread with Tartar sauce or butter, place a thin slice of veal loaf. Press on leaf of lettuce and upper slice. Cut into desired shapes and serve on leaves of lettuce with a garnish of cole slaw.

VEAL LOAF

Mix one cup bread crumbs, one pound raw veal, chopped, two teaspoons butter, two eggs, salt and pepper, one tablespoon sage, and one small onion, ground or grated well. Mold into loaf and bake in moderate oven one hour.

Veal Salad Sandwich

Veal, lettuce, mayonnaise, white bread

Dice or grind very small one cup of cold roast veal and mix with one cup of finely shredded celery or lettuce. Bind together with mayonnaise. Spread on thin slices of white bread. Press on upper slice and cut in two diagonally. Serve on leaves of lettuce.

Veal may be marinated in French dressing and surplus moisture squeezed out if a more piquante mixture is desired.

Veal, celery and chopped pickles, bound together with mayonnaise, make a good combination.

Vegetable Sandwich
See Fresh Vegetable
See Boiled Vegetable

Vegetable Hamburger Sandwich
See Singapore

Venison Sandwich
Venison, bread, butter, currant jelly, lettuce, olives, celery

Cut thin slices of cold roast venison and arrange on very thin slices of bread, spread with butter and currant jelly. Season, press on leaf of lettuce and upper slice. Cut into desired shapes and serve on leaves of lettuce. Garnish with green olives and curled celery hearts. A thin strip of broiled bacon, curled, makes an ideal garnish. Reindeer may be handled the same way.

Ground venison, pickles and ham, bound together with mayonnaise, makes a real sandwich filling.

A slice of roast, grilled or fried venison (seasoned and underdone) placed between two slices of bread is the real hunters' sandwich.

Victoria Sandwich
Toast, butter, crab meat, mayonnaise, egg, lettuce

On thin slices of buttered toast place a thin layer of crab meat mixed with mayonnaise. Arrange four slices of hard-boiled egg on top of crab meat, press on upper slice and cut in two diagonally. Serve on leaves of lettuce. A little curry powder added to mayonnaise will give an added zest to the crab flakes.

Sandwich can be cut into four squares and a little Russian dressing poured over squares; then the tops garnished with four round slices of hard-boiled eggs.

Virginia Ham Sandwich
Virginia ham, bread, lettuce

Cut boiled Virginia ham in thin slices and arrange on slice of rye or plain white bread, buttered. Press on a leaf of heart of lettuce and then the upper slice. Trim and cut diagonally or in finger shapes. Serve on leaf of lettuce. This sandwich does not need a condiment of any kind; it is sufficient unto itself if you are seeking flavor. Served with a few hearts of celery and a glass of milk, it makes a light, well balanced luncheon.

Waldorf Sandwich

Apples, celery, butter, bread, mayonnaise, lemon juice, lettuce

Mix Jonathan, Northern Spy or Snow apples, chopped fine and marinated in lemon juice for fifteen minutes, with one-half the amount finely chopped hearts of celery and enough mayonnaise to bind. Spread mixture on white bread, buttered, and cut in fancy shapes. Serve on lettuce leaves. Chopped walnuts, pecans or pistachios may be mixed with apples and celery for variety.

Walker Sandwich (Open)

Toast, butter, oysters, sauce, bread crumbs, paprika

On two pieces of buttered toast cut diagonally and arranged on a platter in diamond shape place six New York counts or twelve standards, which have been previously poached in a little butter and their own liquor just long enough to set them. Do not cook too long or they will become tough. Make a light sauce of butter, flour, cream, a little of the strained liquor, and salt. Sauce should be just thick enough to coat the oysters. Pour over oysters, sprinkle with bread crumbs, paprika and butter. Brown under a quick broiler and serve at once. Flaked cooked fish or shrimp, lobster, crayfish and scallops can be handled the same way as the above.

Cheese added to bread crumbs before browning gives an added flavor.

Walnut Sandwich
See Black Walnut
See Pickled Walnut

Wedded Nourishment Sandwich

Rye bread, mustard, corned beef, Swiss cheese, slaw

On very, very thin slices of rye bread spread with German made mustard place a very, very thin slice of cold corned beef. On beef place a very, very thin slice of Swiss cheese. Press on upper slice and cut in half. Place the two half sandwiches one on the other, but between the two halves spread a little well made Mexican slaw (not wet). The combined height of the sandwiches should not be more than one inch. Two of these sandwiches cut in half (4 pieces) should be served to an a la carte order.

Welsh Sandwich

Toast, butter, tomato, bacon, Welsh rabbit, cheese

Toast two thin, trimmed slices of white bread and spread with butter. Place three thin slices of peeled

tomato on lower slice and strip with three thin strips
of broiled bacon. Press on upper slice. Pour over
the top of sandwich rabbit and sprinkle it with
grated bread crumbs. Place under a hot broiler and
brown quickly. This is an unusually tasty, savory
sandwich and one of the best sellers.

WELSH RABBIT OR RAREBIT: Dice four ounces of
Herkimer or Old English cheese, well cured (not
processed) and melt in small saute pan. Add one
or two tablespoons of stale beer or ale, three or four
drops of Worcestershire sauce and a little paprika.
Incorporate all and pour this mixture over the tomato and bacon sandwich. When cheese is of the
proper age and cure it will break from the spoon
when melted and poured and will not string. A
little good cream sauce may be added in place of
ale or beer, if desired.

One-fourth part canned tomato soup added to
three-fourths melted cheese makes an ideal tomato
rabbit or rarebit.

Omit second slice of bread for an open sandwich.
Unless one is extremely hungry the open type sandwich is ample.

One tablespoon of tomato paste to four ounces of
cheese makes a good combination.

If you do not have the right kind of cheese use
one teaspoon of flour to one of melted butter and
work this into a paste or roux, then add cheese, ale,
etc. By using this method you will have a creamy,
short mixutre.

Welsh Rabbit Sandwich

Dice one-half pound of American cheese (not
processed and at least one year old). Place it in a
chafing dish and add two tablespoons of good ale or
beer and one-sixth teaspoon of red pepper. Stir
with a wooden spoon until melted, which will take
from eight to ten minutes. Pour over toasted bread
and serve very hot. If cheese is of right vintage it
will melt, and be tender and be of the right consistency and flavor, if not, it will be stringy, tough
and poor.

Do not spoil a good dish by buying poor materials.

If it is impossible to incorporate all into a smooth
creamy mass, make a roux out of one teaspoon of
flour and one of butter. Melt butter and add flour,
mix up into a smooth paste, then add cheese and seasoning and last the ale, whipping all up into a
smooth mixture. Six to eight tablespoons of ale can
be incorporated when flour is used. Half ale or

beer and half tomato catsup gives mixture an additional tang.

This latter mixture allowed to cool and then spread on thin slices of toast and sprinkled with minced pickles makes a fine filling for a sandwich.

Whitefish Sandwich
See Smoked Whitefish

Ye Olden Hunter Sandwich
Bread, venison, Bermuda onion

On a slice of bread place a slice of freshly broiled or roasted venison, seasoned and cut from the round. Place a thin slice of sweet Bermuda onion on top of venison and press on upper slice.

In the eating of this delectable bit you may say of the flavor as Sam Weller did, "It's the gravy as does it."

"The savory sandwich when made aright
'Tis little tid bid of delight.
The exacting guest with smiles galore
Like fathomless Kate will ask for more."

Fancy Butters and Miscellaneous Spreads

[Butters should be beaten with a spatula or thinned down with whipped or raw cream to the proper consistency for spreading.]

Alligator Pear or Avocado Butter

Rub pulp of a ripe alligator pear thru a fine sieve; season with salt and a little lemon juice. Spread on thin slices of white bread, sprinkle with chopped lettuce (which has been dipped in a real French dressing), press on upper slice, trim and cut into desired shapes. Serve at once. This is an excellent item to be served with a variety of fancy sandwiches.

Almond, Walnut, Cocoanut, Hazelnut or Brazil Nuts Butter

Use same method as in Peanut Butter.

Anchovy and Catsup Butter

See Caviar and Catsup

Aromatic Butter

Mix one tablespoon of aromatic vinegar in two ounces of soft butter, incorporating vinegar into butter over ice while butter is hardening. One tablespoon of chopped cress added to the aromatic butter gives zest to the thinly cut sandwich.

Avocado Butter

See Alligator Pear

Bacon Butter

Grind three strips of freshly broiled, crisp bacon and work into two ounces of creamed butter. A few drops of lemon juice may be incorporated in butter by using the same method as in Orange Butter.

Brazilnut Butter

See Almond

Caraway Seed Butter

Grind one tablespoon of caraway seeds and mix with three ounces of soft butter. Work in one teaspoon of lemon juice.

Catsup Butter

See Caviar and Catsup

See Tomato Catsup

Caviar or Anchovy and Catsup Butter

Whip two tablespoons of caviar or two of finely chopped anchovies into a like amount of tomato catsup butter.

Cheese and Garlic Butter

Grate two ounces of Herkimer cheese and work it into two ounces of creamed butter, which has had an atom of garlic worked into it.

Crush a clove of garlic in a bowl, remove the garlic and then use the same bowl to work butter and cheese together. This method will give you your atom of garlic.

Chive Butter

Cream one-fourth cup of butter and add three tablespoons of finely chopped chives. Then work in one teaspoon of lemon juice.

Cocoanut Butter

See Almond Butter

Colored Butters

See Red, Green, Yellow

Cress Butter

Wash lettuce or cress, dry and chop. Cream three or four ounces of butter and work into it as much chopped cress or lettuce as it will take. Season with salt and use as a spread. After the cress has been added to butter a little mayonnaise can be added for flavor; or in case mixture is too stiff; equal amounts of cress and lettuce can be used.

Crushed Raspberry Butter

Rub fresh raspberries thru a fine sieve and add one tablespoon to three ounces of butter. (See method in Orange Butter.) Then mix in one teaspoon of lemon juice.

Crushed Strawberry Butter

Use same method as for raspberries. Make the butter take all the moisture you can incorporate in it.

Fancy Butters

(For Fancy Sandwiches, Appetizers, Hors d'Oeuvres)

Rub four yolks of hard boiled eggs thru a fine sieve; cream three ounces of butter, and work these two ingredients together thoroly; add one or two drops of pure vegetable coloring or enough to give the proper tinge; stir until thoroly blended.

Place colored butter in a fine cornucopia made of

brown wrapping paper, tapering end to a very fine
point. Pipe the butter around edges of canapes;
make fancy rosettes and flowers on top of Hors
d'oeuvres, etc. Two or three colors are necessary
to do effective work. Have a red, yellow and green
mixture made and all placed in separate paper
tubes or cornucopias and then you can pipe out
leaves, rosettes and various little buds and flowers;
that is, if you practice and are somewhat artistic.
The work must be carefully done to be effective and
worth while.

Fruit Butter

See separate heads as Prune, etc.

Garlic Butter

Mash two or three cloves of garlic in a bowl and
remove connective tissue. Cream three ounces of
butter in same bowl to permeate butter with garlic
flavor.

One yolk of a hard boiled egg rubbed thru a fine
sieve and added to any of the fancy butters will
help to hold moisture and will also make butter
stand up when used for garnishing purposes. One
yolk to every three ounces of butter will suffice.

Garlic and Cheese Butter

See Cheese and Garlic

Gherkin Butter

Grind or chop fine two ounces of gherkins and
work into three to four ounces of creamed butter.
Drain off surplus moisture before adding gherkins
to butter. Olives, dill pickles, spiced cantaloup,
piccalilli, burr pickles, etc., may be handled in the
same way.

Green Butter

Wash small bunch chervil, 6 to 8 leaves tarragon,
½, small bunch of cress, 1 tablespoon chives, a few
sprigs of sweet basil and mix with a pint of very
green and fresh clean spinach. Blanch all in hot
water for two minutes. Drain quite dry, chop and
pound in the mortar, then press through a fine sieve
and add to essence a cup of sweet butter (creamed).
Press two yolks of hard boiled eggs through a sieve
and about six boneless fillets of anchovies separately,
then add to the butter. The eggs will hold the butter
up when used for decorating and the anchovies will
give added flavor. A few drops of lemon will

enhance flavor of butter. If butter is not green enough a little green coloring matter can be added or a little additional spinach green.

Green Olive Butter

Use same method as for Ripe Olive Butter, omitting salt.

Green Pepper Butter

Drop two small green peppers into hot grease for one minute. Wipe off outer skin, cut off stalks and remove seeds. Chop very fine, drain and add to one-fourth cup of creamed butter. Season with salt and work in a tablespoon of lemon juice. (See Orange Butter.)

Hazlenut Butter
See Almond

Herb Butter

Sweet basil, burnet, borage, marjoram, balm, dill, tarragon, mint, chervil, fennel, parsley, spearmint, thyme, sage, sweet savory, sorrel, sour grass, cress, peppergrass, nasturtiums, etc.

Any of the above herbs chopped and worked into a soft butter with the addition of lemon juice and then spread on thin slices of bread and rolled or cut in fancy shapes make ideal items to fill in an assortment of sandwiches. Some of these herbs are of a stronger nature than others and should be used accordingly.

Hop Butter

The leaves of the young hop plant chopped and worked into creamed butter, the same as any other herb, make a slightly bitter filling. Half chopped lettuce and half hop gives an ideal combination. Use salted butter.

Dandelions, endive and other bitter herbs lend themselves to the same ideal treatment.

AUTHOR'S NOTE: In 1574 a pamphlet by Reynolde Scott tells of the virtues of the hop. This quaint passage is taken from it: "There will some smell out of the profitable savour of this herbe, some wyll gather the fruit thereof, some will make a sallet therewith (which is goode in one respect for the bellye, and in another for purse) and when the grace and sweetness hereof conceived, some will dippe their fingers therein up to the knuckles, and some will be glad to licke the dishe, and they that disdayne to be partakers hereof, commonly prove to be such as have mountaynes in fantasie, and beggary in possessions."

Hops are valuable according as they contain a yellow powder called lupuline, which is deposited in minute yellow adhesive globules underneath the bracts of the flower tops. This powder has a powerful aromatic smell and is bitter to the taste. It contains hop resin, tannic acid and hop oil, giving a bitter flavor familiar to all beer drinkers and which acts not only as a stimulant, but as a restorative.

Horseradish Butter

Soak two tablespoons of freshly grated horseradish in a cup of cold water for a few minutes. Drain well and add enough aromatic vinegar to moisten. Then work enough sweet butter into horseradish to incorporate all so that it is the right consistency to spread. Bottled horseradish can be drained and enough added to sweet butter to make it the right consistency to spread.

Lemon Butter

Handle the same as Orange Butter.

A little of the chopped lemon pulp added to the creamed butter makes a desirable spread.

Lettuce Butter

See Cress Butter

Liver Butter

Grate two cooked chicken livers, when cold, and mix into two ounces of creamed butter. Season with salt and pepper. This is an excellent, savory item.

Calf's, goose or turkey liver can be grated and mixed with butter in the same manner. Liver simmered slowly in stock until cooked is an excellent item also.

Lobster Butter

Mix one ounce of finely chopped lobster with three ounces of butter and one teaspoon of lemon juice. Cream butter, whip in lemon juice, then work in lobster. Lobster coral, if obtainable, adds to the color. Crabmeat, shrimp, oyster crabs, sardines or anchovies handled the same way make ideal fillers, or if spread on small, fanciful cuts of toast make real appetizing sandwiches. Bread can be spread with a lemon mayonnaise and lemon juice omitted. Shredded lettuce added to butter and lobster gives sandwich additional zest.

Mace and Nutmeg Butter

Into six ounces of creamed butter whip one-fourth teaspoon of ground nutmeg, one-sixth teaspoon of ground mace and one teaspoon of lemon juice.

Mint Butter

Cream three ounces of sweet butter and add one tablespoon of chopped mint leaves; or whip three drops of mint essence into butter. This is excellent for lamb or mutton sandwiches.

Montpelier Butter

Pound an equal amount of parsley, chives, chervil, gherkins and capers together in a mortar and then rub thru a fine sieve. To the combined amount of mortared herbs add an equal amount of sweet butter and rub together, then add to each three ounces of mixture one yolk of a hard boiled egg which has been previously rubbed thru a fine sieve. A little spinach green can be added if color is too light.

Mustard Butter

Mix one teaspoon of Colman's dry mustard with enough aromatic vinegar to make a paste. Then whip the mustard into four ounces of melted butter, using the same method as in orange butter.

To make a milder, less assertive mustard butter use equal quantities of prepared French or German mustard and melted butter.

"Mustard, according to our archaeologists, is older than Methuselah. It was known to man in prehistoric times. Before history was made, the mustard seed was an article of diet among the aborigines.

"The early Egyptians advertised its virtues on papyrus, and for centuries before the Christian era, Hippocrates, the 'Father of Medicine,' knew of and wrote about the medicinal properties of mustard.

"There are a number of uses for mustard. For making mayonnaise and other salad dressings it is indispensable.

Nut Butters
See Almond

Nutmeg and Mace Butters
See Mace and Nutmeg

Olive Butter
See Green Olive
See Ripe Olive

Onion Butter

Whip into three ounces of melted butter one teaspoon of onion juice extracted from a white Bermuda onion. Add one-half teaspoon of chopped
chives for color.

Grind onion into a bowl and strain juice. Use
same method of incorporating juice as in Orange
Butter.

Orange Butter

Soften two or three ounces of sweet butter in a
small bowl until it is the consistency of mayonnaise;
then place bowl on ice and whip in two teaspoons
orange juice, one teaspoon lemon juice and one teaspoon of powdered sugar. The butter will take up
all the moisture if handled this way.

Fruit juices make an ideal spread or filling for
Afternoon Tea sandwiches. Sandwiches should be
placed in ice-box until needed, but the quicker they
are served the better the flavor. A teaspoon of
finely chopped orange peel may be added if desired.
Any fruit juice may be incorporated in butter by
using this method. Partially melted butter should
be placed in bowl, then the bowl placed on ice and
juices whipped in while butter is hardening.

Rub one hard boiled egg yolk thru a fine sieve and
add to any fancy butter. The egg yolk will help
take up the moisture and if butter is to be used for
garnishing purposes it will stand up better. One
yolk to every three or four ounces will suffice. The
egg yolk detracts from the flavor and with the delicate flavored butter where it is not used for garnishing it is better to omit it.

Peanut Butter

Put shelled and skinned peanuts thru a food
chopper and then mash in a mortar. Mix with
enough salt butter to get the proper consistency, then
work in a little raw cream. Set in ice-box until
needed.

Pimento Butter

Wash two or three real red pimentoes in cold
water, dry and rub thru a fine sieve. Work the
pimentoes into one-fourth cup of creamed sweet butter, add one teaspoon of lemon juice and enough
salt to season. A half teaspoon of paprika can be
added for color.

Plum Butter
See Prune Butter

Printemps Butter

Work two ounces of new green pea puree into three ounces of soft butter and add one teaspoon of chopped mint. Use same method of incorporating as in Orange Butter. A little mayonnaise may be added for flavor. Salt should be used in seasoning puree.

Prune Butter
Plum Butter

Rub one ounce of stewed plums or prunes thru a sieve and incorporate in melted butter. Beat prune puree into butter over ice until all juice and substance is incorporated. Add a little lemon juice if mixture is too flat. Oregon prunes are tart.

Raisin Butter

See Seedless Raisin

Raspberry Butter

See Crushed Raspberry

Ravigote Butter

Chop finely one tablespoon each of tarragon, chives, chervil and burnet and mix into four ounces of creamed butter, then work in one tablespoon of Mayonnaise Base No. 3, or one tablespoon of lemon juice. An excellent filling for sandwich rolls or rolls of sandwich bread. Sprinkle with salt.

Raw Spinach Butter

Scald one cup of fresh spinach for one minute; drain dry and chop very fine. Mix with three ounces of creamed butter, season with salt. Add one drop of onion juice and one-sixth teaspoon of grated nutmeg. Use as a filler in fancy small sandwiches.

Spinach chopped raw and mixed with mayonnaise makes an ideal filler. Butter and chopped raw spinach seasoned with salt is also ideal and a fine sandwich for children. Work as much chopped spinach into the butter as you can and then season to taste. Raw spinach and kraut (equal amounts), surplus juice removed and bound together with mayonnaise is also excellent. Dandelion roots and lettuce likewise.

Red Butter—I

Red Butter is made from tomato paste or lobster coral pounded in a mortar, and then rubbed thru a hair sieve, and enough added to the butter to color; or a small can of red tomato pulp boiled down

with an atom of garlic and a few spices to the point
of evaporation, then rubbed thru a fine sieve and
added to the butter. When these butters are used as
a part of a sandwich filling and not for garnatures
(see Orange Butter) a few anchovies, sardinels or
sardines, skinned and boned then rubbed thru a fine
sieve can be added for flavor. Flakes of crab meat
or salmon can be laid on this colored butter and a
few ground capers or gherkins sprinkled over the
flakes.

Red Butter—II

Rub two tablespoons of lobster coral thru a fine
sieve and mix with one teaspoon of lemon juice and
one tablespoon of Mayonnaise Base No. 3. Mix the
above in three ounces of soft butter, using the same
method to incorporate as in Orange Butter. One
tablespoon of tomato paste may be added for additional color. This is very fine for finger or rolled
sandwiches. The outer red skin of lobster flesh
finely chopped and added to butter adds to flavor
and color.

Remoulade Butter

Mix one tablespoon each of finely chopped capers,
chives, parsley, chervil and tarragon with two
tablespoons of Mayonnaise Base No. 3. Incorporate
the above in six ounces of soft butter, using the
same method as in Orange Butter. Excellent for
rolled sandwiches or finger variety.

Ripe Olive Butter

Stone and chop finely twenty large ripe olives
and work them into enough creamed butter to bind.
Add one tablespoon of mayonnaise to every three
ounces of butter used. Season with salt. Mayonnaise should be stiff.

Rose Butter
See Violet Butter

Sardellen Butter

Soak sardellen or sardells in plenty of cold water
over night, changing the water at least twice. Bone
and skin; wipe dry and press in a dry cloth. Place
in a mortar and mash. Add twice the amount of
sweet butter and make into a paste; add a few
drops of onion juice.

Seedless Raisin Butter

Wash and steam for a few minutes one-half cup
of raisins, chop and add to a nut butter using half

nuts and half raisins when mixing with butter. If too stiff add a little raw cream to reduce to proper consistency for spreading.

Singapore Butter

Grind one tablespoon each of pimentoes, green peppers, celery and Major Grey's chutney. Work the above into three ounces of soft butter, using the same method of incorporating as in Orange Butter. One tablespoon of Mayonnaise Base No. 3 may be added for flavor. Very good for finger sandwiches, assorted.

Sorrel Butter

Chop two tablespoons of sorrel and incorporate in two ounces of creamed butter.

Spiced Butter

See Nutmeg, etc.

Spinach Butter

See Raw Spinach

Spreads, Miscellaneous

See footnote to Butters

Strawberry Butter

See Crushed Strawberry

Tarragon Butter

Chop two tablespoons of fresh tarragon and incorporate in three ounces of butter, creamed.

Tartar Butter

Grind or chop fine one tablespoon each of capers, gherkins, parsley, chives, tarragon and add to six ounces of creamed butter and one ounce of Mayonnaise Base No. 3. Whip all together in a porcelain bowl placed on a bed of ice. A very good aromatic butter.

Tomato Catsup Butter

Partially melt six tablespoons of butter and then whip in two tablespoons of tomato catsup and one teaspoon of lemon juice. Place the butter in a bowl and whip catsup and lemon juice into the soft butter by placing the bowl in chopped ice. As the butter hardens during the continued whipping it

will take up all the liquid and become quite light.
A teaspoon of Paoli tomato paste added to **three**
ounces of soft butter, gives color and flavor.

Violet Butter
Rose Butter

Whip fresh butter to a cream. Pack a layer of
violets, rose or nasturtium petals or clover blossoms
on bottom jar, cover with a perforated paper and
place one-half pound of butter on paper. Place
another perforated wax paper on top of butter and
some more of the petals on top of paper. Leave an
air space all around sides of bottom paper only
taking up as much space as the butter; butter to be
molded back into a square or ball allowing air space
all around. Cover jar tight and set in ice-box for
several hours. Use as a spread on fanciful cuts of
bread, lettuced. Serve with the flowers as a garniture, etc.

This is not one of the author's recipes; however,
it may please some.

Walnut Butter
See Almond

Yellow Butter

Rub three yolks of hard boiled eggs thru a fine
sieve and add four ounces of creamed butter, work-
ing it in thoroly. This butter can be seasoned with
a little lemon juice and piped out of a small rubber
pastry sack containing a very fine tube, or out of a
double paper sack with a fine tube. This mixture
can be made any color. The addition of egg yolks
helps to hold the butter in shape.

Spreads and Fillers

Mixtures or Combinations to Be Used as Sandwich Spreads

Cottage cheese mixed with chopped chives.

* * *

Ripe olives and lettuce chopped and bound with mayonnaise.

* * *

Marmalade and chopped almonds on thin slices of bread spread with cream cheese.

* * *

Ground scraps of goose mixed with chopped pickles and a little catsup. Ground scraps of goose mixed with apple sauce.

* * *

Fish flakes and lettuce finely chopped, seasoned and mixed with mayonnaise.

* * *

Chutney sauce spread on thin slices of white bread, buttered.

* * *

Chicken livers and cooked mushrooms.

* * *

Two parts chicken livers and one part chopped and drained broccoli; season.

* * *

Two parts goose livers and one part spinach; season.

* * *

Two parts chicken livers to one part broiled bacon, chopped fine and season.

* * *

Three parts of chopped broiled lamb kidneys; one part chopped cooked mushrooms; one part chopped broiled bacon.

* * *

Two parts cooked veal, chicken or turkey mixed with one part grated, smoked boiled beef tongue, then add enough mayonnaise to bind. Season and sprinkle mixture with chopped pickles when mixture is spread on bread. (Chicken, veal, etc., to be ground or chopped fine.)

* * *

Chop fine three hard-boiled eggs, one-half cup sweet pickles, one cup of lettuce (heart), and add

enough mayonnaise to bind. Add a very little salt
to egg. Use as a sandwich spread.

* * *

Marinate thin slices of white Bermuda onion and
cucumber in a French dressing for twenty-four
hours. Drain, chop fine, then drain again. Sprinkle
with a little salt, add enough mayonnaise to bind
and use as a spread on buttered rye bread.

* * *

Put thru a fine grinder one hard-boiled egg, one
small sour pickle, six stoned green olives and three
ounces of cooked fish flakes. Season and add enough
mayonnaise to bind. Use in making sandwich rolls
or small, fancy shaped sandwiches.

* * *

Chop fine or grind one cup boiled ham, one-half
cup celery and one-half cup sweet pickles. Drain,
mix together, bind with mayonnaise and use as a
spread on rye bread.

* * *

Chopped hard-boiled eggs, lettuce and dill pickles
mixed and bound together with mayonnaise make
another good spread.

* * *

Two parts finnan haddie or cod, one part ham
and tongue, ham and bacon, fat and lean.

* * *

One part bluefish or mackerel, two parts ham or
tongue.

* * *

Cooked brains, salt, lemon juice, chives and lettuce.

* * *

Chicken livers, mushrooms, salt, egg yolks.

* * *

Minced herring, sour apple, bread soaked in vinegar, chopped chives made into a fine spread.

* * *

Sliced tomato, chopped green pepper and cukes;
cover with grated cheese, placed on toast and
browned.

* * *

Grated smoked boiled tongue, mustard, chopped
egg and finely chopped lettuce, mixed with mayonnaise makes a good spread.

* * *

Thin slices of roast grouse or prairie chicken in
combination with a slice of thin boiled ham makes
an excellent filler.

Thin slices of roast young kid on thin slices of white bread spread with caper butter, makes an excellent combination.

* * *

Chopped figs, cream cheese and chopped green grapes is a good combination.

* * *

Cream cheese, chopped onion tops and a few capers makes an ideal filler.

* * *

Take very thin slices of French rye bread or slices of stale rye bread or French rolls and spread with caviar or sprinkle with cheese; brown and melt.

* * *

Chopped onions and chives mixed with rendered chicken fat (cold), salt to taste. Spread on thin slices of toasted rye rolls.

* * *

Ground turkey hash is a good filler for a toasted sandwich.

* * *

All the above can be chopped or ground fine (as well as many other like combinations).

The meat and fish should be seasoned to taste after mixing. Spread bread with mayonnaise or butter. Serve on plain or toasted bread. Cut in plain or fancy shapes. All should be lettuced. If the meats are too lean add just a little fat from the ham or bacon to flavor. Mackerel, trout and salmon are of a fatty nature and the meats mixed with this type of fish should be lean. If mixtures are too stiff add a little French dressing to thin down, using base No. 5. Garnish these with olives, gherkins, scooped out red beets filled with Tartar sauce or heavily garnished vinagrette sauce, pearl onions, dill pickles, etc. Dress on lettuce leaves or beds of cress.

* * *

The following cheeses may be used alone, or in combination with meats, herbs, etc., as fillers. They may be worked into sandwiches either by slicing or spreading as pastes, or grating and adding cream or liquids for reducing to a spreadable mixture.

American	Imperial
Brick	Parmesan
Camembert	Philadelphia Cream
Cream	Pimento
Cheddar	Port Du Salut
Edam	Romano

English Cheshire   Roquefort
Gorganzola   Swiss
Gruyere   Swiss Gruyere
Holland Edam   Switzerland
Liederkranz   Wisconsin Brick

The following sausages may be used in the same manner:

Cervelet

Large German style Salami

A Few Garnitures Described in Detail

See list of Garnitures on page 242

French Fried Onions or Onion Rings, Fried

Slice thin julienned rings of Bermuda onions, dust in salt and flour, then fry the same as French fried potatoes until crisp and brown. Two French fryers are necessary to do justice to these French fried onions. Place the onions in one basket and fry until nearly done, then place the basket in the second fryer of hotter grease and brown up quickly. French fried onions make an ideal garnishing item and they are well liked by all who eat them.

French Fried Onions can be breaded and then fried.

Fried Parsley (Garnish)

Heat lard in a French fryer until smoking. Immerse sprigs of parsley in basket and fry for a few minutes. Drain on cloth and use as a garnish. Parsley should be very dry after frying; all moisture should be evaporated.

Green Pepper Garnishes

See Green Pepper Sandwich

Lilied Radishes

Buy the small strawberry hot house radish with the beautiful green stems, or leaves, red cheeks, and white base. They should be fresh and hard to the touch. Cut off the root right to base of radish, leave intact the green leaves slightly trimmed if they are green and pretty, and then with a small, pointed, sharp knife turn back the stem in five petals making fine and only skin deep incisions, running knife close to the flesh of radish. Lilied radishes are extremely decorative and can be used with mostly any kind of sandwich.

Octopus Pickle

Cut a thin slice of dill pickle straight thru center from end to end, then with a thin pointed sharp knife start at one-fourth of an inch from stem end and cut slice in about 8 thin strips leaving the slice intact at stem end; then weave the thin strips into a sort of an octopus—excellent as a garnish.

Sweet Pickles (Fanned)

Use a very small pickle and with a very small sharp pointed knife make at least six incisions down the length of pickle, starting about one eighth of an inch from stem end and going right thru to the end. These cuts or slices should be straight and of equal thickness and not severed from head or stem end of pickle. After the cuts have been made spread pickle out in a fan shape, and use as a garnish.

Hors D'Oeuvres: Supremes, Canapes, Relishes

When and where does the hors d'oeuvre turn into an appetizer, an appetizer into a relish, and a canape into a hors d'oeuvre, or vice versa? The French dictionary defines hors d'oeuvre as "an out-work, out-building, or side dish"; Funk and Wagnalls as "a dish that does not form part of a regular course, relish, side-dish"; Ude's Cookery, as "small dishes which are served with the first course"; Gancel's Ready Reference of Menu Terms makes no mention of hors d'oeuvres, but lists relishes, canapes, salpicons, etc. Ranhofer's Epicurean defines hors d'oeuvres as "side dishes" signifying out of the work, having no place on the bill of fare. Quoting further, he says "They are certain appetizing dishes placed on the table before dinner, remaining on, in the Russian service, until the dessert; in the French service they pass around a few hors d'oeuvre after the soup, such as melons, olives, radishes, celery, figs, artichokes, canapes, etc."

Francatelli's Cooks Guide says "On the Continent these are generally denominated 'hors d'oeuvre' and are mostly eaten before dinner or breakfast to stimulate the appetite; hence it is that I have here applied to them the term 'appetizers.' Le Guide du Gourmet a Table les hors d'oeuvres froids peuvent etre servis indifferement avant ou apres le potage; en Angleterre se servent toujours avant la soupe; mais en France se passent souvent apres." (The cold hors d'oeuvres may be served either before or after the soup; in England they always serve it before, but in France often after.)

Having gone thru several hundred other books, and finding the same indefiniteness, I believe it should be decided just what these little shoeing horns should be called, according to the position they occupy on the menu. Hors d'oeuvres may be in the form of a canape, or include various relishes such as mixed olives, celery, stuffed or plain, radishes, caviar, anchovies, mangoes and various other items of like nature, as well as various bonne bouchees inclosing highly flavored forcemeats and mixtures of game, fish, fowl, liver, etc.

1. As I see it, any of the above or all, if served as the first course, as we do here in America, whether they be from a buffet table in a separate room, from a roulette or from a compartment plate or platter, as long as there are a variety of them served at the same time, should be headed "hors d'oeuvres" and should occupy first place on the menu.

2. A canape, when it is served separately as a course, should not be listed as an hors d'oeuvre.

3. Items such as celery, olives, radishes, mangoes, salted nuts, spiced fruits, listed as hors d'oeuvres in No. 1, become relishes when served as an accompaniment of soup. The soup being the main dish of the course, these items being lesser in consequence naturally follow, and when listed on a table d'hote dinner should be placed in small type right under the soup and not above it.

4. Items such as fruit, melon or avocado supremes, tomato, clam, fruit or sauerkraut juices served in well iced supreme stands constitute the first course and I believe should come under the heading of "Supremes" and not "Cocktails." The caption "Cocktail" should be eliminated from menus, as the word in the sense we now use it, is a misnomer.

5. All hot hors d'oeuvres should be listed as such.

6. Shrimp, crab flakes, oysters or clams should be termed appetizers. When served with a sauce, as we now serve them under the caption Cocktail, they should be listed as Shrimp, Clam or Oyster Appetizer, Spiced Sauce.

In my research work on this topic I find that two centuries before the birth of Christ, the Romans as well as the Egyptians dipped their celery, chicorum, lettuce or endive in salt and ate it as an appetizer before their meals. In the first century A. D. Martial, the poet, complained about his people eating these appetizers after their meats, when his forefathers had always started their meals with them. Socrates, who lived at this time, said that these appetizers were unnecessary, "for all that was needed for appetite was hunger and thirst; hunger being the sauce for food and thirst the sauce for drink." However, I believe the old philosopher had liquid refreshments in mind rather than hors d'oeuvres when he issued that warning.

Appetizers, Hors D'Oeuvres, Canapes or Relishes do not appear under these names in any of the cookery books before the Seventeenth Century, at least not in the books in my collection, which date back to 1499 from the present time and number some 2,000 volumes. In "The Art of Cookery," by Mollard in 1800 I find the word "Canapes" and on this topic he says, "Cut some pieces of the crumb of bread about four inches long, three inches wide and one inch thick, fry them in boiling lard until a light brown color; then put them in a drainer, and cut into slips some breast of fowl, anchovies picked from the bone, pickled cucumbers and ham and tongue. Then butter the pieces of bread on one side and lay upon them alternately the different articles until filled. Trim the edges, and put the pieces (cut in what form you please) upon a dish with slices of lemons round the rim, and serve a sauce boat of a little mixture of oil, vinegar, cayenne pepper and salt."

In one of the late Seventeenth Century cookery books I find the word hors d'oeuvres for the first time and on page 248 of the "Manuel des Amphitryons," printed in 1808, the author starts one menu with eight hors d'oeuvres, altho there are twenty-five menus listed, all the others start with potage. The book was composed by the author of "L'Almanach Des Gourmonds" and unquestionably was one of the best books published on cookery, foods and manners of the day. The hors d'oeuvres mentioned in this menu are Du boudin et des saucisses, Des petits pates au natural, Des rognons au vin de champagne, Deux andouilles grilles, Des pieds de cochon farcis aux truffes, Des coquilles au gratin, Des huitres sautees and Une grosse anguille a la tartare. In England in the early Nineteenth Century they were called comers-on, pullers-on, shoeing horns etc., called so on account of their highly saline, bitter or acid flavor. Ranhofer in his "Epicurean" calls them "flying dishes" because they were passed in the anteroom, adjoining the dining room, before the guests sat down to dinner.

In the saloons of yester-year many comers-on, pullers-on, relishes, etc., were to be found on the bars to incite men to drink. Parched corn, one of the first foods cooked by man, found its place on the bar as an appetizer. Pretzels, pickles, kraut, wine herring, salted fish etc., formed a combination hors d'oeuvres that incited thirst. The early Germans, as well as the Egyptians, ate cabbage before and after their banquets to overcome the after-effects of drink; and I am wondering if it were from this practice that sauerkraut was first served in the saloons. The appetizers incited thirst as well as hunger and the sauerkraut offered its sobering effect upon those who drank, not wisely but perhaps too well. In early American times the corner grocer hung a piece of salt fish on the side of the ale barrel, and as a bait or puller-on to incite customers to drink after pulling off slivers of salt fish and eating it.

All countries have their special dishes and for appetizers we look to all countries to supply our needs. Norway sends smoked herring and sardines; Russia, caviar; Germany, sausages and Westphalian hams; France, pate de foie gras and sardines; Italy, antipasto and anchovies; India, capers; Spain, ripe and salted olives; England, bloaters and cured cheeses; America, spiced fruits, celery, mangoes, clams, oysters, lobsters etc.

———————••———————

Supremes

Juices, or Liquid Supremes, are placed first upon the menu

Grape Juice Supreme

Serve the same as Orange Juice, only use a three- instead of a four-ounce glass. See Tomato Supreme for service.

Grapefruit Juice Supreme

Serve the same as orange juice. A little sugar or a simple syrup should be added to the squeezed juice, just enough to mellow the acidity. The Florida grapefruit are of finer texture, better flavor and by far the best of any produced in the United States. See Tomato Supreme for service.

Orange Juice Supreme

Squeeze either Florida or California oranges, strain and serve in four-ounce Delmonico glasses in supreme stand, well iced, as in Tomato Juice. The orange juice is a refreshing, healthful morning ap- petizer and to get the best results should be drank at least one-half hour before breakfast. California orange juice is of a better color than that of the Florida orange, but the Florida fruit contains more juice and perhaps a trifle sweeter. A crate of 216 Florida oranges will yield a gallon more juice than the same amount of California oranges the same size.

AUTHOR'S NOTE: Oranges are named amongst the articles of diet consumed by the Lords of the

Star Chamber in 1509 when the prices are quoted at iijd, and ijd respectively, while the charge for strawberries was iiijd. Perhaps, however, they were used as hors d'oeuvres, for Randall Homes, in his instructions how to arrainge a dinner (in that omminum gatherum academy of armory), mentions oranges and lemons as the first item of the course.

Prune Juice Supreme

Thoroly wash some Oregon prunes and allow to soak in cold water for a few hours. Place on the fire and simmer until tender, using about one-third cup sugar to the pound of prunes. Strain the juice and add a few drops of lemon juice for each glass. Serve the same as tomato juice.

Sauerkraut Juice Supreme

Serve ice-cold and use the same method of serving as in Tomato Juice Supreme. Do not season; buy juice already prepared or strain right out of barrel and drink as is. Three ounces is sufficient for a service.

Tomato Juice Supreme

Strain a number two can of Sweetheart Tomatoes (tall can) and push most of the pulp thru also; season with teaspoon of salt and a dash of tobasco sauce. Pour into four-ounce Delmonico glasses and serve in a supreme stand well iced. Garnish side of glass with a galax leaf. In case you do not have a supreme stand place glass in a bowl and heap shaved ice around it, in a sort of mound.

Tomato juice is a very healthful appetizer. The Sweetheart brand is of fine flavor and color, this is why the brand is mentioned. Tobasco sauce can be omitted if you dislike or do not care for food highly seasoned.

Fruit Supremes

Avocado Supreme—I

Cut a ripe avocado in half and remove the stone. Ball out fruit with a very small parisienne scoop. Place balls in bowl, marinate in lemon juice and place in ice box. Serve the same as Honeydew Supreme, plain or with a sauce made of one-fourth chili sauce, one-half catsup and one-fourth of lemon juice and prepared horseradish combined. Serve the sauce on the side.

Avocadoes which are not ripe are unfit for food. If ripe they will give a little to the touch when gently pressed. The pulp which remains in the shell can be scooped out, pureed and then added to the sauce if desired, reducing the amount of catsup or chili sauce used. The shells can be used, if of good color, in place of supreme stands. A little finely chopped celery can be added to avocado, if desired.

Avocado Supreme—II

Cut two medium sized alligator pears (avocado) in half, remove stone and parisienne them out with a small parisienne scoop. Dice three small hearts of celery, twelve sections of orange, skinned, and twelve sections of grapefruit, skinned. Mix all together carefully. Pour two tablespoons of lemon juice over and mix to keep pear from turning black. Set in ice box and thoroly chill.

This amount will make six supremes. In arranging supremes the parisienned pear should be arranged on top of the supreme glasses attractively. The oranges as well as grapefruit can be omitted if desired, but they are added here on account of the citric acid cutting the high oil content of the pear, helping to neutralize, as well as for their blending quality.

The following sauce should be passed and served on supreme at table: 6 tablespoons chili sauce; 6 tablespoons catsup; 1 tablespoon prepared horseradish; ½ teaspoon salt. Thoroly chill and mix.

NOTE: After the pear is parisienned out, there will be a certain amount of pear pulp left. This can be scraped out with the parisienne cutter and rubbed thru a fine sieve and added to the sauce.

An avacado just cut in half and served in the natural shell with a little lemon juice or French dressing is an epicurean item. Serve on leaf of lettuce.

Banana, Orange and Pineapple Supreme
See, Orange, Banana and Pineapple

Basket Supreme
See Orange Wedding Basket

Breakfast Coupe
Sliced seasonable fresh fruit placed in thin stem glass and top garnished with large pieces of the same fruit, placed attractively. Pour over all a lit-

tle grenadine syrup and serve. Top can be sprinkled with grated fresh cocoanut.

Oranges, grapefruit, cherries, berries, pineapple, etc., lend themselves to this attractive coupe.

Cantaloup Filled with Red Raspberries

Cut a ripe cantaloup in half, remove seeds and chill. Fill center with red ripe raspberries and serve on a cold salad plate underlined with two galax leaves. This is an exceptional item to be used as an appetizer or as a dessert.

Edge of cantaloup can be scalloped all around and a few stewed fresh raspberries placed in center for variety. Stewed raspberries should remain in cantaloup at least 5 hours in ice box to chill and for cantaloup to absorb part of liquid of raspberries. An excellent blend of flavors (if this is done) will be developed.

Cantaloup and Honeydew Supreme

Cut a cantaloup in half, remove seeds; also a honeydew melon and remove seeds. Use a parisienne scoop and ball the melons out, using equal proportions in a supreme glass. Honeydew as well as cantaloup should be ice cold and the former seasoned with lemon juice and the latter with a little salt. Insert a galax leaf on side of supreme glass before placing it in the stand and serve well iced. Both of these items are delicious and are right in season.

Cantaloup Supreme

Use the same method as in Honeydew Supreme and serve the same way, but season slightly with salt instead of lemon juice. Use only ripe and sweet cantaloup and do not cut too close to the skin when cutting out the balls. Serve ice cold. The golden and yellow green small cantaloups which come from California early in the season, as well as the Rockyfords, are the melons to use if you can get them. Do not attempt to make this supreme if your materials are not worthy.

Cantaloup Surprise

Cut cantaloups in half and remove seeds. With a small parisienne scoop round out ten or twelve balls from the top edge and fill the holes with balls of honeydew and watermelon, alternately placed and of uniform size. Arrange in a mound in bottom of cantaloup the balls previously removed and top them with a few red raspberries. If desired raspberries may be used to fill the holes instead of watermelon. Serve ice-cold on galax leaves on a cold, dry plate.

Casaba Melon Supreme

Handle the same as Honeydew Supreme.

Fresh Cherry Supreme

Stone cherries and handle the same as Fresh Raspberry Supreme. Garnish top with whole cherries (seeded) arranged attractively. The top cherries may be stuffed with filberts or a little cream cheese.

Fresh Raspberry Supreme

Arrange attractively in a supreme stand fresh raspberries, black and red. Pour over them a little fresh currant juice or grenadine.

Fresh Strawberry Supreme

Handle the same as Raspberry Supreme. Omit the currant juice. A few ripe Thompson seedless grapes and diced fresh pineapple added to the berries enhances the flavor and attractiveness.

Fruit Nabob

Fill glass one-third full of chopped fresh or canned fruit and then arrange sections of orange alternate with berries around edge of glass. Just before serving turn into center of glass a scoop of raspberry or lemon ice. Garnish top of ice with strawberry and pour over all a little grenadine syrup. An excellent item.

Fruit Supreme

See separate listings as Banana, Cherry, Orange, etc.

Fruit Supreme for St. Patrick's Luncheon

Take two large oranges (100-126); two Florida grapefruit (46-54 size); one pint fresh strawberries; four tablespoons of emeraldettes; one cup of grenadine, galax leaf, and four slices of pineapple.

Section out the oranges and grapefruit, cut all sections in three parts, excepting eight of orange and eight of grapefruit, these to be left to garnish top of supreme.

Cut pineapple the same size as the grapefruit and orange. Slice all but six berries. Mix cut up fruit and place in six supreme glasses, then garnish top of supremes with two sections of orange and two of grapefruit alternately; these to be placed around edge of glass. Next place a whole strawberry right in center of supreme and from center berry run four lines of emeraldettes equal distance apart. This will take sixteen emeraldettes. Place one nice slice of strawberry between each line of emeraldettes, the slice of berry to nestle close to center berry. Over the top of all pour enough grenadine syrup to fill the glass. This supreme should be served in a silver supreme stand, iced. Garnish side of glass with a galax leaf. In case you do not have the supreme stands, serve in a tall stem glass. Underline with a galax leaf.

Grapefruit, Orange and Raisin Supreme
See Orange, Grapefruit, etc.

Grapefruit Surprise

Cut in half a Florida grapefruit (Checker brand if obtainable) and detach the sections with a sharp grapefruit knife. Remove three sections in a row and replace the first one with a section of orange, the next with three or four red, ripe berries cut in half and placed in section red side up overlapping one another; in the next section place a piece of pineapple cut like a section of an orange. Allow the fourth section of grapefruit to remain and continue around the grapefruit in the same manner until all the sections have been alternately filled with the various fruits. There are generally eleven sections in a grapefruit, so there would be about three of each different kind of fruit. The removed sections of grapefruit should be diced and placed in a mound in the center of grapefruit where core has been removed. Top this center with two or three red, ripe berries cut in half and placed around mound of grapefruit. Place the berries so that they hide the mound of grapefruit and form a sort of a pyramid. Just before serving sprinkle with powdered sugar and serve ice-cold on a galax leaf underlined with a doily on a cold plate.

Honey Ball Supreme
Handle the same as Honeydew Supreme.

Honeydew Melon Supreme

With a medium sized parisienne vegetable scoop ball out an ice cold, ripe honeydew melon. Place the balls in a bowl and squeeze over them the juice of one lemon. Pile the balls in a supreme glass in a sort of pyramid shape and serve in a supreme stand well iced. Garnish with a galax leaf. They may be served in a stem glass on paper doily and garnished with a galax leaf.

Use nothing but the melon and lemon; anything else is superfluous and will detract rather than enhance. The Honeydew Supreme is a real aristocrat of the dinner table.

Honeydew Melon Surprise

Use the same method as in Cantaloup Surprise, only use about one-fourth or one-fifth of the melon, according to size, in place of a half. The same kind of fruit may be used to plug up holes and a fancy design can be worked out by cutting holes to represent a symmetrical figure and then using the various melons and fruit alternately or a cluster of colors. Do not pile any balls in center, as this method spoils the picture. Serve as in Cantaloup Surprise, only squeeze a little lemon juice over the fruit and serve a section of lemon on the side. Finger bowls should accompany these particular dishes. If the fruit is handled right you will have a real picture.

Mango Supreme

Dice or slice mangoes and place in supreme stand. Garnish the top attractively with raspberries. Pour over a little raspberry juice and serve.

Mangoes and honeydew melons served with lemon juice make a fine combination.

AUTHOR'S NOTE: Mangoes are extremely rare and hard to get. The author tries many times to get them during the season, which is in early July to late September, and is successful only four or five times a season. He has paid as much as $1.50 apiece for them. The Chinese buy them up as fast as they come in and will generally pay most any price to get them. They are of excellent flavor and make one of the finest salads that he knows of.

The mangoes are esteemed as one of the most delicious of tropical fruits. Like the apple of the temperate zones it varies greatly in shape, size, color and flavor; sometimes large and luscious, sometimes small, tough, stringy and tasting like turpentine.

Melon Supreme

See Casaba, Honeydew, etc.

Melon Surprise

Cut a cantaloup in half and remove the seeds and fill it with ice cold raspberries. Serve on cold plate underlined with a galax leaf.

Mixed Melon Supreme

Arrange attractively in a supreme stand watermelon, honeydew and cantaloup. Serve as in Honeydew Supreme. Sprinkle a little salt and lemon juice over cantaloup and honeydew. Omit lemon on the side.

Orange, Banana and Pineapple Supreme

Dice orange sections, pineapple and bananas. Arrange equal amounts of each in supreme glasses in an attractive manner. Top with emeraldettes and rubyettes. Pour over all a grenadine syrup.

Orange, Grapefruit and Raisin Supreme

Section out one orange, one grapefruit and dice. Steam one-half cup of seedless raisins for about three minutes and chill; mix orange sections, grapefruit and raisins together and then arrange attractively in supreme glasses. Pour over all a little grenadine and serve.

Pineapple added to the supreme and the top garnished with halved ripe strawberries and centered with a whole berry makes a pretty picture. (See introduction on Supremes for Service.)

Orange Wedding Basket

Take a 100-size orange and cut from top to center on both sides of the stem end, allowing one-fourth inch in center of the two slits for basket handle. Cut away outer quarters of orange at center to form rim of basket, leaving handle intact. Hollow out orange with a sharp knife to form the basket. Fill basket with diced sections of orange, diced pineapple and half strawberries. Garnish top with one or two red, ripe strawberries and pour a little grenadine over the top. Tie a bow of white baby ribbon on the handle. Serve on a galax leaf. This is a very appropriate appetizer for a wedding breakfast, luncheon or dinner. The rim of basket should be notched all around.

Pineapple, Orange, Banana Supreme
See Orange, Banana, etc.

Pineapple Surprise

Use the same method as in Honeydew Surprise, cutting a small, ripe pineapple in four pieces and without removing the green leaves. (Select a fine specimen with real green leaves if you serve this item. In case some of the leaves are discolored or seared, remove them.) Serve the same as Honeydew Supreme, omitting the lemon. This makes a lively picture.

Raisin, Orange and Grapefruit Supreme
See Orange, Grapefruit, etc.

Raspberry Supreme
See Fresh Raspberry

St. Patrick Supreme
See Fruit Supreme St. Patrick

Strawberry Supreme
See Fresh Strawberry

Supreme Surprise

Take two half Melba peaches and make three deep V-shaped notches in each half peach. Place the two half peaches at the bottom of a Melba glass so that the two halves 'form half a ball. Fill the center of ball with cubed oranges, grapefruit, pineapple and a few whole rubyettes. Use four sections of orange and four pieces of pineapple cut like sections of orange and fit these into the notches of Melba peach, rounding out a perfect ball. Cut six or seven strawberries in very thin slices and wedge in between the orange and pineapple alternately to bring out color effect. Place a red ripe strawberry on top of the top and pour a little grenadine over all. Serve in a supreme stand and garnish with a galax leaf, and of course have stand well iced. This appetizer is very effective, very delicious, something new, in fact it is a sort of stuffed appetizer and should be called a Supreme Surprise. After the supreme is finished, it should represent a perfect ball. Do not fill the peach too full or you will be unable to round it out perfectly.

Sections of orange and grapefruit can be formed into a ball the same way and of course filled or stuffed. A ball of frozen sherbet can be used for center; however, if ice is used they must be prepared after guests sit down, unless you have the electric refrigeration.

In cutting the peach place the half peach flat side down on board and notch it in a V-shape deeply, making at least three notches in each half.

Wedding Basket
See Orange Wedding Basket

Fish Supremes

Cotuits on Half Shell
(*Or any large oyster*)

These oysters are large and are generally served on iced silver platter on flat shell with lemon in the center, as Oysters plain. Condiments such as mentioned in Oysters on Half-Shell should accompany this service with the usual wafers.

Crab Supreme
See Oyster Crab

Crabmeat Supreme

Arrange and serve as Lobster Supreme.

Deep Sea Food Appetizer

On soup plate filled with crushed ice and centered with glass of spiced sauce as in Avacado or Shrimp Supreme, place six shells, one filled with lobster, one with shrimp, one with oyster, one with clam, one with crabmeat and one with cooked fish flakes. Oyster shells are preferable for this service. The different sea foods should be attractively arranged. Serve with lemon and wafers. Any combination may be used or two of each, making three kinds of sea food.

Fish Flakes Supreme

Handle the same as Crab Meat Flakes and serve as shrimp or avocado supreme with sauce.

Little Neck Clams on Half Shell

Serve as Oysters on Half Shell, plain or with sauce as called for. Cherry stone clams are served the same way.

Lobster Supreme

Cut boiled lobster in cubes and place attractively in supreme glasses either plain or mixed with finely chopped hearts of celery. On the side serve sauce such as used for oysters or shrimp. Supreme stand may be garnished with galax leaf and section of lemon. The flesh of the claws may also be arranged attractively on top of lobster to enhance the appearance of the dish.

Olympia Oysters

Olympia oysters are very small Pacific Ocean oysters, are very sweet and make an exceptionally fine supreme. Handle as Oysters Supreme with sauce on the side. (See Avocado or Shrimp Supreme.)

Oyster Crab Supreme

Handle the same as Oysters Supreme. (See Avocado and Shrimp Supreme.)

Oysters on Half-Shell
(Plain or with spiced sauce)

In a soup plate filled with crushed ice, centered with a glass filled with sauce (see Avocado or Shrimp Supreme), place six oysters on half-shell, freshly opened. Additional condiments such as horseradish, tobasco sauce, as well as lemon and wafers should form the accompaniment of this dish. The center glass of sauce may be omitted and a quartered lemon placed in center underlined with an inner leaf of lettuce.

Oysters Supreme

Use the small oyster, as it is the sweetest and best flavored, or just the tenderloin or soft part of the larger oyster. Fill supreme glasses and serve as in Shrimp or Avocado Supreme. Serve sauce on the side. An inner leaf of lettuce placed in the supreme glass first, then the oysters adds to the attractiveness. A few chopped green peppers added to sauce helps the appearance.

Scallops (cooked) Supreme

Steam scallops and cool. Cut in thin slices and serve as in Oyster Supreme. Serve with sauce on the side. (See Shrimp or Avocado for sauce.)

Sea Food Appetizer
See Deep Sea Food

Shrimp Supreme I

In center of a soup plate filled with crushed ice place a sauce glass. Fill glass with sauce such as is used in Shrimp Supreme or a Thousand Island dressing. Surround glass with fine inner leaves of lettuce and on top of lettuce arrange in an attractive, pleasing manner boiled, peeled and cleaned shrimp. This method of serving shrimp is always favorably commented on.

Peel fresh shrimp first and then cook in salted water about fifteen minutes. Peel off the back flap of shrimp and remove the black alimentary tract, wash and chill.

Shrimp Supreme II

Cook shrimp, then remove shell and black alimentary tract. Cut in half lengthwise or across. When cold arrange in a supreme glass in a pleasing manner. Sprinkle with a little finely chopped hearts of celery. On side serve a sauce like that used for Avocado or Oyster Supreme. Serve in supreme stand and garnish with a galax leaf.

------------◆◆------------

Vegetable Supremes

Cooked Vegetable Supreme

Use only the finest and freshest of vegetables to make this supreme. The supreme glass may be lined with thick green heads of asparagus so placed that the heads just pop above the edge of glass. A few chopped artichoke tubers and celery hearts should be placed on the bottom, stringless beans on top of celery and a rosette of white cauliflower in center surrounded by diced connective tissue of red ripe tomato. Serve with a Vinaigrette or Oyster Supreme sauce on the side.

The vegetables must be attractively arranged or ninety per cent of the value is lost.

Raw Vegetable Supreme

Grind or chop up finely, one-fourth cup of each of the following ingredients: cress, celery, peppers, cabbage and pineapple (raw), and add two tablespoons of orange, one of lemon juice, one-half teaspoon of salt. Mix all together and place in supreme glasses; cover with a spiced sauce.

Raw green peas added to mixture in place of celery or artichokes gives a different relish to supreme. The raw green peas can be used to decorate top of supreme and a small pom pom of cress stuck in center of glass in an upright position adds to the appearance. Do not place cress until last minute, for if you do the cress will wilt. This supreme was first served on the first of May, 1928, and was very favorably received. Try it and be convinced. The number of ingredients can be reduced, but the raw pineapple or raw pear should stay, as these items bring out a unique flavor.

Spiced sauce—one-half cup catsup, one-fourth cup chili sauce, one tablespoon of prepared horseradish, a dash of tobasco and one-third teaspoon of salt. Mix all together and either pour sauce over top or serve on side as desired. Ir served on side, top of supreme must be garnished, for the cut up vegetables do not present an appetizing appearance.

Raw sauerkraut and canned tomato juice make good substitutes for a raw vegetable and the orange juice.

Canapes

Ab Ova Canape
See Canape Ab Ova

Anchovy Canape—I
Toast, anchovy paste, butter, lemon juice, pearl onions

Spread toast, cut in various shapes, with one part anchovy paste mixed with two parts creamed butter, and add just enough lemon juice to flavor. Around edge make an extremely fine border of the finest and smallest pearl onions. These pearl onions run about forty to the teaspoon and are imported from Holland. Place a curled anchovy in center and pipe a little rosette of red butter in center of anchovy.

Toast—spread with lemon butter, then covered with thin anchovy fillets, decorated with various colored butters and trimmed to desired shapes makes a real treat.

Anchovy Canape—II
See Sardine Canape

Anchovy-Sardellen Canape
Bread, anchovy, lobster butter

On toasted white bread, cut in 2½-inch squares or in oblongs 2½x1 inch, arrange fillets of anchovies artistically and decorate with rosettes of red and green lobster butter. Sardellen can also be served the same way and garnished with lettuce, slices of lemon and parsley. Anchovies can be boned and mashed and mixed with sweet butter in the ratio of three or four parts of butter to one of anchovy. Squeeze a little lemon juice into mixture and spread on toasted wafers or long thin strips of toasted bread. Round out anchovy mixture and press with a fork to make a nice appearance, then garnish top alternately with red and green peppers cut diamond shape.

Anchovy and Sardine Canape
Anchovies, sardines, butter, lemon juice, olives, toast

Anchovies and sardines (equal parts) can be boned, skinned and rubbed through a fine sieve, then mixed with sweet butter and lemon juice, using one-third butter to two-thirds fish, and afterwards spread on thin, toasted, fanciful cuts of white bread. Garnish with thin slices of stoned ripe or green olives, and rosette of aromatic, or coral butter. Serve on leaves of lettuce.

Antipasto Canape
Antipasto, tomato, butter, toast

Arrange various items contained in a can of antipasto on slices of tomato (peeled) or on thin slices of
fanciful cuts of buttered toast. Decorate top of antipasto with various colored rosettes of butter. Serve
on leaves of lettuce. Antipasto can be drained and
chopped finely and then spread on toast. The juice
added to a mayonnaise can be used as a spread for a
thin rolled sandwich.

Antipasto is an assortment of vegetables and fish
packed in cans and imported from Italy.

Antipasto can be served in an hors d'oeuvre compartment dish as is, in conjunction with various
other appetizers. A Russian or Thousand Island
dressing can be served on the side when Antipasto
is served as a canape.

Artichoke Bottom Appetizer
Artichoke bottoms, caviar, butter, lemon, lettuce

Use either canned or fresh artichokes. If you use
the canned artichokes, take the artichokes out of the
can and wash them in salted water. Then dry them
carefully and pipe a red or green butter around the
edge. Fill the center with caviar and serve on leaf
of lettuce with an assortment of hors d'oeuvres. Garnish with lemon. (See artichoke canape, fresh.)

Artichoke Canape
Artichoke, French dressing, caviar, lemon, lettuce,
butter, onion juice

Wash, tie and steam artichokes until done. Remove leaves and center nest of fine leaves or choke,
and trim bottom in an attractive shape, cutting off all
edges and making outline smooth; or use a canned
artichoke fond or bottom. Marinate artichoke bottoms while they are a little warm in French dressing,
as they will absorb more of the flavor while they are
warm. Allow to remain in dressing thirty minutes.
Drain and wipe dry. Have the bottoms perfectly
cold and dry. Mix Beluga or the Astrakan caviar
with a little fresh butter, squeeze in a little lemon
juice to flavor and spread or fill artichoke bottoms
with caviar. Set one fond in a nest of lettuce and
garnish upper edge of artichoke and center with
rosettes of red butter to which has been added a few
drops of onion juice.

After artichokes are cooked and cooled the leaves
can be spread apart and the choke removed, then the
bottom or fond can be filled with cooked shrimp,

nicely arranged and the top of shrimp covered with a little caviar. Serve Thousand Island dressing on side and place each artichoke in a bed of lettuce. Use the small artichokes and remove the extreme outside leaves.

Artichoke Suedoise
See Lettuce Suedoise

Asparagus Canape
Tomato, asparagus tips, peppers, aspic, lettuce

On half slice of peeled, ripe tomato place two or three short cut asparagus tips. Garnish with strips of red and green peppers and mask with gelatine or aspic. Serve on bed of lettuce. This item along with a little caviar and sardellen or anchovy canape can be served on an individual plate, garnished with lettuce and served as an assorted hors d'oeuvre.

These small canapes can be placed on a raised wire mesh, and a diluted, partially chilled, gelatine poured over to bring out the effect, or, in other words, enhance the appearance. The canapes should be placed immediately in ice box to chill gelatine, so that gloss will be perfect. Do not make gelatine or aspic too stiff.

Avocado Canape
Lettuce, tomato, avocado, mayonnaise, anchovies

On leaf of lettuce place a thick slice of peeled ripe tomato. Garnish top of tomato with parisienne balls of alligator pear (avocado) and mask with a mayonnaise to which has been added some finely chopped anchovies, or mask with a spiced sauce made of chili sauce, catsup, equal amounts, and enough grated horseradish to season highly.

Use a small scoop to make balls with and pile them up on tomato in a pleasing manner. The pulp that is left in the shells of pear after using parisienne scoop can be taken out with a spoon and mixed with cream cheese; this mixture can then be piped around the edge of tomato to hold the balls in place.

Beelzebub Canape
Toast, butter, beets, red cabbage, mayonnaise, pimentoes

On a crescent of buttered toast, spread a mixture of equal amounts of ground pickled red cabbage and red beets. Cabbage and beets should be drained quite dry and then mixed with a highly seasoned mayonnaise. Dip ends of crescent in a mayonnaise and dredge with paprika. Decorate center top with a devil cut out of pimentoes in fine strips. Serve on leaves of lettuce.

Red apple salad can be used in place of beets and cabbage.

RED APPLE SALAD: Make same as Waldorf, using the red apples without peeling. Jonathan apples are excellent for this item. (Apples should be chopped extremely fine.) A few finely chopped red radishes (skins) can be used to add zest and color to canape.

Bloater Canape
See Smoked Cisco

Bon Bouchee
See Lobster Bon Bouchee

Bonne Femme
See Caviar Canape

Canape Ab Ova
Toast, egg, caviar, butter, anchovy

Fill with caviar the half of a hard boiled egg from which the yolk has been removed. Set egg on a slice of toast cut with oval biscuit cutter and set egg in hole. Decorate the edges of toast and the edge of egg with green or red butter. Garnish center with a small curled anchovy.

Hard boiled egg to be cut lengthwise. Egg should set snugly in hole of toast and not protrude beyond the lower part of toast.

Canape Quarte Coins
Toast, tartar sauce, smoked fish, caviar, hard-boiled egg

On an oblong piece of toast, three inches long and one and one-half inches wide, spread tartar sauce, heavily garnished. Place one thin strip of smoked salmon and one thin strip of smoked sturgeon, criss-crossed to the four corners. Fill one section with red caviar, mixed with a little sweet butter, a drop of onion juice and one of lemon. On the opposite section place grey caviar, mixed the same way. Fill the two opposite sections, with whites and yellows of eggs, chopped separately, and serve on a leaf of lettuce. Any mixture can be used on this particular canape, such as sardines, anchovy, fillets, green peppers, antipasto, Major Grey's chutney, ham, bacon, etc.

Canape Tartar

Toast, tartar sauce, green butter, peppers, lettuce

Make a heavy tartar sauce, that is, put a great deal of garnish in the mayonnaise when making sauce. Be sure that the ingredients are well drained and chopped fine. Spread thin slices of toast, cut square, with tartar sauce. Make a border of green butter. In the center of canape make a flower of green and red pepper. Serve on leaves of lettuce. A little chopped lettuce can be added to tartar sauce.

AUTHOR'S NOTE: Lettuce is in constant requisition for salads, canapes, sandwiches, cold meat platters, relishes, hors d'oeuvres, etc. There is no herb or vegetable that I know of that could take its place. Chicory, cabbage, endive, fetticus, cress, spinach, dandelions, etc., have their places and uses, but to enhance the appearance of a dish they are completely outdistanced by lettuce. Even the above named items must call on Miss Cos, Miss Boston or Miss Iceberg to enhance their own beauty when served.

Caviar on Butter Wafers

On small round toasted butter crackers pipe a border of green butter and fill the center with black or red caviar, or a sardine mixture and garnish the center with fancy dots of butter. Serve on doilies with rosettes of cress. Long wafers can be used with two or three mixtures and separated with the butter colors or with strips of red and green peppers, truffles, black olives, mangoes or capers, in dotted lines.

Caviar Canape

Toast, egg, anchovy, caviar, green butter

Make a round of toast the size of a round slice of white of egg, or nearly so. Spread toast with anchovy butter. Place the round white on toast and fill center with caviar. Dot center of caviar with rosette of green butter.

Caviar Canape, Bonne Femme

Toast, caviar, colored butter, pearl onions, crawfish, lettuce, lemon

On a piece of toast, cut with a small doughnut cutter, spread fine, grey caviar mixed with a little sweet butter, onion and lemon juice. Pipe the inner edge of toast with a green butter. On the outer edge proper pipe a border of red butter and garnish top with fine pearl onions. In the center place a small trussed crawfish or a crawfish head piped with green eyes, as a garniture. Serve on leaf of lettuce or doily, with slice of lemon. The crawfish head should be small enough to just fit in center hole without spoiling garniture of canape butter.

Caviar Canape Trimalchio

Carve out a square 15-pound block of ice by searing it all around with an ice pick or shaver. Cut a hole in top center large enough to receive a can of Beluga or Astrakan caviar, grayish or gold egg, large type. Cut four smaller holes on all sides of can large enough to admit a small cut glass bowl or fancy sauce dish. These holes can be made by placing a small tin can filled with boiling water on the particular spot you intend to place bowls in and sponging out water as it accumulates. In these sauce dishes place finely minced onions, white and yolks of eggs chopped separately and fanciful cut lemons, garnish with sprigs of cress around center can. These holes should be at equal distances apart and center can should be raised up above the other four dishes. Cut a square hole in bottom of ice piece and place a small battery to illuminate.

The ice masterpiece should be placed on a silver tray and underlined with a napkin. Thin slices of toasted French rye, very small, and very thin pancakes or toasted fanciful cuts plain white bread, to form an accompaniment with caviar. The toast can be kept warm in a chafing dish and guests can either serve themselves or an atttendant can perform service for them.

The ice piece can be made out of colored water if you have your own refrigeration. A pinkish or greenish piece of ice makes a very effective showing such as Trimalchio would undoubtedly serve.

Caviar Combination
Sardellen, butter, toast, caviar, pimento, green peppers

Rub ten or twelve sardellens or anchovies thru a fine sieve, mix with enough sweet butter to spread and add a few drops of lemon juice to flavor. Cut finger strips' of toast and spread both ends of toast with the mixture, using up two-thirds of toast. In the center third spread Beluga black and golden caviar in equal proportions longitudinally on toast. Separate the red and black longitudinally with a strip of pimento and the red and black horizontally from the brown ends with two strips of green peppers. In the center of each section dot with various colored butters. The dividing lines of pepper will form an H in center of canape. Serve on lettuce leaves.

Caviar and anchovies, caviar and sardines, caviar and lobster, caviar and crab, or any such combinations can be made and handled as above. The same combination can be worked out on top of a tomato or artichoke bottom, using the center and sides of tomato to carry out the same arrangement.

Caviar and Pearl Onions
Bread, butter, caviar, onions

Cut circular pieces of bread and brown in oil or on broiler, on one side. Spread white side of bread with sweet butter and then with grey caviar. In the center place a little mound of red caviar and in center of caviar pipe a rosette of green butter and on outer edge of grey caviar make a dotted line of the finest pearl onions. It will take about 40 onions to make border, as these onions are only as large as the very finest sifted pea. Serve on leaves of lettuce and garnish with lemon.

Caviar Salad Canape
Tomato, caviar, pearl onions, green butter, beets,
anchovy

Take a slice of ripe, peeled tomato and remove center with a half-inch column cutter, spread tomato all the way around with grey or black caviar. Pipe outer edge of tomato with green butter and stud with small pearl onions to make a border. Cut julienned strips of very red beets which have been baked and pickled. Run these strips of beets from edge of center hole of tomato to outer edge like spokes of a wheel. Decorate the center hole with a curled anchovy to form the hub, and pipe a border of green butter around base of anchovy. Serve on lettuce or doily.

Anchovy can be curled around a piece of red pimento, giving hub a better appearance. Anchovy should fit in hole of tomato very snug.

Caviar Unique
Egg, caviar, colored butters, lettuce, cress, lemon

Cut a hard boiled egg in half lengthwise and remove yolk. Fill center of egg with caviar. Decorate the border of egg with green and red butter and make a handle out of a lobster feeler, inserting the ends of fine lobster feelers into caviar to form handle. Serve on bed of lettuce with a slice of lemon and garnish with cress.

Celery
See Stuffed Celery

Cherry Tomato Stuffing

Mix together thoroly one teaspoon salt, one teaspoon sugar, one-third teaspoon paprika and three tablespoons of tomato catsup. Then whip in eight ounces of olive oil gradually just like you would in making mayonnaise, until all is incorporated and sauce is of the consistency of mayonnaise. Have ready three sheets of French gelatine dissolved in four tablespoons of boiling aromatic vinegar. Pour boiling vinegar over broken pieces of gelatine and stir until dissolved. Whip gelatine and vinegar into the sauce. Set the bowl of sauce in crushed ice and whip until it is real stiff, then stuff tomatoes.

A dozen chopped anchovies, one-third cup of grated Roquefort cheese, or one-third cup of whipped cream and one-half cup of ground blanched almonds can be added to dressing for variety. A little chopped cress and sweet savory added to thickened dressing gives it an added zest. In stuffing cherry tomatoes cut the tomato partially in two at stem end and remove seeds with a small, sharp Parisienne scoop; then stuff tomato, using an A.D. spoon. Press tomato together and serve with an assortment of hors d'oeuvres.

Cherry tomatoes (red or yellow) served plain with green stems make a real garnish, or one item to be included in an assortment of hors d'oeuvres. Radishes: The small hot house radish with leaves on and lilied adds to the appearance of these assortments.

Chicken and Ham Savory
See Ham and Chicken

Cigarettes a la Russe
Bread, caviar, chaud-froid sauce, lettuce

Spread very thin slices of new bread (Pullman) with caviar and roll into cigarettes. Trim ends and cover or mask with a white chaud-froid sauce, excepting one end which is masked with a pink chaud-froid sauce. Sprinkle pink end with paprika and serve three or four of these dainty appetizers on leaves of lettuce. See Sandwich Rolls.—*Courtesy of E. E. Amiet, Chef, Palmer House, Chicago.*

Clams Hacheé
Clams, cheese, seasoning, toast

Mince one dozen steamed clams and arrange on thin slices of toast, cut round. Sprinkle with grated herkimer cheese, paprika, butter and brown. Serve at once.

Clams (Hot)

Handle same as oysters Rockefeller, only leave out the spinach. Strip with a thin piece of bacon and brown.

Codfish-Finnan Haddie
See Finnan Haddie

Crab Meat Canape
Crab meat, tomato, lettuce, mayonnaise

Arrange flaked crab meat on a slice of peeled tomato; place tomato on leaves of lettuce and serve on cold plate. Mask with mayonnaise or Russian dressing and dot with various colored butters. Crab meat should be mounded up on the tomato in pyramid shape. Cherry tomatoes can be stuffed with crab meat salad.

Crab and lobster salad can be mixed in equal proportions and arranged on toast, then decorated with dots of fancy butters. Crab meat Newburg served in small pastry shells or on toast makes an ideal hot hors d'oeuvre.

Crabmeat and Tomato
See Tomato and Crabmeat

Cucumber Marinate
*Cucumbers, French dressing, Garlic, Bermuda
onions or chives*

Peel and score cucumbers with a fork from top to bottom. Slice very thin. Place them in a good French dressing base No. 5. Bowl should be rubbed with garlic. Allow to stand in ice-box for at least four hours. Finely shredded Bermuda onions may be added in the ratio of six of cucumbers to one of onions, or a few chopped chives may be sprinkled over the top.

Cucumber Suedoise
See Lettuce Suedoise

Eastern Star Canape
Eggs, toast, caviar, gherkins, capers, chervil, butter,
mayonnaise, lettuce

With a five-pointed star cutter cut a piece of
bread (white) one-fourth inch thick and either
brown it quickly in a pan with a little olive oil or
place it between a fine wire broiler and brown
quickly. It may be toasted first and then cut in star
shape. Mix finely chopped yolks and whites of
eggs, chopped separately, with just enough creamy
white mayonnaise and a little lemon juice to bind.
Use knife and mound two points, one with the
whites and one with the yolks of eggs. Mix black
caviar with lemon juice and fresh butter for the
third point; red caviar, butter and lemon juice for
the fourth point and for the last point finely chopped
gherkins, capers and chervil mixed with a little
green butter. In the center pipe a rosette made of
yellow butter and dot the center of yellow butter
with a dot of green butter. Serve on lettuce.

In place of caviar chopped red beets mixed with
mayonnaise or chopped ripe olives, or pickled walnuts mixed with a little butter may be substituted.

Eggs, Stuffed
See Stuffed Eggs—I and II

Favorite Canape
Boston lettuce, tomato, alligator pear, caviar, yellow
butter, green peppers

On a base of Boston lettuce, place a slice of peeled
tomato, and on the tomato place a slice of alligator
pear; in the center place a small mound of caviar
and pipe a border of yellow butter around the edge.
Place six diamond cut green peppers equal distance
apart and pipe a little strip of butter from caviar to
border. This gives sort of a wheel effect. It is an
unusually fine looking appetizer. Very tasty and
easy to make.

Finnan Haddie-Codfish
Haddock, tomato, mayonnaise, capers, onions, lettuce,
Russian dressing

Boil haddie or cod in a herb stock with a little
lemon juice. Flake and place in a mortar, pound
to a paste, season and add enough mayonnaise to
moisten and press into shapes. Cover a slice of
peeled tomato with a thin mixture and work into
shape with a fork, making criss-crosses with the
prongs of fork. Garnish edge of tomato with capers

and pearl onions alternately. Serve on lettuce. Make a little flower out of strips of gherkin and place in center. A Russian dressing should be served on side and passed at table. This mixture can be served on fancy cuts of toast also.

The mayonnaise can be omitted and the mixture thinned with raw cream, newberg, or a papillotte sauce, then sprinkled with butter and grated cheese and browned in oven on shells or on toast.

Fresh Mushroom Hors d'Oeuvres
Mushroom, butter, forcemeat, peppers

Peel a large fresh mushroom and trim it well. Wash in salted cold water and dry. Cook slowly in butter, allow to cool and then pipe a border of red, green or yellow butter around the edge and fill the center with a forcemeat made out of chicken liver and anchovies. Decorate top with red and green peppers.

CHICKEN LIVER FORCEMEAT, either plain or with sardines: Cook the livers slowly either with butter or with a little stock until done. Allow them to cool, then grate them. Mix equal amounts of sardines mashed to a paste with the chicken livers, add a very little butter and season. Then place this forcemeat in the mushroom and decorate the top with colored butter, and strip with green peppers and pimentoes.

Gens Grieben
Goose fat, salt
(An excellent Jewish appetizer)

Cut the fine white fat from the breast of a fat goose about two inches square; roll into a roll and skewer together with a toothpick. Lay the fat in an iron skillet and sprinkle with salt. Place on fire and put about a cup of water in with grieben, cover and cook slowly until all water is evaporated and brown up cracklings. A little inside fat can be added to cracklings to help brown. When cracklings are brown and crisp remove and place on a small baking pan, then place in oven for a few minutes to dry off surplus grease. Salt again and serve as an appetizer.

Roast breast of goose for sandwiches: Allow the neck skin to remain intact with the breast of goose and either sew or skewer it on to protect breast while roasting. Roast slowly in oven with a little onion or garlic and a few sprigs of celery. Excellent for sandwiches, or marinate and use as a hors d'oeuvre.

Goose Liver Unique

*Goose livers, filbert, cream sauce, toast, gelatin,
lettuce*

Take one or two goose livers and cook slowly
under cover in butter until thoroly done. When
cold rub through a fine sieve, season with salt and
pepper and roll into a small ball or apple shape,
with a filbert in the center. Place on a small round
of toast and mask with a cream sauce to which has
been added a little French gelatine. To one cup of
cream sauce add one leaf of French gelatine, dissolved in a tablespoon of boiling water.

The cream sauce is to be poured over canape
cold, the gelatine is added to cream sauce to hold
sauce in shape.

This hors d'oeuvre is called "Pomme d'Amour."
The sides of this apple can be colored with a little
red coloring matter and shaped into a small apple.
A mint stalk with leaf can be stuck into base of apple
for effect. The coloring matter should be done
artistically and with a little fine cloth.

Grecian Hors d'Oeuvres

1 pint of water, ¼ pint oil, 1 teaspoon salt, 1 tablespoon lemon juice, ½ teaspoon coriander seed, 6 or
8 small whole hearts of celery, 1 green pepper, 6 or
8 fresh mushrooms, 2 dozen spinach roots.

Rub a small stewpan with garlic and pour the oil
and water in, add the lemon juice, salt and coriander seed; peel, clean and wash mushrooms. Clean
the spinach roots, skin the green pepper, take the
seeds out, clean up celery. Wrap the 8 stalks of
celery in a fine linen rag very carefully and place
in the olive oil and water. Add the mushrooms,
spinach and green peppers, peppers to be cut into
julienne strips. Simmer for three-quarters of an
hour, or until celery is done. Remove from fire
and allow to chill. Then serve in the liquid. The
majority of water will be evaporated in three-
quarters to one hour's time. The pot should be
small, and should be covered with a cloth during the
process of simmering. The liquid can be used again
for boiling this or similar vegetables by adding
enough oil and water to make up for the loss of
evaporation as well as for the oil that adheres to
the side of vegetables. The Greeks generally eat
all the oil as the sauce.

Grilled Sardines
See Sardines Grilled

Ham and Chicken Savory

Ham, chicken, mayonnaise, aspic, lettuce, toast, chives

Cut boiled ham in rounds at least one-eighth inch thick and two inches in circumference. On top of ham spread a chicken paste, made from white meat of chicken pounded in a mortar, seasoned and mixed with a creamy mayonnaise to which has been added a few finely chopped chives. On top of chicken arrange a slice of tomato aspic. Paint sides with tomato aspic and serve on leaves of lettuce.

Hearts of Palm

Hearts of palm, crab meat, Russian dressing, lettuce

Arrange crab meat flakes on a slice of heart of palm and mask with Russian dressing. Serve on cold plate underlined with leaves of lettuce. Garnish with slice of lemon. Caviar, lobster or shrimp can be substituted for the crab meat flakes. Use a little gelatine in mayonnaise to stiffen it, then garnish mayonnaise with various colored butters.

Hearts of palm sliced and marinated in French dressing and striped with fillets of anchovies and pimentoes is used as an item for a hors d'oeuvre roulette or platter.

Herring Canape—I

Herring, toast, butter, olive

On pieces of freshly made toast, about 3½ by 2 inches spread with a ravigote butter, place several small, thin fillets of boned and skinned herring. Pipe a fine edge of green or ravigote butter around the outer edges. Place a very thin slice of fluted green olive in center of herring and fill center of olive with a starred pimento or black caviar.

Herring Canape—II

See Smoked Herring

Herring Canape III

See Wine Herring

Hors D'Oeuvres a La Russe

(To be served on a platter or roulette)

Hard boiled eggs cut in half and stuffed with fresh caviar, then decorated with fancy colored butters. Canapes foie gras (slices of goose livers on fanciful cuts of toast). Ripe olives (colossal) stoned and stuffed with tuna fish, tuna to be mixed with mayonnaise. Cornucopias of Westphalian ham (thin slices of ham rolled into cornucopias) and a sprig of cress or parsley to be inserted into the horn. Fillets of anchovies in oil and capers, and crab meat mounded upon fanciful cut pieces of toast and masked with sauce ravigote. This makes a fine selection of hors d'oeuvres and a variety to satisfy the most exacting epicure.

Courtesy Lucien Raymond, Chef, Congress Hotel

Italian Olives
See Olives Italian

Lettuce Suedoise
Lettuce, eggs, celery, beets, anchovies

Make a mixture of six hard boiled eggs, three small hearts of celery, two boiled beets, two ounces of fillets of anchovies, all chopped separately and very fine. Squeeze out celery and beets in a cloth until very dry and mix all ingredients together. Add two teaspoons of anchovy sauce and the juice of two lemons. For Lettuce Suedoise, spread this mixture on about ½ inch thick and from 2 to 2½ inches long on hearts of lettuce leaves. Serve on cold plate and garnish the sides of the mixture with chopped hard boiled egg yolks on one side, and chopped whites on the other. Run a little strip of mayonnaise down the center of the top by making a furrow and filling it.

Garnish top of mayonnaise with fanciful cut beets and green peppers.

The same mixture can be placed in a fairly large mushroom or artichoke (Suedoise) cooked in oil, or raw cucumbers cut boat fashion. Serve on leaves of lettuce and garnish much like Lettuce Suedoise.

In boiling artichokes or mushrooms for Suedoise, use one cup of good olive oil and enough water to cover. One teaspoon of coriander seed, bayleaf, one pepper, one clove and one clove of garlic tied up in a little cloth and dropped into the oil and water with enough salt to season. Boil mushrooms or artichokes very slowly for at least thirty minutes or until cooked. Do not get them too well done. Allow to cool and then stuff as in Suedoise.

Lobster Bon Bouchee (Hot)
Toast, mashed potatoes, lobster Newburg, lemon, cress, crumbs and butter

On a thin slice of freshly made buttered toast pipe a thin border around edge of toast with finely mashed potatoes mixed with cream and seasoned highly. This border should be about one-fourth inch high. Fill the center with lobster, crab, shrimp, or oyster crabs in a thick, highly seasoned Newburg sauce. Sprinkle with bread crumbs and butter. Brown in hot oven and serve on doilies immediately. The same mixture can be placed in lobster claws, tails, oyster and clam shells and garnished with lemon cut fancifully and cress. This makes an ideal hot appetizer.

Instead of using a Newburg sauce a little chili, curry or Creole sauce will answer and give satisfaction.

Lobster Canape—I

Tomato, lobster, aspic, lettuce, Thousand Island dressing

On half or whole slices of ripe, peeled tomato place three or four slices of cooked lobster and glaze with aspic for effect. Serve on leaves of lettuce and with a Thousand Island dressing on side. Aspic can be omitted and top piped with various colored butters.

Lobster Canape—II

Lettuce, tomato, lobster, butter, mayonnaise

On inner leaves of lettuce, place a peeled slice of ripe tomato. Arrange small, thin slices of boiled lobster on top of tomato artistically, using the tail part and allowing slices to overlap. In the center, place a little lobster coral on a perfectly round piece of lobster, cut from the end of the tail or a portion cut round from the heavy part of the large claw. Lobster can be marinated before arranging on top of tomato, if desired. Serve with mayonnaise, Thousand Island or Russian dressing on the side, and pass at the table when service is being made. If desired, dressing can be poured over the lobster and top garnished with red butter, and fancifully cut red and green peppers. If the sauce is passed at the table, each slice of lobster can be alternately decorated with a little green and red rosette of lobster butter and the center piece with a trio of rosettes. Shrimp, crab meat, crawfish and, in fact, any fish can be handled much as the above for canapes.

Lobster Canape or Sandwich

Lobster, shrimp, crab meat, salmon or halibut, tomato, lettuce, mayonnaise

On a leaf of lettuce place a thick slice of peeled tomato. Place slice of cold boiled lobster on top of tomato, and coat with a lemon mayonnaise, Thousand Island or Russian dressing. Garnish with an eighth of a lemon cut lengthwise and a sprig of parsley. Crab meat, shrimp, salmon, in fact any kind of sea food can be handled the same way. For effect the canape can be decorated with crawfish tails or trussed crawfish, small lobster claws, feelers, etc. Sandwich to be made of white bread toasted, cut in finger strips or fancy shapes, and after the center is filled the edges should be piped with a stiff fanciful colored mayonnaise, or the center of sandwich can be spread with mayonnaise and then sprinkled with some very finely chopped hearts of celery; this is to be a very thin layer, and then the celery covered with thinly sliced pieces of fanciful arranged lobster, shrimp, flakes or crab meat or any fish or combination you may desire. A sauce boat of mayonnaise, Thousand Island or Russian dressing should accompany these toasted tid bits. At least two or three pieces to an order or a combination of three or four makes an ideal luncheon or supper order. When three or four are served they should be arranged on a platter similar to "My Ladies' Salad Sandwich" (see frontispiece of The Edgewater Beach Salad Book), and in the center place a hollowed out small red ripe tomato and fill with a sauce desired by the guest. Garnish with crabs trussed, with lobster feelers, tails, olives, etc.

Lobster and Shrimp Canape
Toast, butter, shrimp, lobster, aspic, lettuce

On round slices of white bread toasted on one side and spread with anchovy butter, place a row of shrimps, cut in half the red side up, around the outer edge. In the center place three thin slices of lobster, all slices overlapping, and in a sort of circle; if necessary, use four slices, but cover the toast. Paint with aspic and set in box to glaze. Dot backs of shrimp with green butter and the lobster slices with red butter. Serve on leaf of lettuce.

Aspic can be omitted and shrimps and lobster can be masked with mayonnaise or Thousand Island dressing.

Marinate of Shrimp
Shrimp, Thousand Island dressing

Cook, clean and chill fresh shrimp, cut them in half lengthwise, marinate them and serve in compartment hors d'oeuvre dish. They can also be mixed with Thousand Island or Russian dressing and served the same way.

Shrimp can be diced and mixed with an equal amount of diced celery, then bound together with mayonnaise and stripped with pimentoes or julienned strips of anchovies. This shrimp salad is often used as an item in an assortment of hors d'oeuvres.

Mushroom Hors d'Oeuvres
See Fresh Mushrooms

Olives Italian

Two cloves of garlic, ½ pint of oil, 24 colossal ripe olives. Mash the garlic very fine in a bowl, place the olives on top of the garlic and cover them with the oil. Stir olives and oil up thoroly and chill for one hour. Olives should be served right in the olive oil and passed at the table. They make a very delicious item and if once tried they will always be called for.

AUTHOR'S NOTE: "At Rome, olives made their appearance in the first course, at the beginning of the repast; but sometimes, after their introduction, the gluttony of the guests caused them to be served again with the dessert, so that they opened and closed the banquet."

See Jumbo Ripe Olives in Relishes

Oysters, Panned
See Panned Oysters

Oysters Rockefeller
Oysters, chives, garlic, spinach, cream, lemon

Open six oysters on deep shell and season with a drop of cayenne, then sprinkle with finely minced chives, an atom of garlic and butter. Mix a little chopped spinach with cream, oyster liquor and seasoning. Cover oysters with a little spinach mixture, sprinkle with butter, bread crumbs and paprika. Bake quickly in hot oven in pan on salt base and serve as a hot appetizer with quartered lemon.

At certain places in the South a filee is used in addition to other herbs to season oysters with before baking. Filee is the fresh sassafras leaves dried and powdered, with the addition of other savory herbs.

Palmer Square
Tongue, chicken, anchovies, pickles, mustard, cayenne, butter, chives, bread, ham

Dice very fine, one cup each of beef tongue, boiled

ham, boiled chicken, and mix with one-third cup each of dill pickles and anchovies. Add one cup of creamed butter to which has been added one teaspoon of dry mustard, one-tenth teaspoon cayenne and two tablespoons of chopped chives. Mix all together very thoroly. Cut the end off a small French loaf of bread and remove the center, and fill with the above mixture. Place the loaf or loaves in ice box. When chilled cut into thin slices with a sharp knife. Serve on leaves of lettuce. Slices can be garnished with fanciful cut beets, pickles, peppers or butters.—*Courtesy of E. E. Amiet, chef, Palmer House, Chicago.*

Panned Oysters
Oysters, butter, crumbs, bacon, cress, lemon

Open oysters on deep shell, season with butter, salt, pepper and sprinkle with bread crumbs. Strip with a small piece of bacon and roast in pan on a salt base in quick oven. Serve on doily with a little cress and lemon.

Parmesan Canape
Macaroni, ham, cheese, sauce, toast, butter

Macaroni cooked, chopped, seasoned and mixed with chopped ham or broiled bacon and bound together with a good cream sauce, then spread on squares of toast, sprinkled with parmesan, paprika and butter and browned under a salamander or in a hot oven makes an ideal tasty canape. Spaghetti, noodles and Italian pastes of all kinds cooked and bound together with just enough sauce, whether it be Bechamel, Creole, Italian or cream, and browned off as in recipe with macaroni make acceptable hot luncheon sandwiches. Serve one or two slices to the order. These should be considered canapes or open sandwiches.

Spaghetti, grated chicken livers and tomato catsup or sauce handled as above makes a real tasty item.

Pickled Walnuts
Pickled walnut, egg, butter, pimento, green pepper

On a slice of hard boiled egg, cut round, place a slice of pickled walnut. Garnish border of egg with a green colored butter and strip the walnut with julienned lines of red and green peppers. Pipe a rosette of red butter in center to hold peppers in place. Serve on lettuce leaves.

Potato Chips a la Swiss

Grate three ounces of Swiss cheese and add just enough raw cream to the cheese to make a paste, season with a little additional salt.

Take two freshly made potato chips and stick them together with a little of the paste. Serve as an individual dish of sandwiches or as an item with an assortment of hors d'oeuvres. These little tidbits can be sprinkled with celery salt and grated cheese and used as a garniture for a platter of sandwiches.

Prune Hors d'Oeuvres I

Prunes, cream cheese, French dressing, almonds

Wash and soak the largest prunes in cold water for 24 hours, changing water three times. Remove seeds by cutting off top and using a small, thin, sharp knife. Marinate the prunes in French dressing for two days, then drain and dry. Stuff with cream cheese thinned down with French dressing and mixed with chopped, blanched almonds.

Prune Hors d'Oeuvres II

Prunes, French dressing, ham, bacon, pickles

Soak prunes at least 24 hours in three waters (use prunes, size 18 to 30) until soft. Partially cut the top off and remove the seeds with a sharp knife. Place in a good French dressing and allow to marinate one day. Drain and dry. Make paste of equal proportions of boiled ham, sweet pickles and broiled bacon by grinding and mashing in a mortar. Roll into balls and stuff the prunes. Then wrap a slice of bacon around it and skewer it together with a toothpick and brown off in the oven. Allow to cool and serve in a compartment hors d'oeuvre dish. Dates can be handled in the same way, only use the black dates. Prunes handled the same way and stuffed with fine chopped walnuts and almonds mixed with a little cream sauce make an excellent hors d'oeuvre.

Quarte Coins Canape

See Canape Quarte Coins

Roe Canape

See Shad Roe

Russe

See Hors d'Oeuvres Russe

Salad Canape Sandwich De Luxe

*Chicken salad, Vegetable salad, Lobster salad, Cook's
salad, Waldorf diced fruit salad and
Chiffonade dressing salad*

Line a finger shaped chou paste shell with the
inner leaves of lettuce and fill with any of the
above salads. The mixture should be about ¼ inch
thick and the paste shells are to be about 3 inches
long and from 1 to 1¼ inches wide. Garnish the
plate or platter with pieces of stuffed celery, cherry
tomatoes or ripe and green olives. Salads can be
served in lightly browned, freshly baked finger rolls
or on milk bread freshly toasted and cut in finger
shapes, or diagonally. Serve on lettuce leaves.

Salmon Bellies

See Salted Salmon Bellies

Salmon Canape

Bread, gherkins, smoked salmon, cheese, paprika

Spread thin rounds of fried bread with chopped
gherkins mixed with butter. Chop a small piece of
smoked salmon and mix with grated Herkimer
cheese. Then cover gherkins with salmon and
cheese. Brown or melt cheese under a quick broiler
and serve on doilies piping hot. Sprinkle with paprika for color.

Salmon Combination

*Toast, salmon, butter, eggs, beets, green peppers,
lettuce*

On a round piece of bread toasted on one side
and spread lightly with anchovy butter, place a very
thin slice of smoked salmon, cut round to shape.
Make four equal divisions on top of salmon by
piping a little green butter thru the center, then cross-
ing it with a line in the opposite direction. Fill
one section with finely chopped pickled red beets,
another with chopped green peppers, the third with
chopped whites of eggs and the fourth with chopped
egg yolks. See that these items are placed evenly
or the picture will be spoiled. After placing the
fillers, if lines are not exactly straight, pipe another
dividing line on top of the first one, so the lines of
demarcation will be straight and visible. Serve on
lettuce leaves with a little rosette of cress.

Salted Salmon Bellies (Boiled)

This is one of the real epicurean northwestern
dishes. Portland excels in this item. As a breakfast

dish with boiled potatoes it is exquisite. As a cold item sliced and served with an assortment of hors d'oeuvres it makes a real treat.

Sandwich De Luxe
See Salad Canape

Sardellen Canape—I
See Anchovy Canape—I

Sardellen Canape—II
See Sardine Canape—I

Sardine Canape—I
Sardines, wafers, anchovy butter, lettuce, olive, gherkin

Split, skin and bone French oil sardines, lay on toasted and buttered wafers, pipe a small fine border of anchovy butter around outer edge. Place three wafers on a salad plate on a bed of julienned lettuce and garnish with an olive, a fanned gherkin and a slice of lemon.

Sardines, boned and skinned, can be arranged on finger pieces of toast. Squeeze a few drops of lemon juice over and serve as above.

A sardine paste can be piped on toasted wafers, sprinkled with grated cheese, browned quickly and served hot.

A sardine butter can be spread on toasted wafers and dotted with diamonds cut out of sour gherkins or with capers.

Author's Note: The French sardine is a handsome little fish, and its beauty is not entirely lost in the cooking. The French sardines as a rule improve with age, and are considered at their best at from four to six years in the can. Many particular establishments will not sell their stock if it is less than one year old, as that time is considered necessary for the proper blending of the fish, oil and flavor.

Sardels (Holland) specie of sardines come in small kegs, salted.

Sardine Canape II
Toast, sardines, butters

On toasted or plain white or rye bread, cut in fancy shapes, spread with sweet butter, place boned and skinned halved sardines, fillets of anchovies or sardellen. Squeeze a little lemon juice over the fish. Pipe around edges of toast a very fine border of butter, colored with a little lobster coral or tomato paste flavored slightly with lemon juice. The anchovy fillets should be flattened out and laid evenly on toast. If sardines are used, use the small French oil sardines, bone and skin before using. These open sandwiches can be used as appetizers and are termed canapes or hors d'oeuvres. They should be made just before serving and served on toasted bread.

The sardellen should be carefully freed of bones, skin and any other foreign matter, then soaked in clear cold water for at least two hours, then rinsed in more clear water and afterwards placed in olive oil until ready to use.

Sardine and Anchovy Canape
See Anchovy and Sardine

Sardines (Hot) Grilled
French skinless sardines, paprika, lemon butter, lemon, cress, toast

Use the large skinless and boneless sardines. Arrange on fine wire broiler and dust with paprika. Broil quickly and arrange one sardine on each thin piece of toast. Toast to be cut same length and width as the sardine, and spread with lemon butter. Serve on hot plate underlined with paper doily. Garnish with fanciful cut slices of lemon and sprigs of cress.

Savory Canape I
Mushrooms, livers, butter, cheese, toast, lettuce, gherkins

Saute equal amounts of mushrooms and chicken, turkey or goose livers slowly in butter until done, allow them to cool and rub livers thru a fine sieve and chop the mushrooms finely. Mix with a little sweet butter, season and spread on toasted pieces of whole wheat or white bread. Cut in fancy shapes. The livers must be free from gall and perfectly fresh.

These canapes can be sprinkled with grated cheese and a little butter, and toasted or browned under a broiler. The butter can be omitted and the mixture placed on untoasted bread and pressed into a toaster and browned. These canapes or sandwiches are very rich and are to be garnished with lettuce, green olives, gherkins, etc.

Savory Canape II

*Turkey, goose liver, ham, crab meat, mayonnaise,
lettuce*

On a thin round slice of roast turkey, spread with
a pate de foie gras paste (or a slice of goose liver),
place a thin round slice of Virginia ham and on ham
place a mound of crab meat. Mask with mayonnaise and serve on leaves of lettuce.

Savory Hors d'Oeuvres

Cut thin slices of bread and toast very crisp.
Spread the cheese, pickles and bacon mixture on
these toasted sippets and brown under a hot broiler.
This makes a very appetizing hors d'oeuvre.

Savory Sturgeon

See Sturgeon Savory

Sea Food Canape

Toast, caviar, anchovies, colored butter

On fancy cuts of thin buttered toast (toasted on
one side), spread a thin layer of best caviar mixed
with a little lemon juice. Cut fillets of anchovy in
three pieces lengthwise and lattice them over top of
caviar. Fillets should be cut the size of toast so
they do not extend beyond the border. Dot or pipe
in each opening a small rosette of red butter. Pipe
edge with a penciled line of green butter.

Toast to be buttered on the side which is not
browned.

Shad Roe Canape

*Bacon, roe, anchovy paste, butter, lemon, toast,
lettuce, gherkins*

Bake a pair of shad roe, wrapped in an oiled piece
of paper, in the oven, or broil over a slow fire until
done. Allow to cool, season lightly with salt and
pound in a wooden bowl or mortar, then add one-
third teaspoon of anchovy butter, two ounces of
fresh butter and one ounce of finely ground broiled
bacon. Stir all together into a fine paste and add a
few drops of lemon juice. Whip butter into a cream
before adding. Spread mixture on toast, cut into
fancy shapes and garnish top center of canapes
with four thin slices of sweet or sour gherkins overlapping each other. The outer edge of canape to be
piped with a very fine line of green butter.

Serve on cold plates and underline canape with
lettuce. Anchovy paste can be omitted.

Shrimp Canape I
Toast, shrimp, mayonnaise, colored butter

On thin slices of white or brown bread, toasted or plain, cut round, and spread with anchovy mayonnaise, lay five small shrimp which have been shelled and cleaned. Place shrimp on toast like you were making a flowered wheel, ends together in center and crescents of shrimp at equal intervals apart, in order to complete wheel. Place a little rosette of Ravigote or Venetian butter in center and dot between shrimp. Shrimp should be placed red side up. Shrimp can be split in two if desired. One teaspoon of anchovy paste whipped into half cup of mayonnaise will give additional flavor to mayonnaise. Additional mayonnaise or T.I.D. can be passed at table.

Shrimp Canape II
Shrimp, toast, peppers, mayonnaise, lettuce, capers, Thousand Island dressing

Boil fresh shrimp and allow to cool. Remove shells and clean, then cut in half lengthwise. Place at least eight or ten of these half shrimp on a thick slice of peeled ripe tomato or round of toast underlined with a leaf of lettuce. Place the shrimp in a sort of circle like spokes of a wheel with the red side up. In between each half shrimp place a very thin julienne strip of green pepper. Pipe a rosette of stiff mayonnaise in the center of canape and dot it with green capers. Serve on ice cold plates with Thousand Island dressing on the side.

Shrimp and Lobster Canape
See Lobster and Shrimp

Shrimp Marinate
See Marinate of Shrimp

Smoked Cisco Canape
Toast, smoked fish, butter, lettuce, pimentoes

Remove fillets from herring, bloater or whitefish and trim to small uniform pieces. Brown oblong pieces of bread on both sides, either by sauteing in olive oil or between fine wire broiler over fire. Spread with a green or lemon butter and lay on fillets the length of toast. Place several thin slices of pimentoes across fish diagonally, at equal distances apart, and pipe green butter across the pimentoes diagonally in the opposite direction, making a latticed effect. Serve on julienned lettuce.

Smoked Herring Canape

Herring, toast, butter, hard boiled egg, gherkin

Separate the meat carefully and cut in thin fillets. Fillets should be cut all the same size. Arrange on oblong pieces of toast, which have been spread with a little fresh butter. Make a border of chopped whites and yolks of hard boiled eggs. Serve on lettuce leaves. Arrange a little rose in the center of canape made out of a small gherkin and place a fancy piece of pimento, cut round, in the center of the rose.

Smoked Sturgeon Canape

Smoked sturgeon, toast, butter, horseradish, lettuce, olives

Spread thin pieces of toasted whole wheat or white bread, cut into squares, with a sweet butter mixed with enough freshly grated horseradish to flavor. Cover with a thin slice of smoked sturgeon and garnish with colored butters. Serve on lettuce with three slices of olives ringed together and laid on top of sturgeon.

Aspic is added to give a gloss to canape; it can be omitted if you so desire.

Sot l'y Laisse

Turkey fillets, anchovy paste, colored butter

Trim the fillets out of a roast turkey. These fillets are to be found in the two large indentations of the backbone, close to where the leg articulates with backbone. Cut small pieces of toast just a little larger than fillet and the same shape (cone shaped). Spread toast with anchovy butter and place the fillet on top. Pipe a little colored butter around edge and serve on leaf of lettuce. It is only possible to list this item where a great many turkeys are roasted, as each turkey yields but two. This hors d'oeuvre can be served hot or cold. When hot replace anchovy butter with a hot well seasoned lobster paste, sprinkle with a little grated cheese, brown and serve quickly. The French "Sot l'y Laisse" is translated "The fool leaves them."

The fillet is the most delicious morsel on the whole turkey carcass, and is generally overlooked excepting by the epicure, or by the boy who gets the backbone, the day after.

These fillets served plain or marinated and served on a fancy piece of toast spread with cranberry sauce are quite acceptable.

Strawberry Hors d'Oeuvres
Lobster, butter, bread crumbs

Chop up very finely one-half pound of cooked lobster, shrimp or crab meat, and season. Mix in one-fourth the amount of butter to the meat and roll into a strawberry shape. Grate one cup of bread crumbs and add one or two drops of red coloring matter (vegetable) to the crumbs to color. Roll lobster meat mixture into crumbs to bring out color. Insert an artificial leaf and stem into berry and serve as one of an assortment of fancy hors d'oeuvres.

Use the lobster, shrimp or crab meat and fill Rose Apples, inserting an artificial leaf and stem in same.

Rose apples come in cans and run about 27 to 30 to the can. These apples or peppers can be stuffed with any highly flavored forcemeat, fish or chicken.

Stuffed Celery
Celery, Roquefort cheese

Take the inner white small stalks of celery, thoroly cleaned and dried, and pipe a Roquefort cheese mixture into the hollows. Cheese should be rubbed thru a sieve and mixed with a little raw cream, to reduce to the proper consistency for piping. Two of these small branches can be stuck together and the bottom trimmed short and placed in an upright position in center of an hors d'oeuvre dish as garnish.

The very inner stalks (cut like matches) with their tiny foliage can be piped with cheese and then rolled in a very thin slice of fresh bread and afterwards tied with baby ribbon. These dainty tit bits can be placed in an upright position in the center of a platter of assorted sandwiches giving the platter a gala appearance. These little rolls of sustenance should be handled very carefully, rolled compactly and trimmed exactly or they will destroy rather than enhance the appearance of your offering. The foliage should protrude above the bread, and the bottom part cut flat so that it will stand up straight. Five or six in center is sufficient. The assortment of sandwiches piled around center will hold these little masterpieces in place.

Cream cheese thinned down with a little cream and garnished with chopped pickles can be used as a filler in place of Roquefort. Herkimer or any of the tangy types can be worked into a paste and used as a filler.

When using the stalks in the rolled sandwiches, spread the slices of bread first with butter, then with cheese.

Stuffed Eggs I

Eggs, slaw, Thousand Island dressing, butter, lettuce

Cut hard boiled eggs in half, remove the yolks. Mix equal quantities of chopped Mexican slaw, green olives, and mashed hard yolks with Thousand Island dressing to bind. Stuff whites with mixture and place on a bed of shredded lettuce. Do not add too much Thousand Island dressing, but just enough to bind ingredients together. Pipe edge of egg with various colored butter and cut the bottoms of the eggs so that they will remain in position.

Stuffed Eggs II

Chow chow, eggs, peppers, butter

Drain and chop one-half cup of chow chow. Cut four hard boiled eggs in half lengthwise, remove and grate the yolks and add the finely chopped chow chow. Stuff the eight halves of eggs with the mixture and serve as one of an assortment on hors d'oeuvres platter. The top of halved eggs can be decorated with strips of red and green peppers, and rosettes of varied colored butter.

Sturgeon Canape

See Smoked Sturgeon

Sturgeon Savory

Sturgeon, tartar sauce, toast, aspic, lettuce

Cut smoked sturgeon or salmon in rounds, same as ham savory. Spread rounds of toast with a heavily garnished tartar sauce. Cover with a round of tomato aspic and paint sides with aspic. Set in ice box to harden. Serve on leaves of lettuce.

Sweetbread Canape

Sweetbreads, tomato, lettuce, walnut, mayonnaise

On a slice of peeled ripe tomato, place a slice of veal sweetbread (cooked). On this place a slice of walnut and mask with tomato aspic mayonnaise and decorate with fancy colored butters. Serve on leaves of lettuce.

Sweetbreads, Hot

Curry powder, mustard, Roquefort cheese, Worcestershire sauce, butter, sweetbreads, cheese, toast

One-half teaspoon of curry powder, one-third teaspoon of dry mustard, one ounce of Roquefort cheese, one teaspoon of Worcestershire sauce and three ounces of creamed butter. Mash cheese and add curry powder and mustard, then mix in sauce and add butter. Spread on thin slices of fanciful cut toast and garnish top with thin slices of sweetbreads. Sprinkle with cheese, brown and serve at once.

Swiss Nuts Appetizer

Grated Swiss cheese (two ounces); whipped or raw cream, shelled pecans (three ounces)

Stir into 1½ ounces of the grated cheese, 2 table-spoons of whipped cream, or 1 tablespoon raw cream and make cheese and cream into a paste. Take a little of the paste and stick 2 pecans together with it. After you have stuck all pecans together, roll them in the ½ ounce of dry grated cheese you have left and also sprinkle them with salt. Serve these Swiss nuts as appetizers. They are very delicious and something new. They are to be eaten out of hand as you would celery or olives.

The 1½ ounces of Swiss cheese is enough for 90 medium sized pecans. Don't forget to sprinkle the remainder of the dry cheese over the stuffed nuts and roll them about so the dry cheese adheres to them. This gives the nuts a very nice appearance.

Tartar Canape

See Canape Tartar

Tid Bits

Butter crackers, cream cheese, bar le duc, cress, olives

On toasted butter crackers spread a mixture of one-half package of cream cheese, thinned with a little raw cream, and two tablespoons of bar le duc. Do not thin cheese too much. Serve on paper doi-lies. Garnish with cress and olives.

Tomato and Crab Meat

Tomato aspic, mayonnaise, crab meat, tomato, lettuce, butter

Add enough tomato aspic mayonnaise to bind one cup of crab meat and stuff small peeled, ripe, sea-soned tomato shells with it. Allow to thoroly chill and cut into quarters with a thin sharp knife. Serve quarters on leaves of lettuce and decorate with fancy colored butters. A little partially chilled tomato aspic can be poured over the quarters to glaze and then quarters can be decorated with fancy butter.

Note: Peel tomato and cut off stem and remove all the seeds and juice and turn upside down to drain shells for an hour in the ice box before stuffing.

Note: Hard boiled eggs cut in half lengthwise and stuffed with the same mixture and then turned upside down on freshly made ovals of toast piped with fancy butter border make a real treat.

Chicken and lobster seasoned with curry and Major Grey's Chutney and used as a filling for egg and tomato also make a really tasty item.

Tomato Savory Canape

Hard-boiled eggs, butter, anchovies, lemon juice, toast, tomato, French dressing

Rub thru fine sieve two yolks of hard-boiled eggs and whip into eggs two ounces of creamed butter. Add one ounce of skinned and boned anchovies mashed to a paste, one teaspoon of lemon juice and one teaspoon of French dressing base No. 5. Spread on thin rounds of toast. Place a thin slice of peeled ripe tomato on top of toast and decorate top of tomato with fancy rosettes of the above mixture piped out of a small paper tube.

Tomato should be selected so that rounds are not too large and toast should be cut so that tomato just fits the top. Tomato can be sprinkled with grated Herkimer cheese and browned. Serve the canape hot if this method is used.

Tongue Canape

Tongue, chicken, mayonnaise, aspic, lettuce

Cut smoked tongue in rounds at least one-fourth inch thick. On top of tongue spread a chicken paste, made from white meat of chicken pounded in a mortar, seasoned and mixed with a creamy mayonnaise. Pour over canape a partially chilled tomato aspic perfectly clear. Set in box to cool and glaze. Serve on leaves of lettuce.

Tongue should be very well cooked and tender.

Tuna Fish Cups

Tuna fish, peppers, aspic, butter, lettuce

Rub six ounces of tuna fish thru a sieve and season. Add enough French dressing or lemon juice to make a soft mass and fill small red pepper cups. Cut cup in half and glaze with aspic. Garnish round side with fanciful colored butters. Serve on lettuce round side up. Sweet red peppers can be bought in cans.

Canapes made of tuna fish, crabmeat, lobster or shrimp can be mounded on a slice of tomato or artichoke bottom underlined with lettuce and masked with a Thousand Island dressing or mayonnaise.

Whitefish Canape
See Smoked Cisco

Wine Herring

Serve with a little of sauce which comes with it and sour cream dressing on side. Wine herring comes in cans.

Fillets cut to shape on slices of tomato or toast and masked with a Russian dressing make a tasty titbit.

To Glaze Hors d'Oeuvres
One cup of clear consomme, one or two sheets of silver label French gelatine

Dissolve gelatine by pouring boiling consomme (clear) over it. Allow it to chill (but not to harden) and color it if you wish. Place a wire base in pan (to catch the aspic which does not adhere) and on this wire base place the fancy hors d'oeuvres. Pour the chilled aspic over these, a portion of which will adhere to them and form a coating. If the consomme is strong one sheet of gelatine to one pint of consomme will suffice.

Relishes

Relishes

Any finely cut salad can be used as a relish.

Almonds
See Salted Almonds

Ann Cook

To a cupful of Cook's or Chiffonade Salad add three diced fillets of anchovy and a tablespoon of capers. Serve in a Hors d'Oeuvre compartment dish, on leaves of lettuce, enough on each leaf so that leaf and all can be lifted out to make a service.

AUTHOR'S NOTE: Cook's or Chiffonade salad can be stripped with two anchovy fillets, the fillets to be crisscrossed over each individual portion of salad.

Artichoke Tubers

Clean and peel tubers and place in ice water. Cut them in uniform shapes and serve in a dish of cracked ice, the same as you would celery. This is an excellent nutty relish.

Tubers fluted and then filled with Roquefort cheese as used in stuffed celery make a desirable relish. Use a very small flute or column cutter.

Beets
See Pickled

Breakfast Relish

"The flesh of a cold roast fowl and an equal quantity of smoked tongue cut in fine particles and then pounded in a mortar with a teaspoonful of salt, half a teaspoon of cayenne, and the same of ground mace and nutmeg will make an acceptable breakfast dish."
—*Epicures Almanac*, 1841.

The above ingredients mixed with enough French dressing Base No. 5 to reduce it to the proper consistency and flavor makes an ideal sandwich filler. The breakfast relish was evidently made into a cake and fried in the Colonial days, much as we use the sausage cakes of today.

Carrot Relish

Clean thoroly and scald small, new carrots; then rub off skin. Boil slowly for about fifteen minutes in salted water. Drain and cover with a boiling aromatic vinegar. Drain off vinegar, boil it again and pour it over the carrots for the second time. Cork and allow to nearly cool, then seal. These carrots add greatly to an assortment of hors d'oeuvres. Carrots can be immersed in olive oil to which a few cloves of garlic, crushed, have been added. This adds a unique flavor to the carrots.

Celery, Curled
See Frizzled Celery

Celery, Frizzled
See Frizzled Celery

Cherry Tomatoes
Marinate whole, small, yellow, cherry tomatoes in a bowl rubbed with garlic and filled with French Dressing. Serve as a relish. Tomatoes cut in half and marinated 24 hours make an excellent hors d'oeuvre.

The red and yellow tomato peeled and marinated, then served together, enhances the appearance of any hors d'oeuvre offering.

Chives and Cucumbers
See Cucumbers and Chives

Cod Cheeks Relish

Cod Flakes Relish
Boil cod and flake. Between each layer of flakes place a few thin slices of onion and sweet peppers, one or two cloves (whole), one bay leaf, and a few drops of oil. When dish is filled pour over a little aromatic vinegar. Marinate for several hours. Serve as an item with an assortment of hors d'oeuvres.

Cod cheeks can be handled the same way. They are delicious.

AUTHOR'S NOTE: "Black strap was a mixture of rum and molasses. In early Colonial times casks of it stood in every country store, a salted and dried codfish slyly hung alongside as free lunch to be stripped off and eaten, and thus tempt, through thirst, the purchase of another draught of black strap."

Corn Relish
Corn, tomatoes, chopped pickles, celery.

Cucumber and Chives
Peel, scar with a fork and slice thinly young green

cucumbers. Sprinkle with salt and allow to marinate in water for at least three hours. Drain off the
salty liquor and cover with oil, then add one-fourth
the amount of vinegar as you did oil. Sprinkle with
freshly ground black pepper and chopped chives.
Serve on leaves of lettuce (without sauce). This is
an excellent item for an assortment of hors d'oeuvres,
to be served in a roulette or from an hors d'oeuvres
platter or wagon.

Cucumbers Japanese

Peel and score cucumbers with a fork from top
to bottom and slice thin. Soak in enough slightly
salted water to cover, for one hour. Drain dry and
place in a bowl. Cover with a Sour Cream Dressing
No. 3.

Mix one-half cup of fresh sweet and one-half cup
of whipped cream together, add one-fifth teaspoon
of freshly ground pepper and one-half teaspoon of
salt, and, lastly one teaspoon of lemon juice. An
additional teaspoon of lemon juice can be added if
cream is perfectly fresh. Then add one tablespoon
of chopped chives. This sauce can be soured by adding one-half cup of buttermilk. This makes an
exceedingly fine relish. Serve toasted sippets of
bread with this sort of relish.

Cucumber Novelty

Cut hard boiled eggs in slices. Remove the yolks,
fill white centers with finely ground cucumbers (surplus moisture drained) and bound with mayonnaise. Arrange 2 or 3 rings on bed of lettuce and
sprinkle with chopped chives. Garnish with cress.
French dressing.

Egg slices must be cut thick and cucumbers arranged in rings very carefully.

Cucumber Shells

After peeling and scoring carefully with a fork
cut cucumbers into one-inch slices and with a column cutter, remove enough of the cucumber so that
the shell or ring will have a wall not over $\frac{1}{4}$ inch
thick. Marinate shells of cucumber in French Dressing for at least one hour. Mix equal quantities of
Cook's Salad, chopped fine, with finely cut lobster
and shrimp, which has been marinated in French
dressing for an hour. Fill shells and mask top with
a little Thousand Island Dressing. Caviar may be

mixed with the Cook's Salad for the filling of cucumbers. Cucumbers may be cut into quarters and then into boats, seared on outside, hollowed out and filled with mixture and masked. Serve on shredded lettuce and watercress.

Curled Celery
See Frizzled Celery

Eggs, Herbal
See Oeufs Herbal

Eggs, Pickled
See Pickled Eggs—I

Egg Relish
Cut hard boiled eggs in quarters or slices, season with salt and white pepper and dress with French Dressing Base No. 5. Sprinkle with chopped chives, chervil, tarragon and sweet basil. Serve in relish tray on leaves of lettuce.

Eggs, Spiced
See Spiced Eggs

Eggs, Stuffed
See Stuffed Eggs—III

Frizzled Celery
Curled Celery
Clean and wash celery carefully, cut the inner white branches in half lengths, saving the outside green stalks and roots for other purposes. Take these inner branches and with a small sharp knife start at one end and cut each piece from three to five times from the top to within an inch of the bottom; leave this part intact. Place these pieces in ice water (plenty of water and ice), and allow them to remain two or three hours. This treatment will frizzle and curl them and give you an added attraction and item for garnishing dishes as well as for a relish.

Italienne Olives
See Jumbo

Julienned Vegetables
See Marinated Vegetables

Jumbo Ripe Olives, Italienne

Rub a porcelain or china bowl well with garlic (using two cloves of crushed garlic), place a pint of ripe olives in bowl and cover olives with olive oil. Place in a cool place for an hour and then serve as a relish. Olives should be served right in the oil; they are delicious. If you ever serve ripe olives this way you will never be pleased with them served any other way.

Lamb Tongue, Pickled
See Pickled Ox Palates

Love Nuts
See Swiss Nuts in Canape Section

Marinated Julienned Vegetables

Boil peeled carrots in slightly salted water. Bake large beets with tops on to preserve all their juices. Drop large green peppers in smoking grease for a minute and remove and wipe off skins. Julien a large Bermuda onion and boil in a little salted water until just under done. Cut equal amounts of carrots, beets and peppers in julienned strips as soon as they are cold. Cut all about the same size and mix an equal amount of onions. Place all in a French Dressing Base No. 5 and marinate in ice-box for twenty-four hours. Drain, sprinkle with chopped olives and serve as a relish. Large onions can be cut in thin rings and then in half.

AUTHOR'S NOTE: An aromatic vinegar (mild) can be used to marinate fish, meat, or vegetables. It was perhaps thru the use of aromatic vinegars that perfume came into being; at least the idea of toilet vinegar arose from it.

Mexican Slaw

Finely shred a small cabbage, chop 1 green pepper very fine and 1 or 2 whole canned pimentos; mix the red and green pepper into the cabbage and add enough French dressing to this cabbage and pepper mixture to moisten. Season with a little salt.

Nasturtium Pods
See Pickled Nasturtium Pods

Nuts, Salted
See Salted Almonds

Oeufs—Herbal

Cut hard boiled eggs in half, remove yolk and cut a slice off round sides. Place on bed of lettuce and fill center with a mayonnaise which has been heavily garnished with chopped tarragon, chervil, cress, gherkins and chives. Season egg before filling with mayonnaise. Serve on leaves of lettuce.

Olives

See Italienne

See Jumbo Ripe

See Salted Spanish

Ox Palates

See Pickled Ox Palates

Peanuts, Salted

See Salted Almonds

Pecans, Salted

See Salted Almonds

Pickled Beets

Bake until done two dozen young beets with short stemmed tops. Peel, slice, then cover with a very mild aromatic vinegar. Add one bay leaf, two whole cloves, one slice of onion, small stick of cinnamon and one-fourth cup sugar to each quart of liquid used. Allow them to marinate for at least twenty-four hours. If beets are put in whole allow them to marinate at least three days, in ice-box.

Pickled Eggs—I

Boil eggs hard and peel. Place in French Dressing Base No. 5, while hot, and allow them to remain in marinade for several days in ice-box. Serve on leaves of lettuce, either quartered or whole. Bantam eggs are best.

Pickled Eggs—II

See Spiced Eggs

Pickled Lamb Tongues

See Pickled Ox Palates

Pickled Nasturtium Pods

Pick the nasturtium pods, green, and place in a salt brine of four parts water and one part salt, for two or three days. Drain and wash in clear water. Place in a jar and pour boiling aromatic vinegar over them. Use in six or eight weeks. Fine for a hors d'oeuvre.

Fancifully cut celery roots can be boiled in salted water for about ten minutes, then drained and a boiling aromatic vinegar poured over them. The vinegar should have a tablespoon of dry mustard added for each pint used. Cover roots with the vinegar and allow to stand, sealed, at least three weeks before using.

Pickled Ox Palates
Pickled Lamb's Tongue

Diced or thinly sliced pickled ox palates or lamb's tongue mixed with mayonnaise and a little finely chopped celery are excellent as a relish.

Sliced fresh ox palates or lambs' tongues cooked and mixed with julienned red beets and onions and then marinated in French Dressing for twenty-four hours make a real relish.

Ripe Olives
See Jumbo Olives

Salted Almonds

Place almonds in hot water and blanch or simmer for a few minutes. Pour off water and remove skins. Dry. Use a French fryer, place nuts in basket and brown in hot grease until a delicate brown. Dump out on a dry towel and sprinkle with fine salt. If you do not happen to have a French fryer place almonds in hot grease in a frying pan, stir them around until brown and remove them with pierced skimmer.

Salted Nuts
See Salted Almonds

Salted Spanish Olives

These olives are ripe and cured in salt. When bought in casks they have a certain amount of oil on them. The skin is rather wrinkled, but if well cured and olives are of good quality they make a very tasy relish.

AUTHOR'S NOTE: "One cannot wax enthusiastic about the flavor of salt itself, but only of the zest, or relish, it can impart to innumerable aliments as a seasoning agency. To salt, indeed, we owe not merely that last edge on the flavor of so many meats, fish, vegetables, olives, etc., but to a veritable cornucopia of the good things of the table."

There are certain tribes who use salt as a legal tender or a medium of exchange, deeming it the most rare and most precious of all commodities.

Shrimp Relish

Chop two cups of shrimps, one cup of celery, one-half cup of olives (green), and one-half cup of green peppers. Add equal proportions of French dressing and mayonnaise to moisten. Arrange with an assortment of hors d'oeuvres and garnish with strips of pimentos.

Lobster, salmon or crab meat can be handled in the same way. One cup of julienned boiled ham or smoked tongue can be added or used in place of shrimp, lobster or crab.

Slaw
See Mexican

Spanish Olives
See Salted Spanish

Spiced Eggs
Pickled Eggs

Marinate hard boiled eggs in Aromatic French Dressing for five days in ice-box. Slice or quarter and mask with mayonnaise. Serve on leaves of lettuce or on rounds or ovals of toast. Mayonnaise can be sprinkled with chopped gherkins. Eggs can be marinated in spiced vinegar, which should be poured over eggs boiling hot and allowed to cool and stand for at least three days in ice-box.

Warm eggs take on flavor and color quicker than eggs that are cold.

Stuffed Eggs III

Boil eggs hard and allow to cool; cut in halves and remove the yolks carefully, placing the whites together in pairs. Mash yolks and add one teaspoon of prepared horseradish, one-half teaspoon of made mustard, and one tablespoon of chopped pickles for each six yolks. Season highly, roll mixture into balls and replace in paired whites. If balls are too soft add another mortared yolk. Serve on leaves of lettuce.

Tomato Combination Relish

Very small red tomatoes peeled and hollowed out, stuffed with Cook's salad, chiffonade or Mexican slaw, make ideal relishes.

Tongue, Pickled Lamb
See Pickled Ox Palate

Vegetables, Marinated
See Marinated Vegetables

The Makings

Various canned items—fish, vegetables and condiments—used in the manufacturing of hors d'œuvres, salads and sandwiches.

Anchovies, fillets of—in cans—2 to 27 oz., Italian, Spanish or Portuguese, with or without capers.

Anchovy fillets in oil.

Anchovy rings—French pack—in bottles—3-4-5-or 6-ring.

Anchovies in salt.

Antipaso in 4½ to 7-ounce cans.

Artichoke bottoms.

Artichoke hearts.

Bloaters.

Cantaloupe spiced.

Capers.

Carciofini.

Caviar—Russian—fresh Beluga—fresh Malossol—Romanoff salted—Maximoff whole grain—Gorky pressed.

Colorings—green, red, yellow.

Crabmeat.

Cucumber rings.

Eggs.

Fish, cured—Canadian cured, 30 lb. box.
    Codfish bits.
    Codfish middles, 25 lb. box.
    Codfish threads, 3 lb. box; 20 lb. box.
    Salt herring, 10 lb. pail; 20 lb. pail.
    Salt mackerel, 10 lb. pail.
    Large salt mackerel, 20 lb. pail.

Fish pastes—anchovy paste, 8 oz. jar; bloater paste, 2 oz. tube; lobster paste, 3 oz. tin; salmon paste, 2 oz. jar; sardellen butter, 2 oz. jar; anchovy and shrimp paste, sardine paste.

French cockscombs—Rognon de coq; Financieres.

French snails.

French sprats.

German cervelat sausage.

Hams, German; Westphalian Kugel; Prager; American.

German senfgurken.

Hearts of palm.

Herring—kippered, Norwegian, Scotch, French or German.

Lambs tongues, pickled.

Lobster.
Mackerel.
Mackerel roe.
Olives farcies.
Olives, ripe, queen, salt, stuffed, stuffed queen, stuffed
  manzanilla.
Palm hearts.
Pate de foie gras.
Pearl onions.
Potted meats, corn beef, etc.
Rose apples.
Salmon.
Salt sardellen.
Sardines—French, Norwegian, Italian, Portuguese,
  Royans, Spanish, American.
Sauces — condiments — Newburg (sherry) ; Major
  Grey's chutney; Brand's A1 sauce; Lea & Perrins;
  Bercy sauce; Chili sauce; catsup; Harvey sauce;
  Chop suey sauce.
Shad roe.
Shrimp.
Slices of smoked goose breasts.
Slices of smoked pork loin.
Smoked fish—bloaters, 50 count.
  Boneless herring, 10 lb. box.
  Finnan haddie, medium; (Red tag) ; fillets, 15 lb.
    box.
  Halibut.
  Salmon.
  Scotch kippers.
Sweet pickled fruits and beets.
Tomato paste.
Tongue.
Tripe a la mode de Caen.
Trout.
Truffles.
Tuna.
Vinegar, French tarragon; malt.
Watermelon rind.
Whole natural goose livers.
Wine herring.
Yankee relish.

Garnitures

Garnitures selected from the following list may be used to enhance the appearance of sandwiches, appetisers, hors d'œuvres, etc.

Anchovies—rings, fillets, butter, paste, salt.

Angelica.

Apple—baked, spiced, colored.

Bacon.

Bamboo shoots—marinated and sliced.

Beans—marinated string or small green butter.

Beets—pickled, spiced, baked and hollowed out; cut into flowers, baskets and other fancy shapes.

Broccoli.

Butters—fancy.

Cabbage—red, white, slaw.

Candied orange peel, Canton ginger, violets, etc.

Cantaloup—spiced.

Canton ginger.

Capers.

Carrots, baby (whole or flowered) flowers, fancy shapes.

Celery—stalks, hearts, curled, salad, leaves.

Cherries—candied, maraschino, etc.

Chervil.

Chicory.

Clover blossoms—fresh.

Cockscombs.

Cornucopias, ham—filled with salad, etc.

Cos.

Crabs—spiced.

Crabapples—spiced.

Crawfish (boiled)—trussed, claws.

Cress.

Croustades, cases.

Crupoos.

Cucumbers—sliced, squeezed, marinated, rings.

Daffodils.

Daisies.

Eggs, hard boiled—chopped whites or yolks, pickled, stuffed, basketed, colored, sliced, quarters.

Emeraldettes.

Endive.

Ginger, candied, Canton.

Ham cornucopias—filled with salad, etc.

Hop buds.

Lemons and limes—sliced, quartered, twists, basketed, flowered, etc.

Lettuce—leaves, shredded, nests, etc.

Lobster (boiled) claws, feelers, heads, butterfly, etc.
Mangoes.
Mint.
Mung bean—sprouted, marinated.
Mushrooms.
Nasturtium.
Noodles—fried, Chinese fried.
Nuts—salted, almonds, pecans, peanuts, walnuts.
Olives—green, ripe, salted, pimolas, Italienned.
Onions—green, pearl, fried rings, white Bermuda, sliced, French fried, whole.
Orange—twists, slices.
Parsley—green or fried.
Peppers—green, red, small finger, stuffed sweet; cut in diamonds, hearts, strips, flags, flowers, etc.
Piccalilli.
Pickles—gherkins, dill, burr, pin-money; fanned, sliced, octopussed, etc.
Pickled fruit.
Pineapple—fried, rings, crushed, etc.
Potato—chips, fried, mashed, julienned, shoestring, salad, etc.
Prunes—cooked without sugar, spiced, stuffed, or plain.
Radishes, lilied, sliced.
Romaine.
Rosebuds.
Rubyettes.
Shrimp (boiled) halved, sliced, whole, or salad.
Slaw—red, white, plain, Mexican, without juice.
Sorrel.
Spiced crabs.
Spiced crabapples.
Spiced fruits.
Tomatoes—sliced, quartered, baskets, flowered; cherry tomatoes, etc.
Tomato relish.
Truffles.
Vegetables, marinated macedoine of.
Violets.
Watermelon rind—pickled, spiced.
Walnuts, pickled.

Sauces and many other items are sometimes served in small cases and placed at the side of sandwich for a garnish, such as tartar sauce, apple sauce, etc., but strictly speaking they are not garnitures. Sauces should be served on the side.

Dressings or mayonnaises are sometimes served in small cases.

Bibliography

Acetaria—Discourse on Sallets, by John Evelyn, London, 1699.

Adam's Luxury and Eve's Cookery, London, 1744.

American Home Diet, E. V. McCullum & Nina Simmonds, 1921.

Antiquitates Culinariæ, Reverend Richard Warner, London, 1791.

Aromatics and The Soul, Dan McKenzie, London, 1923.

Art of Cookery, William King, LL.D., London, 1708.

Art of Modern Cookery Displayed, 1757.

Atlanta Women's Club Book, Mrs. Newton C. Wing, Atlanta, 1921.

Blue Book of American Dishes, Alfred Fries, Chef Pompeian Rooms, Congress Grill.

Book of Children's Parties, Mary and Sara White, New York, 1903.

Book of Corn Cookery, Mrs. Mary I. Wade, Chicago, 1907.

Book of Food, P. Morton Shand, 1928.

Book of Hors D'Oeuvres, Lucy G. Allen, Boston, 1925.

Bread Making, T. N. T., New York, 1884.

Character Analysis and Correct Diets, Marie Winchell Walker, M.D., 1921-1927.

Chemistry of Food and Nutrition, Sherman, 1923.

Child Life in Colonial Days, Alice Morse Earle, 1899.

Choice Recipes of a Georgia Housekeeper, New York, 1880.

Chronicles of Fashion, Mrs. Stone, 1845.

Clarisse or The Old Cook, A. B. Walkley, New York.

Colonial Dames and Good Wives, Alice Morse Earle, 1895.

Comments on Corpulency, 1829.

Conduct of the Kitchen, X. Marcel Boulestin, 1925.

Cookery, Its Art and Practice, J. L. Thudichum, M.D., 1895.

Cooks Own Book and Housekeepers Register, Boston, 1838.

Cottage Economy, William Cobbett, 1822.

Creative Chemistry, Edwin E. Slosson.

Cuisine Bourgeoise of Ancient Rome, H. C. Coote, 1868.

Culinary Chemistry, Scientific Principles of Cookery, Frederick Acum, 1821.

Day Book MS. Cookery, 1700.

Diet and Regimen, 1800.

Dining and Its Amenities, 1907.

English Housewife, G. Markham, 1675.

Epicure's Year Book and Table Companion, 1868.

Feeding the Family, Mary Swartz Rose, Ph.D., 1925.

Fifteenth Century Cookery—Books Harleian MS. 279; MS. 4030; MS. 1450, T. Austin, 1848.

Fire as an Agent in Human Culture, Walter Hough, 1926.

Follies and Fashions of Our Grandfathers, Andrew W. Tuer (1807) ; 1886-7.

Food for the Diabetic, Mary Pascoe Huddleson, 1924.

Food of London, Dodd, 1856.

Food Products, Sherman, 1915.

Gombo Zhebes, Lafcadio Hearn, 1885.

Good Housekeeping Book, 1905.

Gracious Art of Dining, Mrs. John Alexander King.

Hand-Book of Cookery for a Small House, Jessie Conrad, 1923.

Haven of Health, Thomas Cogan, M.D., 1612.

Health of the Run About Child, William Palmer Lucas, 1923.

Health's Improvement, Thomas Muffet, M.D., 1655.

Histoire de la Table, Louis Nicolardot, 1868.

History of Clubs and Club Life, John Timbs, 1872.

Home Life in the Colonial Days, Alice Morse Earle, 1899.

Honours of the Table, 1791.

Hotel Management, Lucius M. Boomer.

Ideas for Refreshment Rooms, Hotel Monthly Press.

Indian Domestic Economy and Receipt Book, Madras, 1860.

International Jewish Cook Book, Florence Kresler Greenbaum.

Jewish Cookery, Mrs. Esther Levy, 1871.

Kitchenette Cookery, Anna Merritt East, 1917.

La Cuisine Creole, 1885.

Lady's Assistant, Charlotte Mason, 1777 (first sandwich recipe).

L'Arte di Ben Cucinare, Bartolomeo Stefani, Bologna, 1672.

Leaves from Our Tuscan Kitchen, Janet Ross, 1899.

Louisiana Plantation Cook Book, Mrs. J. E. Smitherman.

Magic of Herbs, Mrs. C. F. Leyel, 1926.

Manuel des Amphitryons, 1808.

Merrie England in the Olden Time, George Daniel, 1841.

MS. 1750-1820 Cookery.

MS. 1790 Cookery.

Newer Knowledge of Nutrition, McCullum and Simmonds, 1925.
Old English Plate, Cripps, 1878.
Our Viands, Anne Walbank Buckland, 1893.
Pamphlets or Bulletins U. S. Government Department of Agriculture, No. 487 on Cheese, 391 on Meat, 807 on Bread and Bread Making, 712 on School Lunches, and 567 on Corn Meal as a food and ways of using it.
Petronius Cena Trimalchionis.
Primeval Diet of Man.
Pythagorean Diet of Vegetables Only, Antonio Cocchi, 1745.
Queen-Like Closet, Hannah Wooley (perhaps the first woman to write a cook book), 1681.
Royal Cookery Book, Jules Gouffe, 1868.
Salads and Sandwiches, Liberty Magazine, Ethel Somers.
Salads and Sandwiches, Marion H. Neil, 1916.
Salads, Sandwiches and Chafing Dishes, Janet M. Hill, 1914.
Salads and Sandwiches and Specialty Dishes, Emory Hawcock, 1928.
Sandwiches, Mrs. S. Rorer, 1912.
Social England, Trail.
Technology of Bread Making, Jago, 1921.
The Table, Alessandro Filippini of Delmonicos, 1889.
Treasurie of Hidden Secrets, 1627.
Treatise of Foods in General, M. L. Lemery, M.D., Paris, 1704.
Uncooked Food, Christian, 1904.
Up-to-Date Sandwich Book, Eve Green Fuller, 1924.
Valentine's Manual of Old New York, Henry Collins Brown.
Virginia Housewife, Mrs. Mary Randolph, 1836.
Vital Vegetables, Ida C. Bailey Allen, 1927.
What to Do with Cold Mutton, 1865.
Woman's Life in Colonial Days, Carl Holliday, 1922.
Wooings and Weddings in Many Climes, Louise Jorden Miln, 1900.
Ye Old Cheshire Cheese, 1913.
Your Foods and You, Ida C. Bailey Allen, 1926.

Magazines—American Dietetics, American Restaurant, Club Management, Journal of Home Economics, The Hotel Monthly, Hotel Bulletin, Hotel World, Hotel Management, Nation's Chefs.

General Index

Classified Index

Supremes, Etc.

A CATALOGUE OF SELECTED DOVER BOOKS
IN ALL FIELDS OF INTEREST

A CATALOGUE OF SELECTED DOVER BOOKS
IN ALL FIELDS OF INTEREST

LEATHER TOOLING AND CARVING, Chris H. Groneman. One of few books concentrating on tooling and carving, with complete instructions and grid designs for 39 projects ranging from bookmarks to bags. 148 illustrations. 111pp. 7⅞ x 10.
23061-9 Pa. $2.50

THE CODEX NUTTALL, A PICTURE MANUSCRIPT FROM ANCIENT MEXICO, as first edited by Zelia Nuttall. Only inexpensive edition, in full color, of a pre-Columbian Mexican (Mixtec) book. 88 color plates show kings, gods, heroes, temples, sacrifices. New explanatory, historical introduction by Arthur G. Miller. 96pp. 11⅜ x 8½.
23168-2 Pa. $7.50

AMERICAN PRIMITIVE PAINTING, Jean Lipman. Classic collection of an enduring American tradition. 109 plates, 8 in full color—portraits, landscapes, Biblical and historical scenes, etc., showing family groups, farm life, and so on. 80pp. of lucid text. 8⅜ x 11¼.
22815-0 Pa. $4.00

WILL BRADLEY: HIS GRAPHIC ART, edited by Clarence P. Hornung. Striking collection of work by foremost practitioner of Art Nouveau in America: posters, cover designs, sample pages, advertisements, other illustrations. 97 plates, including 8 in full color and 19 in two colors. 97pp. 9⅜ x 12¼.
20701-3 Pa. $4.00
22120-2 Clothbd. $10.00

THE UNDERGROUND SKETCHBOOK OF JAN FAUST, Jan Faust. 101 bitter, horrifying, black-humorous, penetrating sketches on sex, war, greed, various liberations, etc. Sometimes sexual, but not pornographic. Not for prudish. 101pp. 6½ x 9¼.
22740-5 Pa. $1.50

THE GIBSON GIRL AND HER AMERICA, Charles Dana Gibson. 155 finest drawings of effervescent world of 1900-1910: the Gibson Girl and her loves, amusements, adventures, Mr. Pipp, etc. Selected by E. Gillon; introduction by Henry Pitz. 144pp. 8¼ x 11⅜.
21986-0 Pa. $3.50

STAINED GLASS CRAFT, J.A.F. Divine, G. Blachford. One of the very few books that tell the beginner exactly what he needs to know: planning cuts, making shapes, avoiding design weaknesses, fitting glass, etc. 93 illustrations. 115pp.
22812-6 Pa. $1.50

AUSTRIAN COOKING AND BAKING, Gretel Beer. Authentic thick soups, wiener schnitzel, veal goulash, more, plus dumplings, puff pastries, nut cakes, sacher tortes, other great Austrian desserts. 224pp. USO 23220-4 Pa. $2.50

CHEESES OF THE WORLD, U.S.D.A. Dictionary of cheeses containing descriptions of over 400 varieties of cheese from common Cheddar to exotic Surati. Up to two pages are given to important cheeses like Camembert, Cottage, Edam, etc. 151pp. 22831-2 Pa. $1.50

TRITTON'S GUIDE TO BETTER WINE AND BEER MAKING FOR BEGINNERS, S.M. Tritton. All you need to know to make family-sized quantities of over 100 types of grape, fruit, herb, vegetable wines; plus beers, mead, cider, more. 11 illustrations. 157pp. USO 22528-3 Pa. $2.25

DECORATIVE LABELS FOR HOME CANNING, PRESERVING, AND OTHER HOUSEHOLD AND GIFT USES, Theodore Menten. 128 gummed, perforated labels, beautifully printed in 2 colors. 12 versions in traditional, Art Nouveau, Art Deco styles. Adhere to metal, glass, wood, most plastics. 24pp. 8¼ x 11. 23219-0 Pa. $2.00

FIVE ACRES AND INDEPENDENCE, Maurice G. Kains. Great back-to-the-land classic explains basics of self-sufficient farming: economics, plants, crops, animals, orchards, soils, land selection, host of other necessary things. Do not confuse with skimpy faddist literature; Kains was one of America's greatest agriculturalists. 95 illustrations. 397pp. 20974-1 Pa. $3.00

GROWING VEGETABLES IN THE HOME GARDEN, U.S. Dept. of Agriculture. Basic information on site, soil conditions, selection of vegetables, planting, cultivation, gathering. Up-to-date, concise, authoritative. Covers 60 vegetables. 30 illustrations. 123pp. 23167-4 Pa. $1.35

FRUITS FOR THE HOME GARDEN, Dr. U.P. Hedrick. A chapter covering each type of garden fruit, advice on plant care, soils, grafting, pruning, sprays, transplanting, and much more! Very full. 53 illustrations. 175pp. 22944-0 Pa. $2.50

GARDENING ON SANDY SOIL IN NORTH TEMPERATE AREAS, Christine Kelway. Is your soil too light, too sandy? Improve your soil, select plants that survive under such conditions. Both vegetables and flowers. 42 photos. 148pp. USO 23199-2 Pa. $2.50

THE FRAGRANT GARDEN: A BOOK ABOUT SWEET SCENTED FLOWERS AND LEAVES, Louise Beebe Wilder. Fullest, best book on growing plants for their fragrances. Descriptions of hundreds of plants, both well-known and overlooked. 407pp. 23071-6 Pa. **$4.00**

EASY GARDENING WITH DROUGHT-RESISTANT PLANTS, Arno and Irene Nehrling. Authoritative guide to gardening with plants that require a minimum of water: seashore, desert, and rock gardens; house plants; annuals and perennials; much more. 190 illustrations. 320pp. 23230-1 Pa. $3.50

THE MAGIC MOVING PICTURE BOOK, Bliss, Sands & Co. The pictures in this book move! Volcanoes erupt, a house burns, a serpentine dancer wiggles her way through a number. By using a specially ruled acetate screen provided, you can obtain these and 15 other startling effects. Originally "The Motograph Moving Picture Book." 32pp. 8¼ x 11. 23224-7 Pa. $1.75

STRING FIGURES AND HOW TO MAKE THEM, Caroline F. Jayne. Fullest, clearest instructions on string figures from around world: Eskimo, Navajo, Lapp, Europe, more. Cats cradle, moving spear, lightning, stars. Introduction by A.C. Haddon. 950 illustrations. 407pp. 20152-X Pa. $3.50

PAPER FOLDING FOR BEGINNERS, William D. Murray and Francis J. Rigney. Clearest book on market for making origami sail boats, roosters, frogs that move legs, cups, bonbon boxes. 40 projects. More than 275 illustrations. Photographs. 94pp. 20713-7 Pa. $1.25

INDIAN SIGN LANGUAGE, William Tomkins. Over 525 signs developed by Sioux, Blackfoot, Cheyenne, Arapahoe and other tribes. Written instructions and diagrams: how to make words, construct sentences. Also 290 pictographs of Sioux and Ojibway tribes. 111pp. 6⅛ x 9¼. 22029-X Pa. $1.50

BOOMERANGS: HOW TO MAKE AND THROW THEM, Bernard S. Mason. Easy to make and throw, dozens of designs: cross-stick, pinwheel, boomabird, tumblestick, Australian curved stick boomerang. Complete throwing instructions. All safe. 99pp. 23028-7 Pa. $1.75

25 KITES THAT FLY, Leslie Hunt. Full, easy to follow instructions for kites made from inexpensive materials. Many novelties. Reeling, raising, designing your own. 70 illustrations. 110pp. 22550-X Pa. $1.25

TRICKS AND GAMES ON THE POOL TABLE, Fred Herrmann. 79 tricks and games, some solitaires, some for 2 or more players, some competitive; mystifying shots and throws, unusual carom, tricks involving cork, coins, a hat, more. 77 figures. 95pp. 21814-7 Pa. $1.25

WOODCRAFT AND CAMPING, Bernard S. Mason. How to make a quick emergency shelter, select woods that will burn immediately, make do with limited supplies, etc. Also making many things out of wood, rawhide, bark, at camp. Formerly titled Woodcraft. 295 illustrations. 580pp. 21951-8 Pa. $4.00

AN INTRODUCTION TO CHESS MOVES AND TACTICS SIMPLY EXPLAINED, Leonard Barden. Informal intermediate introduction: reasons for moves, tactics, openings, traps, positional play, endgame. Isolates patterns. 102pp. USO 21210-6 Pa. $1.35

LASKER'S MANUAL OF CHESS, Dr. Emanuel Lasker. Great world champion offers very thorough coverage of all aspects of chess. Combinations, position play, openings, endgame, aesthetics of chess, philosophy of struggle, much more. Filled with analyzed games. 390pp. 20640-8 Pa. $4.00

HOUDINI ON MAGIC, Harold Houdini. Edited by Walter Gibson, Morris N. Young. How he escaped; exposés of fake spiritualists; instructions for eye-catching tricks; other fascinating material by and about greatest magician. 155 illustrations. 280pp. 20384-0 Pa. **$2.75**

HANDBOOK OF THE NUTRITIONAL CONTENTS OF FOOD, U.S. Dept. of Agriculture. Largest, most detailed source of food nutrition information ever prepared. Two mammoth tables: one measuring nutrients in 100 grams of edible portion; the other, in edible portion of 1 pound as purchased. Originally titled Composition of Foods. 190pp. 9 x 12. 21342-0 Pa. $4.00

COMPLETE GUIDE TO HOME CANNING, PRESERVING AND FREEZING, U.S. Dept. of Agriculture. Seven basic manuals with full instructions for jams and jellies; pickles and relishes; canning fruits, vegetables, meat; freezing anything. Really good recipes, exact instructions for optimal results. Save a fortune in food. 156 illustrations. 214pp. 6⅛ x 9¼. 22911-4 Pa. $2.50

THE BREAD TRAY, Louis P. De Gouy. Nearly every bread the cook could buy or make: bread sticks of Italy, fruit breads of Greece, glazed rolls of Vienna, everything from corn pone to croissants. Over 500 recipes altogether. including buns, rolls, muffins, scones, and more. 463pp. 23000-7 Pa. $3.50

CREATIVE HAMBURGER COOKERY, Louis P. De Gouy. 182 unusual recipes for casseroles, meat loaves and hamburgers that turn inexpensive ground meat into memorable main dishes: Arizona chili burgers, burger tamale pie, burger stew, burger corn loaf, burger wine loaf, and more. 120pp. 23001-5 Pa. $1.75

LONG ISLAND SEAFOOD COOKBOOK, J. George Frederick and Jean Joyce. Probably the best American seafood cookbook. Hundreds of recipes. 40 gourmet sauces, 123 recipes using oysters alone! All varieties of fish and seafood amply represented. 324pp. 22677-8 Pa. **$3.50**

THE EPICUREAN: A COMPLETE TREATISE OF ANALYTICAL AND PRACTICAL STUDIES IN THE CULINARY ART, Charles Ranhofer. Great modern classic. 3,500 recipes from master chef of Delmonico's, turn-of-the-century America's best restaurant. Also explained, many techniques known only to professional chefs. 775 illustrations. 1183pp. 6⅝ x 10. 22680-8 Clothbd. **$22.50**

THE AMERICAN WINE COOK BOOK, Ted Hatch. Over 700 recipes: old favorites livened up with wine plus many more: Czech fish soup, quince soup, sauce Perigueux, shrimp shortcake, filets Stroganoff, cordon bleu goulash, jambonneau, wine fruit cake, more. 314pp. 22796-0 Pa. $2.50

DELICIOUS VEGETARIAN COOKING, Ivan Baker. Close to 500 delicious and varied recipes: soups, main course dishes (pea, bean, lentil, cheese, vegetable, pasta, and egg dishes), savories, stews, whole-wheat breads and cakes, more. 168pp.
USO 22834-7 Pa. $1.75

How to Solve Chess Problems, Kenneth S. Howard. Practical suggestions on problem solving for very beginners. 58 two-move problems, 46 3-movers, 8 4-movers for practice, plus hints. 171pp. 20748-X Pa. $2.00

A Guide to Fairy Chess, Anthony Dickins. 3-D chess, 4-D chess, chess on a cylindrical board, reflecting pieces that bounce off edges, cooperative chess, retrograde chess, maximummers, much more. Most based on work of great Dawson. Full handbook, 100 problems. 66pp. 7⅞ x 10¾. 22687-5 Pa. $2.00

Win at Backgammon, Millard Hopper. Best opening moves, running game, blocking game, back game, tables of odds, etc. Hopper makes the game clear enough for anyone to play, and win. 43 diagrams. 111pp. 22894-0 Pa. $1.50

Bidding a Bridge Hand, Terence Reese. Master player "thinks out loud" the binding of 75 hands that defy point count systems. Organized by bidding problem—no-fit situations, overbidding, underbidding, cueing your defense, etc. 254pp. EBE 22830-4 Pa. $3.00

The Precision Bidding System in Bridge, C.C. Wei, edited by Alan Truscott. Inventor of precision bidding presents average hands and hands from actual play, including games from 1969 Bermuda Bowl where system emerged. 114 exercises. 116pp. 21171-1 Pa. $1.75

Learn Magic, Henry Hay. 20 simple, easy-to-follow lessons on magic for the new magician: illusions, card tricks, silks, sleights of hand, coin manipulations, escapes, and more —all with a minimum amount of equipment. Final chapter explains the great stage illusions. 92 illustrations. 285pp. 21238-6 Pa. $2.95

The New Magician's Manual, Walter B. Gibson. Step-by-step instructions and clear illustrations guide the novice in mastering 36 tricks; much equipment supplied on 16 pages of cut-out materials. 36 additional tricks. 64 illustrations. 159pp. 6⅝ x 10. 23113-5 Pa. $3.00

Professional Magic for Amateurs, Walter B. Gibson. 50 easy, effective tricks used by professionals —cards, string, tumblers, handkerchiefs, mental magic, etc. 63 illustrations. 223pp. 23012-0 Pa. $2.50

Card Manipulations, Jean Hugard. Very rich collection of manipulations; has taught thousands of fine magicians tricks that are really workable, eye-catching. Easily followed, serious work. Over 200 illustrations. 163pp. 20539-8 Pa. $2.00

Abbott's Encyclopedia of Rope Tricks for Magicians, Stewart James. Complete reference book for amateur and professional magicians containing more than 150 tricks involving knots, penetrations, cut and restored rope, etc. 510 illustrations. Reprint of 3rd edition. 400pp. 23206-9 Pa. $3.50

The Secrets of Houdini, J.C. Cannell. Classic study of Houdini's incredible magic, exposing closely-kept professional secrets and revealing, in general terms, the whole art of stage magic. 67 illustrations. 279pp. 22913-0 Pa. $2.50

THE RED FAIRY BOOK, Andrew Lang. Lang's color fairy books have long been children's favorites. This volume includes Rapunzel, Jack and the Bean-stalk and 35 other stories, familiar and unfamiliar. 4 plates, 93 illustrations x + 367pp.
21673-X Paperbound $3.00

THE BLUE FAIRY BOOK, Andrew Lang. Lang's tales come from all countries and all times. Here are 37 tales from Grimm, the Arabian Nights, Greek Mythology, and other fascinating sources. 8 plates, 130 illustrations. xi + 390pp.
21437-0 Paperbound $3.50

HOUSEHOLD STORIES BY THE BROTHERS GRIMM. Classic English-language edition of the well-known tales — Rumpelstiltskin, Snow White, Hansel and Gretel, The Twelve Brothers, Faithful John, Rapunzel, Tom Thumb (52 stories in all). Translated into simple, straightforward English by Lucy Crane. Ornamented with headpieces, vignettes, elaborate decorative initials and a dozen full-page illustrations by Walter Crane. x + 269pp.
21080-4 Paperbound $3.00

THE MERRY ADVENTURES OF ROBIN HOOD, Howard Pyle. The finest modern versions of the traditional ballads and tales about the great English outlaw. Howard Pyle's complete prose version, with every word, every illustration of the first edition. Do not confuse this facsimile of the original (1883) with modern editions that change text or illustrations. 23 plates plus many page decorations. xxii + 296pp.
22043-5 Paperbound $4.00

THE STORY OF KING ARTHUR AND HIS KNIGHTS, Howard Pyle. The finest children's version of the life of King Arthur; brilliantly retold by Pyle, with 48 of his most imaginative illustrations. xviii + 313pp. 6⅛ x 9¼.
21445-1 Paperbound $3.50

THE WONDERFUL WIZARD OF OZ, L. Frank Baum. America's finest children's book in facsimile of first edition with all Denslow illustrations in full color. The edition a child should have. Introduction by Martin Gardner. 23 color plates, scores of drawings. iv + 267pp.
20691-2 Paperbound $3.00

THE MARVELOUS LAND OF OZ, L. Frank Baum. The second Oz book, every bit as imaginative as the Wizard. The hero is a boy named Tip, but the Scarecrow and the Tin Woodman are back, as is the Oz magic. 16 color plates, 120 drawings by John R. Neill. 287pp.
20692-0 Paperbound $3.00

THE MAGICAL MONARCH OF MO, L. Frank Baum. Remarkable adventures in a land even stranger than Oz. The best of Baum's books not in the Oz series. 15 color plates and dozens of drawings by Frank Verbeck. xviii + 237pp.
21892-9 Paperbound $2.95

THE BAD CHILD'S BOOK OF BEASTS, MORE BEASTS FOR WORSE CHILDREN, A MORAL ALPHABET, Hilaire Belloc. Three complete humor classics in one volume. Be kind to the frog, and do not call him names . . . and 28 other whimsical animals. Familiar favorites and some not so well known. Illustrated by Basil Blackwell. 156pp. (USO) 20749-8 Paperbound $2.00

DECORATIVE ALPHABETS AND INITIALS, edited by Alexander Nesbitt. 91 complete alphabets (medieval to modern), 3924 decorative initials, including Victorian novelty and Art Nouveau. 192pp. 7¾ x 10¾.   20544-4 Pa. $4.00

CALLIGRAPHY, Arthur Baker. Over 100 original alphabets from the hand of our greatest living calligrapher: simple, bold, fine-line, richly ornamented, etc. —all strikingly original and different, a fusion of many influences and styles. 155pp. 11⅜ x 8¼.   22895-9 Pa. $4.50

MONOGRAMS AND ALPHABETIC DEVICES, edited by Hayward and Blanche Cirker. Over 2500 combinations, names, crests in very varied styles: script engraving, ornate Victorian, simple Roman, and many others. 226pp. 8⅛ x 11.

22330-2 Pa. $5.00

THE BOOK OF SIGNS, Rudolf Koch. Famed German type designer renders 493 symbols: religious, alchemical, imperial, runes, property marks, etc. Timeless. 104pp. 6⅛ x 9¼.   20162-7 Pa. $1.75

200 DECORATIVE TITLE PAGES, edited by Alexander Nesbitt. 1478 to late 1920's. Baskerville, Dürer, Beardsley, W. Morris, Pyle, many others in most varied techniques. For posters, programs, other uses. 222pp. 8⅜ x 11¼.   21264-5 Pa. **$5.00**

DICTIONARY OF AMERICAN PORTRAITS, edited by Hayward and Blanche Cirker. 4000 important Americans, earliest times to 1905, mostly in clear line. Politicians, writers, soldiers, scientists, inventors, industrialists, Indians, Blacks, women, outlaws, etc. Identificatory information. 756pp. 9¼ x 12¾. 21823-6 Clothbd. $30.00

ART FORMS IN NATURE, Ernst Haeckel. Multitude of strangely beautiful natural forms: Radiolaria, Foraminifera, jellyfishes, fungi, turtles, bats, etc. All 100 plates of the 19th century evolutionist's Kunstformen der Natur (1904). 100pp. 9⅜ x 12¼.   22987-4 Pa. $4.00

DECOUPAGE: THE BIG PICTURE SOURCEBOOK, Eleanor Rawlings. Make hundreds of beautiful objects, over 550 florals, animals, letters, shells, period costumes, frames, etc. selected by foremost practitioner. Printed on one side of page. 8 color plates. Instructions. 176pp. 9³/₁₆ x 12¼.   23182-8 Pa. $5.00

AMERICAN FOLK DECORATION, Jean Lipman, Eve Meulendyke. Thorough coverage of all aspects of wood, tin, leather, paper, cloth decoration — scapes, humans, trees, flowers, geometrics — and how to make them. Full instructions. 233 illustrations, 5 in color. 163pp. 8⅜ x 11¼.   22217-9 Pa. $3.95

WHITTLING AND WOODCARVING, E.J. Tangerman. Best book on market; clear, full. If you can cut a potato, you can carve toys, puzzles, chains, caricatures, masks, patterns, frames, decorate surfaces, etc. Also covers serious wood sculpture. Over 200 photos. 293pp.   20965-2 Pa. $3.00

SLEEPING BEAUTY, illustrated by Arthur Rackham. Perhaps the fullest, most delightful version ever, told by C.S. Evans. Rackham's best work. 49 illustrations. 110pp. 7⅞ x 10¾. 22756-1 Pa. **$2.00**

THE WONDERFUL WIZARD OF OZ, L. Frank Baum. Facsimile in full color of America's finest children's classic. Introduction by Martin Gardner. 143 illustrations by W.W. Denslow. 267pp. 20691-2 Pa. **$3.00**

GOOPS AND HOW TO BE THEM, Gellett Burgess. Classic tongue-in-cheek masquerading as etiquette book. 87 verses, 170 cartoons as Goops demonstrate virtues of table manners, neatness, courtesy, more. 88pp. 6½ x 9¼.
22233-0 Pa. **$2.00**

THE BROWNIES, THEIR BOOK, Palmer Cox. Small as mice, cunning as foxes, exuberant, mischievous, Brownies go to zoo, toy shop, seashore, circus, more. 24 verse adventures. 266 illustrations. 144pp. 6⅝ x 9¼. 21265-3 Pa. **$2.50**

BILLY WHISKERS: THE AUTOBIOGRAPHY OF A GOAT, Frances Trego Montgomery. Escapades of that rambunctious goat. Favorite from turn of the century America. 24 illustrations. 259pp. 22345-0 Pa. **$2.75**

THE ROCKET BOOK, Peter Newell. Fritz, janitor's kid, sets off rocket in basement of apartment house; an ingenious hole punched through every page traces course of rocket. 22 duotone drawings, verses. 48pp. 6⅞ x 8⅜. 22044-3 Pa. **$1.50**

PECK'S BAD BOY AND HIS PA, George W. Peck. Complete double-volume of great American childhood classic. Hennery's ingenious pranks against outraged pomposity of pa and the grocery man. 97 illustrations. Introduction by E.F. Bleiler. 347pp. 20497-9 Pa. **$2.50**

THE TALE OF PETER RABBIT, Beatrix Potter. The inimitable Peter's terrifying adventure in Mr. McGregor's garden, with all 27 wonderful, full-color Potter illustrations. 55pp. 4¼ x 5½. USO 22827-4 Pa. **$1.00**

THE TALE OF MRS. TIGGY-WINKLE, Beatrix Potter. Your child will love this story about a very special hedgehog and all 27 wonderful, full-color Potter illustrations. 57pp. 4¼ x 5½. USO 20546-0 Pa. **$1.00**

THE TALE OF BENJAMIN BUNNY, Beatrix Potter. Peter Rabbit's cousin coaxes him back into Mr. McGregor's garden for a whole new set of adventures. A favorite with children. All 27 full-color illustrations. 59pp. 4¼ x 5½.
USO 21102-9 Pa. **$1.00**

THE MERRY ADVENTURES OF ROBIN HOOD, Howard Pyle. Facsimile of original (1883) edition, finest modern version of English outlaw's adventures. 23 illustrations by Pyle. 296pp. 6½ x 9¼. 22043-5 Pa. **$4.00**

TWO LITTLE SAVAGES, Ernest Thompson Seton. Adventures of two boys who lived as Indians; explaining Indian ways, woodlore, pioneer methods. 293 illustrations. 286pp. 20985-7 Pa. **$3.00**

JEWISH GREETING CARDS, Ed Sibbett, Jr. 16 cards to cut and color. Three say "Happy Chanukah," one "Happy New Year," others have no message, show stars of David, Torahs, wine cups, other traditional themes. 16 envelopes. 8¼ x 11.
23225-5 Pa. $2.00

AUBREY BEARDSLEY GREETING CARD BOOK, Aubrey Beardsley. Edited by Theodore Menten. 16 elegant yet inexpensive greeting cards let you combine your own sentiments with subtle Art Nouveau lines. 16 different Aubrey Beardsley designs that you can color or not, as you wish. 16 envelopes. 64pp. 8¼ x 11.
23173-9 Pa. $2.00

RECREATIONS IN THE THEORY OF NUMBERS, Albert Beiler. Number theory, an inexhaustible source of puzzles, recreations, for beginners and advanced. Divisors, perfect numbers. scales of notation, etc. 349pp. 21096-0 Pa. $4.00

AMUSEMENTS IN MATHEMATICS, Henry E. Dudeney. One of largest puzzle collections, based on algebra, arithmetic, permutations, probability, plane figure dissection, properties of numbers, by one of world's foremost puzzlists. Solutions. 450 illustrations. 258pp. 20473-1 Pa. $3.00

MATHEMATICS, MAGIC AND MYSTERY, Martin Gardner. Puzzle editor for Scientific American explains math behind: card tricks, stage mind reading, coin and match tricks, counting out games, geometric dissections. Probability, sets, theory of numbers, clearly explained. Plus more than 400 tricks, guaranteed to work. 135 illustrations. 176pp. 20335-2 Pa. $2.00

BEST MATHEMATICAL PUZZLES OF SAM LOYD, edited by Martin Gardner. Bizarre, original, whimsical puzzles by America's greatest puzzler. From fabulously rare Cyclopedia, including famous 14-15 puzzles, the Horse of a Different Color, 115 more. Elementary math. 150 illustrations. 167pp. 20498-7 Pa. $2.50

MATHEMATICAL PUZZLES FOR BEGINNERS AND ENTHUSIASTS, Geoffrey Mott-Smith. 189 puzzles from easy to difficult involving arithmetic, logic, algebra, properties of digits, probability. Explanation of math behind puzzles. 135 illustrations. 248pp. 20198-8 Pa. $2.75

BIG BOOK OF MAZES AND LABYRINTHS, Walter Shepherd. Classical, solid, and ripple mazes; short path and avoidance labyrinths; more —50 mazes and labyrinths in all. 12 other figures. Full solutions. 112pp. 8⅛ x 11. 22951-3 Pa. $2.00

COIN GAMES AND PUZZLES, Maxey Brooke. 60 puzzles, games and stunts —from Japan, Korea, Africa and the ancient world, by Dudeney and the other great puzzlers, as well as Maxey Brooke's own creations. Full solutions. 67 illustrations. 94pp. 22893-2 Pa. $1.50

HAND SHADOWS TO BE THROWN UPON THE WALL, Henry Bursill. Wonderful Victorian novelty tells how to make flying birds, dog, goose, deer, and 14 others. 32pp. 6½ x 9¼. 21779-5 Pa. $1.25

COOKIES FROM MANY LANDS, Josephine Perry. Crullers, oatmeal cookies, chaux au chocolate, English tea cakes, mandel kuchen, Sacher torte, Danish puff pastry, Swedish cookies — a mouth-watering collection of 223 recipes. 157pp.

22832-0 Pa. $2.00

ROSE RECIPES, Eleanour S. Rohde. How to make sauces, jellies, tarts, salads, potpourris, sweet bags, pomanders, perfumes from garden roses; all exact recipes. Century old favorites. 95pp.

22957-2 Pa. $1.25

"OSCAR" OF THE WALDORF'S COOKBOOK, Oscar Tschirky. Famous American chef reveals 3455 recipes that made Waldorf great; cream of French, German, American cooking, in all categories. Full instructions, easy home use. 1896 edition. 907pp. 6⅝ x 9⅜.

20790-0 Clothbd. $15.00

JAMS AND JELLIES, May Byron. Over 500 old-time recipes for delicious jams, jellies, marmalades, preserves, and many other items. Probably the largest jam and jelly book in print. Originally titled May Byron's Jam Book. 276pp.

USO 23130-5 Pa. $3.00

MUSHROOM RECIPES, André L. Simon. 110 recipes for everyday and special cooking. Champignons à la grecque, sole bonne femme, chicken liver croustades, more; 9 basic sauces, 13 ways of cooking mushrooms. 54pp.

USO 20913-X Pa. $1.25

FAVORITE SWEDISH RECIPES, edited by Sam Widenfelt. Prepared in Sweden, offers wonderful, clearly explained Swedish dishes: appetizers, meats, pastry and cookies, other categories. Suitable for American kitchen. 90 photos. 157pp.

23156-9 Pa. $2.00

THE BUCKEYE COOKBOOK, Buckeye Publishing Company. Over 1,000 easy-to-follow, traditional recipes from the American Midwest: bread (100 recipes alone), meat, game, jam, candy, cake, ice cream, and many other categories of cooking. 64 illustrations. From 1883 enlarged edition. 416pp.

23218-2 Pa. $4.00

TWENTY-TWO AUTHENTIC BANQUETS FROM INDIA, Robert H. Christie. Complete, easy-to-do recipes for almost 200 authentic Indian dishes assembled in 22 banquets. Arranged by region. Selected from Banquets of the Nations. 192pp.

23200-X Pa. $2.50

Prices subject to change without notice.
Available at your book dealer or write for free catalogue to Dept. GI, Dover Publications, Inc., 180 Varick St., N.Y., N.Y. 10014. Dover publishes more than 150 books each year on science, elementary and advanced mathematics, biology, music, art, literary history, social sciences and other areas.